Fodor's

BERMUDA

WELCOME TO BERMUDA

Just a two-hour flight from most East Coast U.S. cities, Bermuda is one quick getaway that feels worlds away. Tranquil and prosperous, this island nation of pastel houses and manicured gardens also displays a deep British heritage with crisp colonial architecture. A comfortable climate provides year-round opportunities for outdoor recreation on pink-sand beaches, at championship golf courses, and in cerulean waters. Add excellent, varied shopping and dining, and it's easy to see why this small-in-size country looms large on many itineraries.

TOP REASONS TO GO

★ **Beaches:** Sand and sea come together in beautiful pink and blue crescents.

★ **Island Culture:** A rich heritage of British traditions with a calypso twist.

★ **Shopping:** Boutiques, galleries, and upscale department stores in walkable districts.

★ **Dining:** Superb independent and resort restaurants serve Bermudian and global cuisine.

★ **Water Sports:** Warm, clear waters are perfect for diving, snorkeling, boating, and more.

★ **Golf:** Greens designed by the greats include cliff-top holes and expansive ocean vistas.

13 ULTIMATE EXPERIENCES

Bermuda offers terrific experiences that should be on every traveler's list. Here are Fodor's top picks for a memorable trip.

1 Relax on a Blushing Beach

With a gently-curving crescent of pink sand lapped by turquoise waters and backed by uncluttered South Shore Park, Horseshoe Bay Beach is the perfect spot to swim, play, and soak up the sun. *(Ch. 6)*

2 Stroll St. George

In Bermuda's 400-year-old settlement you can step into
St. Peter's, an Anglican church completed in 1612, and wander
alleys lined with traditional shops, pubs, and cottages. *(Ch. 2)*

3 Charter a Boat

There are 120 tiny islands scattered around Bermuda's
shores. Rent your own boat or charter one for a scenic tour
of the surrounding coves, lagoons, and islets. *(Ch. 6)*

4 Sleep Pretty

No high-rises here, just elegant beachfront resorts and inland sanctuaries. Choose among luxurious hotels, cottage colonies, and flower-filled guesthouses. (*Ch. 4*)

5 Catch Cup Match Fever

A spirited two-day celebration, the annual Cup Match Cricket Festival is the highlight of Bermuda's summer calendar with plenty of Bermudian food and music. (*Ch. 6*)

6 Explore Underwater Treasures

The superior water clarity here affords divers and snorkelers technicolor views of coral and marine life, underwater caves, and shallow wrecks. (*Ch. 6*)

7 Tour Crystal Caves

Easy-to-explore, Crystal Caves is an impressive underground passage with long stalactites and thin limestone straws above, and stalagmites in clear emerald pools below. (*Ch. 2*)

8 Shop Fashionable Front Street

High-end, fashionable retail dominates the island's shopping scene. The lack of sales tax provides a bit of savings for a vacation splurge on quality clothing, jewelry, and more. *(Ch. 7)*

9 Get Lost Along the Railway Trail

Escape Bermuda's busy streets on a car-free trail for walkers, joggers, and cyclists. It spans the island end-to-end, overlooking rocky coastlines and passing through green countryside. *(Ch. 6)*

10 Tee Off on Ocean-View Greens

On courses designed by the world's best golf architects, pros and high-handicappers alike are treated to sweeping ocean vistas and landscaping with spectacular blooms. *(Ch. 6)*

11 Visit Bermuda Aquarium Museum and Zoo

BAMZ brings Bermuda's undersea habitat up close with a towering 140,000-gallon tank. Also on display is area wildlife, including more than 300 birds, reptiles, and mammals. *(Ch. 2)*

12 Hit Bermuda's Top Attraction

Formerly a British military stronghold, the Dockyard is now home to museums, forts, water activities, a craft market, and great shops and eateries. *(Ch. 2)*

13 Sample a Rum Swizzle

Two must-have Bermudian cocktails, the Rum Swizzle and the Dark 'n Stormy, share a secret weapon: Gosling's Black Seal Rum, loved by locals since 1806. *(Ch. 7)*

CONTENTS

MAPS

ABOUT THIS GUIDE

Fodor's Recommendations

Everything in this guide is worth doing—we don't cover what isn't—but exceptional sights, hotels, and restaurants are recognized with additional accolades. **Fodor's Choice★** indicates our top recommendations. Care to nominate a new place? Visit Fodors.com/contact-us.

Trip Costs

We list prices wherever possible to help you budget well. Hotel and restaurant price categories from $ to $$$$ are noted alongside each recommendation. For hotels, we include the lowest cost of a standard double room in high season. For restaurants, we cite the average price of a main course at dinner or, if dinner isn't served, at lunch. For attractions, we always list adult admission fees; discounts are usually available for children, students, and senior citizens.

Hotels

Our local writers vet every hotel to recommend the best overnights in each price category, from budget to expensive. Unless otherwise specified, you can expect private bath, phone, and TV in your room. For expanded hotel reviews, facilities, and deals visit Fodors.com.

Top Picks	Hotels & Restaurants
★ Fodor'sChoice	⌧ Hotel
Listings	↩ Number of rooms
✉ Address	¶Ol Meal plans
✉ Branch address	✕ Restaurant
☏ Telephone	⚓ Reservations
⎙ Fax	⌂ Dress code
⊕ Website	▭ No credit cards
✉ E-mail	Ⓢ Price
◩ Admission fee	**Other**
⊙ Open/closed times	⇨ See also
Ⓜ Subway	☞ Take note
⊹ Directions or Map coordinates	⚐ Golf facilities

Restaurants

Unless we state otherwise, restaurants are open for lunch and dinner daily. We mention dress code only when there's a specific requirement and reservations only when they're essential or not accepted. To make restaurant reservations, visit Fodors.com.

Credit Cards

The hotels and restaurants in this guide typically accept credit cards. If not, we'll say so.

EUGENE FODOR

Hungarian-born Eugene Fodor (1905–91) began his travel career as an interpreter on a French cruise ship. The experience inspired him to write *On the Continent* (1936), the first guidebook to receive annual updates and discuss a country's way of life as well as its sights. Fodor later joined the U.S. Army and worked for the OSS in World War II. After the war, he kept up his intelligence work while expanding his guidebook series. During the Cold War, many guides were written by fellow agents who understood the value of insider information. Today's guides continue Fodor's legacy by providing travelers with timely coverage, insider tips, and cultural context.

EXPERIENCE
BERMUDA

WHAT'S WHERE

1 Hamilton and Central Parishes. The city of Hamilton, in the heart of Pembroke, is a bustling little capital referred to as "town" by locals. Along with major historic sites, Hamilton has the broadest array of restaurants, shops, bars, and museums. Paget Parish, adjoining Pembroke to the south, is best known for its enviable selection of south-shore beaches and Paget Marsh and the Botanical Gardens. Sleepy Devonshire Parish, adjoining Pembroke to the east, is the geographical center of the island, but most travelers merely pass through it. Serious sports enthusiasts are the exception, because the National Sports Centre, National Equestrian Centre, Bermuda Squash Racquets Association, and Ocean View Golf Course are all there. Warwick has Bermuda's longest beach; Warwick Long Bay Beach is rarely crowded, even in peak season.

2 St. George's and Eastern Parishes. Air travelers first touch down in St. George's, just as the crew of the *Sea Venture* did in 1609. Their shipwreck kick-started Bermuda's settlement, and the town is today a UNESCO World Heritage site. In the East you'll also find Hamilton Parish (not the city of Hamilton), which

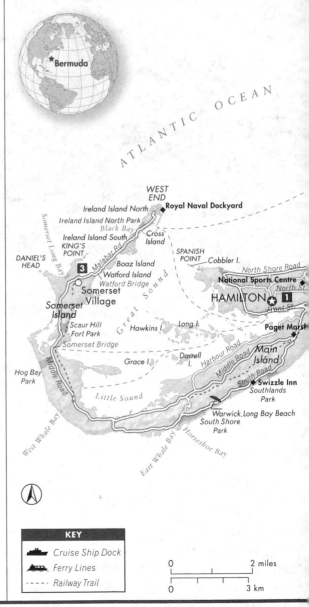

Bermuda

ATLANTIC OCEAN

WEST END
Ireland Island North · Royal Naval Dockyard
Somerset Long Bay
Ireland Island North Park
Black Bay
Ireland Island South
Cross Island
KING'S POINT
DANIEL'S HEAD
Malabar Rd
SPANISH POINT · Cobbler I.
3 Boaz Island
Watford Island
Watford Bridge
Somerset Village
Somerset Island
North Shore Road
National Sports Centre
North St.
HAMILTON **1**
Front St.
Great Sound
Scaur Hill Fort Park
Hawkins I.
Long I.
Paget Marsh
Somerset Bridge
Darrell I.
Grace I.
Harbour Road
Main Island
Middle Road
Hog Bay Park
Little Sound
Middle Road
South Road
Swizzle Inn
Southlands Park
Warwick Long Bay Beach
South Shore Park
West Whale Bay
East Whale Bay
Horseshoe Bay

KEY
🚢 *Cruise Ship Dock*
🚌 *Ferry Lines*
---- *Railway Trail*

0 ———————— 2 miles
0 ———————— 3 km

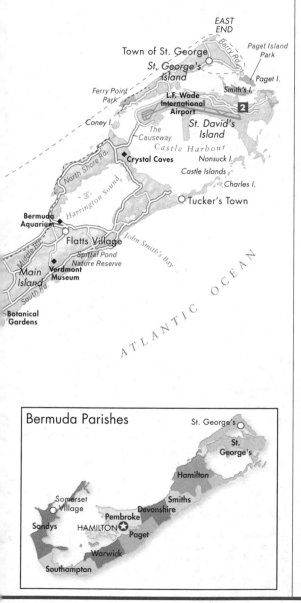

is home to the Bermuda Aquarium, Museum and Zoo, the Crystal Caves, Shelly Bay Park, and the infamous Swizzle Inn. In Smith's Parish, which borders Harrington Sound, you'll find Spittal Pond Nature Reserve, the Verdmont Museum, and John Smith's Bay.

3 Dockyard and Western Parishes. At the farthest West End tip in the parish of Sandys (pronounced *Sands*) you will find Bermuda's single largest tourist attraction: the Royal Naval Dockyard. A former British bastion, the complex has been converted to house the Bermuda Maritime Museum, Dolphin Quest, and Snorkel Park Beach, plus shops and restaurants. You'll also find Cross Island, the product of a 9-acre land reclamation project and home of the America's Cup Village during the 35th America's Cup in 2017. Southampton is home to Horseshoe Bay, the most popular pink-sand beach.

NEED TO KNOW

Atlantic Ocean

BERMUDA

● Hamilton

AT A GLANCE

Capital: Hamilton

Population: 65,300

Currency: Bermudian dollar; pegged to U.S. dollar

Money: ATMs are common; credit cards and U.S. dollars widely accepted.

Language: English

Country code: 1 441

Emergencies: 911

Driving: On the left

Electricity: 120v/60 cycles; plugs are U.S. standard two- and three-prong

Time: One hour ahead of New York

Documents: All visitors must carry a valid passport; immigration preclearance returning to U.S.

Mobile phones: GSM (1900 bands)

Major mobile companies: CellOne, Digicel

WEBSITES

Bermuda Department of Tourism: ⊕ www.gotobermuda.com

Bermuda.com: ⊕ www.bermuda.com

Bermuda 4u: ⊕ www.bermuda4u.com

GETTING AROUND

✈ **Air Travel:** L.F. Wade International Airport is the sole airport in Bermuda.

🚌 **Bus Travel:** Bermuda has a great public transport system, with buses covering the entire island. Buses are clean, safe, and reliable.

🚗 **Car Travel:** You can't rent a car in Bermuda; only full-time residents are issued driver's licenses. You can, however, rent a two-person electric car or a scooter, the island's most popular mode of transportation.

⛴ **Ferry Travel:** Travel within Bermuda by fast ferry. The principal ferry terminal is located in Hamilton at Albuoy's Point.

PLAN YOUR BUDGET

	HOTEL ROOM	MEAL	ATTRACTIONS
Low Budget	$275	$15	Bermuda Botanical Gardens, Free
Mid-Budget	$375	$30	Crystal and Fantasy Caves, $30
High Budget	$475	$50	Whale-watching cruise, $80

WAYS TO SAVE

Order takeout. Take out meals from a restaurant and forgo spending on gratuity and drinks.

Visit in low or value season. You can shave about 40% off your hotel bill by visiting Bermuda in low season, which is sun-kissed yet cool and ideal for tennis, golf, and shopping.

Explore by bus. Buying a daily or weekly travel pass for unlimited use of the public bus system is perhaps the cheapest way to sightsee.

Snorkel at Tobacco Bay. You don't have to pay big bucks to rent a boat to get a close-up look at some wonderful marine life here.

PLAN YOUR TIME

Hassle Factor	Low. Direct flights to Bermuda are frequent.
3 days	Relax poolside or beachside. Explore the island by bike or bus, and don't miss pink-sand stunner Horseshoe Bay.
1 week	Split your time between a resort and the capital city of Hamilton to indulge in big-city sophistication, island style.
2 weeks	Explore the country by bike, scooter, and/or ferry. Visit the Dockyard in the far west to St. George's in the east and every beach in between.

WHEN TO GO

High Season: High season is May through September when the temperatures are the warmest. The island teems with activity, and the events calendar is full.

Low Season: November through March, the pace is much slower. Temperatures range from 55 at night to 60s in early afternoon.

Value Season: Shoulder season of October and April offers good weather for outdoor pursuits, though the beaches can get chilly. Hotel rates are cheaper, and the island remains lively.

BIG EVENTS

January: Bermuda International Race Weekend has a marathon, half marathon, and a 10k charity walk. ⊕ www.bermudaraceweekend.com

March: The Bermuda International Film Festival shows independent feature, documentary, and short films. ⊕ www.biff.bm

May: The Bermuda Day holiday celebrates the official start of summer with a half marathon, parade, and islandwide festivities. ⊕ www.bermudamarathon.bm

July–August: The Cup Match Cricket Festival is a two-day celebration and match between Somerset and St. George's cricket clubs. ⊕ www.bermudacupmatch.com

November: During the World Rugby Classic, former players represent their respective countries in matches. ⊕ www.worldrugby.bm

READ THIS

■ **Bermuda Moods,** Various authors. Compilation of Bermuda snapshots.

■ **The Story of Bermuda and Her People,** William Sears Zuill. Accounts of the island, from 1609 to present.

■ **Shakespeare, an Island and a Storm,** David F. Raine. Historical research and poetic storytelling.

WATCH THIS

■ **The Deep.** 1977 film adaptation of Peter Benchley's novel.

■ **Rare Bird.** A documentary on Bermuda's national bird.

■ **When Voices Rise.** Critically acclaimed film on overcoming segregation in 1950s Bermuda.

EAT THIS

■ **Dark 'n' Stormy:** dark rum and ginger beer.

■ **Codfish cakes:** panfried and mashed with potatoes and seasoning.

■ **Mussel pie:** baked with potatoes, onions, and curry.

■ **Cassava pie:** cassava, eggs, sugar, and pork or chicken.

■ **Steamed salt cod:** with potatoes, bananas, and a hard-boiled egg or tomato sauce.

■ **Rum Swizzle:** a fruit cocktail with dark and light rum.

ABOUT BERMUDA

Bermuda has always been a land of adventure. Since it was first discovered in 1503, explorers and castaways have sought their fortune on the island. Today's adventurers head to Bermuda for water sports, golf, and scooter riding. Great shopping, pink sand, and spas provide retreat for those in search of relaxation. As in much of the world, tourism is struggling in Bermuda, and many large-scale developments are on hold. Thankfully the international business sector remains stable, and in true Bermudian spirit, locals continue to smile as they enjoy the island's rich natural bounty.

Today's Bermuda

...is not just one island. Most visitors wrongly assume Bermuda is just one island, when in fact there are islands everywhere you look. It has six principal islands, which are linked by bridges to create the main land, and a staggering 120 other islands scattered around the shore. Island hopping isn't really an option in Bermuda though, as there is no scheduled boat service, and many of the islets are surrounded by hazardous reefs. Some of the islands are also private residences, while others are mere rocks.

...is still very British. Bermuda's British traditions are obvious, from driving on the left side of the road to afternoon tea, to wig-wearing lawyers strolling to court. The national sports are cricket and football, there are "bobbies on the beat" (policemen on foot), and red letterboxes on street corners. Bermuda is one of the oldest British Overseas Territories, but that said, it's completely self-governing, with its own laws. Everyone, including Britons, is treated as a foreigner, as only Bermudians can own property, land, or vote.

...is not cheap. The World Bank rates Bermuda as one of the most affluent countries in the world, and it won't take long to understand why. Start saving your dollars for Bermuda's high cost of living. Hotel accommodations are expensive, a bag of groceries costs more than $50, and gasoline is three times more expensive than in the United States. That being said, budget travelers should note that free walking tours are offered in Hamilton and St. George's, the Botanical Gardens have free entry, and the Gibbs Hill Lighthouse is a bargain at just $2.50.

...is crammed full of people. Bermuda is the third most densely populated place on earth. There's an average of more than 3,000 people per mile, which means there are more than enough happy faces to welcome you. For a bit of breathing space, head to Tucker's Town in St. George's Parish, the least populated spot on the island.

...is strict about cars. Bermuda has several laws governing the size and quantity of vehicles on the road. Only Bermudians or full-time residents are allowed driver's licenses, and even then they can only have one car per household. Licensing fees are determined by the length of the vehicle.

...is crazy about golf. Bermuda has golf courses everywhere you look, so it's no surprise that it's a popular pastime for many locals. There's a wide selection of government and privately owned golf courses across the island, making it a golfer's paradise. The Pro Sports World Championship of Golf is held here in September, but there are also several annual tournaments, such as team knockouts, couples' classics, and par-3 championships.

LIKE A LOCAL

Enjoy Salt Cod Fish and Potatoes

The custom of eating this traditional Sunday brunch dish dates back to the 18th century, when Bermuda sloops traded with Newfoundland and brought cheap and plentiful salt cod back to Bermuda to feed the slaves. The fish is served with hard-boiled eggs, bananas, avocado, and boiled potatoes with a tomato-and-onion-based sauce on the side.

Save Summer for after May 24

Bermuda Day—May 24—marks the official start of summer, and the date is forever etched on a Bermudian's mind. Regardless of the rising temperatures, true Bermudians would rather swelter in long pants than switch to their summer wardrobe before the all-important date. Bermudians won't even dip their toes in the water or take their boats out a day earlier than May 24. It's a public holiday and is celebrated with a running and cycling race, followed by a parade.

Speak Bermudian

Despite the island's close ties to Britain, you won't hear many true English accents here. In fact, most locals speak with a distinctly Caribbean-esque cadence, their sentences sprinkled with a new lingo of often confusing "Bermewjan Vurds." The native tongue strings words together and has a tendency to swap the letter *w* for the letter *v*. "Up the country" means anything west of Hamilton and "down the country" means anywhere east of Hamilton. If you're "going shrew de trees," you're getting married. If you like the taste of something, it's "well." An empty cocktail is at "low tide," and depending on how drunk you are, you will be labeled anything from "hot" to "full hot."

Give Color-Coded Instructions

Every cottage here is proudly painted in a pastel color, and no one dares to paint his or her home a color like that of a neighbor. Names and numbers of buildings are often irrelevant, as directions are dished out in a color-by-numbers kind of way. You'll be told to take a right at the pink building and then a left when you get to the yellow house. It's much the same story when ordering a taxi; the operator will take an address, but "What color is your place?" will automatically be asked.

Mind your Manners

You won't get very far in Bermuda until you learn the unwritten rule of greeting complete strangers with a "Good Morning" or a "Good Afternoon," followed quickly with "How are you?" It doesn't matter where you are, every conversation has to be started with those all important words—a simple hi won't cut it. Try to get on a bus or buy something in a store without a friendly greeting and see what happens. You have been warned.

Catch Cup Match Fever

On the Thursday and Friday before the first Monday in August, Bermuda takes a two-day holiday ostensibly to watch the Cup Match: an annual cricket game pitting the West End against the East End. Locals clearly take the event seriously. Cup Match fever, for instance, takes hold weeks in advance, when team colors start flying from houses and vehicles islandwide. Cup Match is also an excuse to party. While the players concentrate on whacking a leather ball through a wicket, the spectators focus on food (anyone for mussel pie?), fun fashions, pulsating music, and the 19th-century betting game, Crown and Anchor.

IF YOU LIKE

Life in the Past Lane

You don't have to be here long to realize there's much more to Bermuda than sea, sand, and Rum Swizzles. As one of Britain's oldest colonies, the island has more than 400 years of history and, thanks to thoughtful preservation policies, the architecture to prove it.

The jewel in the crown, in terms of period charm, is the UNESCO-designated **Town of St. George**. As Bermuda's original capital, it has a distinctly colonial feel, and wandering its crooked, cottage-lined lanes is akin to time travel. See the statue of Sir George Somers (who was shipwrecked here in 1609), and view a replica of his vessel before ambling over to King's Square to catch a "ducking stool" reenactment.

The British, keenly aware of Bermuda's strategic significance, kept it well protected from 1612 to 1956—which is why this tiny country has the world's highest concentration of **historic forts**. Start working through the list at the National Museum of Bermuda, a converted fortress that's now the centerpiece of the Royal Naval Dockyard. Fort St. Catherine, a 17th-century edifice, complete with moat and sprawling ramparts, is another must-see.

The **African Diaspora Heritage Trail**, part of the international Slave Route Project, shows that Brits weren't the only ones who helped shape Bermuda. This self-guided tour crisscrosses the island, identifying 11 sites related to black Bermudians. Highlights include the poignant slave graveyard at St. Peter's Church and Cobb's Hill Methodist Church, which was built by and for blacks before Emancipation.

Tee Time

Bermuda is a renowned golfing destination and close enough to the United States and Canada to be pitched as "putting distance" from the Eastern Seaboard. The courses are as scenic as the island itself. But don't let their pretty appearance fool you. Many have holes by the sea or atop ocean-side bluffs, so wind and that big water hazard (the Atlantic!) can play havoc with your game.

Laid out by Charles Blair Macdonald in 1921, the classic course at **The Mid Ocean Club** in Tucker's Town is one of the most spectacular on the island—and one of the most highly regarded in the world. If you can wrangle an introduction from a member (or have your concierge do it on your behalf), you might find yourself on the links with visiting celebrities.

Port Royal Golf Course in Southampton Parish is understandably popular. The affordable public property, fresh from a $14 million makeover, has an impressive pedigree: It's a Robert Trent Jones design and a favorite of Jack Nicklaus. Plus, it boasts Bermuda's most recognizable hole (the sublime 16th), which has been photographed for countless glossy golfing magazines.

You can see why they say, "Good things come in small packages" at the **Fairmont Southampton Resort's Golf Course.** The property's 18-hole, par-3 executive course, designed by Ted Robinson, is on a hillside, and its challenging terrain offers a good warm-up for Bermuda's full-length courses. Better still, playing at Turtle Hill Golf Club for an afternoon won't break your piggy bank.

Just Add Water

Boat-loving Bermudians like to drop anchor, crack open a case of beer, and float the day away—an activity that should not be knocked until it is tried. Yet seeing what lies beneath the turquoise waves can be equally enjoyable. Warm, clear water with visibility up to 150 feet, rich marine life, unique topography, and perhaps most important, reliable outfitters, combine to make Bermuda an ideal place for underwater exploration.

Wreck divers know that not all of Bermuda's history lessons can be learned on dry land. Due to the island's treacherous coral reefs, hundreds of shipwrecks from various eras lie in its waters—and companies like **Dive Bermuda** and **Blue Water Divers** will take you out to see them. Both operate wreck tours for experienced scuba enthusiasts as well as lesson-and-dive packages for first-timers.

Not ready to dive in? Consider taking an underwater walk. **Hartley's Undersea Walk** lets you don a specially designed helmet, then descend about 10 feet for some face time with fish. Although the equipment may look strange, the science is sound (helmets operate on the same principal as a tumbler overturned in water) and the experience is unforgettable.

From April to November all you need are fins and a mask to enjoy the Dockyard's **Snorkel Park Beach.** This sheltered, easy-to-access inlet features exotic sea creatures, submerged artifacts (such as centuries-old cannons), and even floating rest stations. You can rent snorkel gear—along with an assortment of other equipment, including kayaks, pedalos (paddleboats), and Jet Skis—at the site.

Suite Dreams

The island is dotted with one-of-a-kind accommodations, where luxury lodgings are interspersed with posh family-run resorts, old-school cottage colonies, and quaint, sometimes quirky, bed-and-breakfasts. Many properties received renovations, or at least a little lipstick, powder, and paint to host the 2017 America's Cup.

Gracefully perched on Bermuda's south shore, **The Loren at Pink Beach** is the newest and chicest addition to the island's hotel scene. Splurge-worthy suites and villas feature private balconies or terraces, with sweeping ocean views and tasteful modern decor. Lose yourself in the beauty of the turquoise waters from the comfort of the spa's relaxation room, the sleek, spacious sundeck, or the jaw-dropping infinity pool.

The **Hamilton Princess Hotel & Beach Club** completed a three-year, $100 million overhaul, which updated and expanded rooms (some with balconies overlooking the harbor), added the new Exhale spa, a new marina, two additional restaurants, an infinity pool, upscale shopping options, and a collection of art, including works by Banksy and Damien Hirst.

Fourways Inn in Paget offers the convenience of a centrally located hotel with the charm of a cottage colony. Guests in these deluxe accommodations are treated to the seclusion of a tranquil garden and the impeccable hospitality one would expect in old-world Bermuda. A lavish Sunday brunch, set in its 18th-century main dining area, has been attracting generations of adoring patrons for as long as anyone can remember.

GREAT ITINERARIES

BUMMING AROUND BERMUDA: SEA, SAND, AND SIGHTS

Day 1: Horseshoe Bay

Chances are you came for that legendary pink sand, so don't waste any time finding it. Spend the day bouncing from beach to beautiful beach along the south shore (the No. 7 bus will get you there and back from the city of Hamilton), or just choose one and settle in. Our pick is the flagship beach at **Horseshoe Bay**: a gently curving crescent lapped by turquoise water and backed by South Shore Park. It does get crowded here—but for good reason. Unlike most Bermudian beaches, Horseshoe Bay has lifeguards (in season), changing rooms, and on-site food, drink, and beach-gear rentals available at **Rum Bum Beach Bar**. There's also a protected inlet, dubbed Horseshoe Baby Beach, which is perfect for young children. Looking for something more private? Picturesque trails through the park will lead you to secluded coves like Stonehole and Chaplin bays. When the sun goes down—and you have sand in every crevice—stroll over to the lively **Henry VIII pub and restaurant** for an evening bite.

Day 2: The Town of St. George

Founded in 1612, **St. George's** qualifies as one of the oldest towns in the Western Hemisphere and deserves a place on any traveler's itinerary. This UNESCO World Heritage site has a smattering of worthwhile museums including the Bermuda National Trust Museum at the Globe Hotel and Tucker House. Historic buildings such as St. Peter's Church also should not be missed. Organized walks and road train tours cover the highlights. Yet the real delight here is simply wandering the walled lanes and quaint alleys lined with traditional shops, pubs, and cottages. All those roads eventually lead to **King's Square,** where you can try out the replica stocks. Nearby is another device formerly used to punish unruly folk—the seesaw-like ducking stool—which serves as the focal point for reenactments starring the Town Crier and a wet wench. (These are staged at 12:30 May through October, Monday through Thursday and Saturday; other months on Wednesday and Saturday only.) If you have time, continue your history lesson outside St. George's at **Fort St. Catherine,** a hilltop defense built in the 17th century. Stop for a swim just below it in snug **Achilles Bay** or at **Fort St. Catherine Beach**; then cap the day back in town with a meal at the **White Horse Tavern** on the water's edge.

Day 3: The City of Hamilton

Since there's a little bit of everything here, you can plot a course according to your individual tastes. Shoppers should make a beeline for the **Front Street** area to spend a few hours in the stores and galleries. Prefer sightseeing? Pick up a brochure for a self-guided tour at the Visitor Information Centre (VIC). Outside the city, visit **Fort Hamilton**: a must for history buffs and a great spot for photo ops. Alternatively, you can investigate sunken treasure and seashells without ever getting wet at the **Bermuda Underwater Exploration Institute** (about a 15-minute walk from the city center), or get out on the water itself. Excursion options from Hamilton range from archipelago tours and glass-bottom-boat trips to low-cost ferry rides. Afterward, gear up to see Hamilton by night. Pubs and clubs start filling around 10 pm, leaving plenty of time for dinner at one of the area's surprisingly diverse restaurants.

Day 4: The Dockyard

Once a military stronghold and now a magnet for tourists, the **Royal Naval Dockyard** offers a full day of history with a side of shopping and adventure. Its centerpiece is the **Bermuda Maritime Museum**, where you can find exhibits on whaling, sailing, shipbuilding, and shipwrecks set within an imposing stone fortress. Once you've taken in the stunning views from the ramparts, head to the **Old Cooperage**. This former barrel-making factory is the perfect place to stock up on unique souvenirs, because it houses both the Bermuda Craft Market (perhaps the island's best-stocked, best-priced craft outlet) and the Bermuda Arts Centre (a high-end co-op with gallery and studio space). After lunch in an area eatery, join one of the educational in-water programs offered by **Dolphin Quest** at the Keep Pond, or swim right next door at the inexpensive **Snorkel Park Beach**. Spring through fall, adrenaline junkies can Jet Ski with H2O Sports. For a more placid on-the-water experience, take the slow, scenic ferry to Somerset Island and disembark at **Watford Bridge**. From there, explore quiet Somerset Village before sitting down for dinner at the **Somerset Country Squire**, a traditional tavern overlooking Mangrove Bay.

Day 5: Go Green

While dedicated duffers spend at least one day putting the island's top greens, neophytes can get into the swing of things at the **Bermuda Golf Academy**. Other essential "greens" include the **Botanical Gardens** and **Paget Marsh Nature Reserve**, both near the city of Hamilton. The former is a Victorian venue with formal flowerbeds and subtropical fruit orchards; the latter a 25-acre tract that covers five distinct ecosystems (including primeval woodlands that contain the last surviving stands of native palmetto and cedar). From November to May, **Spittal Pond**, on Bermuda's south shore, is a major draw for bird-watchers, thanks to the 30-odd species of waterfowl that stop here; in April it attracts whale-watchers hoping to spy migrating humpbacks from the preserve's oceanfront cliffs. You can access more "undiscovered" spots by traversing all or part of the **Bermuda Railway Trail**. With its lush greenery and dramatic lookouts, this 18-mile recreational route is best seen on foot or by pedal bike. If you like packaged excursions, **Fantasea Bermuda** has a surf-and-turf deal that combines a shoreline cruise with a guided cycle tour along the trail, and a cool-down swim at a Somerset beach.

ON THE CALENDAR

Bermuda is a year-round destination with an active events calendar, so we've highlighted the top annual offerings. For more options, consult **The Bermuda Tourism Authority** (☎ *800/237–6832* ⊕ *www.gotobermuda.com*). Local publications like the free, widely distributed tourist magazine **The Bermuda.com Guide** provide a monthly overview, while the island's newspaper, the **Royal Gazette** (⊕ *www.royalgazette. com*) typically highlights upcoming events in print and online. Further info can be found at ⊕ *www.bermuda.com*, ⊕ *www.bernews.com*, and ⊕ *Bermynet.com*.

WINTER

December

Bermuda Goodwill Tournament. Foursomes made up of professional and amateur golfers swing into action during the Bermuda Goodwill Tournament. First held in 1922, it's the world's oldest pro-am competition, and spectators are invited to watch the event for free. ☎ *441/295–4640* ⊕ *www.bermudagoodwillgolf.bm*.

Christmas Boat Parade. Every other year the Christmas Boat Parade sees decorated vessels of every size and description float through Hamilton Harbour. The event, which can draw 20,000 spectators, usually takes place on the second Saturday of December and is topped off by fireworks. The event will take place in 2019 and following odd years.

Santa Claus Parade. Father Christmas visits Front Street in the Santa Claus Parade, usually held the last week of November. The energy level is high as Santa cruises through Hamilton, accompanied by marching bands, majorettes, Bermuda Gombeys, and floats.

Annual Christmas Walkabout in St. George's. The Annual Christmas Walkabout in St. George's is an early-evening event hosted by the Bermuda National Trust. Properties specially decked out for the holiday season open their doors to the public. Choir concerts, Christmas-theme readings, and eggnog sipping are also on the agenda. ☎ *441/236– 6483* ⊕ *www.bnt.bm*.

Boxing Day. Following Commonwealth tradition, Bermuda makes December 26 a public holiday: Boxing Day. Pugilists need not apply, but many other sporting activities—like harness racing and motocross competitions—are scheduled, and Gombey troupes mark the day by dancing in the streets.

January	**Bermuda Festival of the Performing Arts.** For more than 40 years the Bermuda Festival of the Performing Arts, the largest of its kind on the island, has featured international artistes. Plays, ballets, chamber orchestras, and jazz jams are staged over two months at the City Hall Theatre (now named The Earl Cameron Theatre) and other venues. Lunchtime concerts, book readings, and crafts workshops are also not to be missed. ☎ *441/295–1291* ⊕ *www.bermudafestival.org.*
	Bermuda International Race Weekend. On your mark! Bermuda International Race Weekend kicks off the third weekend of the month. The event begins Friday night with the Front Street Mile. It also includes a marathon, half marathon, and a 10k (6.2-mile) charity walk. Top runners participate, but most races are open to all. ☎ *441/296–0951* ⊕ *www.bermudaraceweekend.com.*
	Bermuda Regional Bridge Tournament. The almost-60-year-old Bermuda Regional Bridge Tournament attracts more than 400 players from both home and abroad. Sanctioned by the American Contract Bridge League, the round-robins are an elegant, exciting, and unique event hosted at the Fairmont Southampton Resort the last week of January. ⊕ *www.bermudaregional.com..*

SPRING

March and April	**Bermuda Men's and Ladies' Match Play Championships.** The island golf association swings into gear with the Bermuda Men's and Ladies' Match Play Championships. Both are played at the exclusive Mid Ocean Club in Tucker's Town. ☎ *441/295–9972* ⊕ *www.bermudagolf.org.*
	The Agricultural Exhibition. Much like a state fair, Bermuda's Agricultural Exhibition fosters a fun, educational environment with a variety of livestock competitions, horticultural displays, and homemade, farm-fresh food contests. This three-day event at the Botanical Gardens typically runs the third weekend in April and is great for kids. ☎ *441/524–7469* ⊕ *www.theagshowbda.com.*
April	**Bermuda International Film Festival.** This prestigious festival shows dozens of independent feature, documentary, and short films from around the world, awarding prizes in various categories. In addition to seven days of screenings,

you can expect panel discussions, parties, and popcorn. ☏ *441/293–3456* ⊕ *www.biff.bm.*

Peppercorn Ceremony. Members of St. George's Masonic Lodge pay their rent on the Old State House with great pomp and circumstance during the Peppercorn Ceremony. A single peppercorn is solemnly passed over to the mayor in a stylish (if somewhat surreal) display that includes a march by the Bermuda Regiment. ☏ *441/297–1532.*

May — **Bermuda Heritage Month.** May is Bermuda Heritage Month, when a host of commemorative, cultural, and sporting activities are scheduled. The climax is Bermuda Day (May 24), a public holiday that includes a parade around Hamilton, a cycling race, and dinghy races in St. George's Harbour. Traditionally, this is also the first day that locals swim, swearing the water is too cold earlier in the year—though most visitors don't seem to mind. ☏ *441/292–1681.*

Open Houses & Gardens Event. Prepare to go green with envy. Tuesday afternoons in May and June, the Garden Club of Bermuda leads to-die-for tours through private properties during its yearly Open Houses & Gardens Event. These walkabouts offer a rare glimpse into unique architectural and horticultural landmarks at the peak of the island's growing season. ☏ *441/292–4086* ⊕ *www.gardenclubbermuda.org.*

SUMMER

June — **Newport–Bermuda Race.** Seasoned yachtsmen chart a challenging 635-mile course from Rhode Island to St. David's Lighthouse during the biennial Newport Bermuda Race. One of the sailing world's preeminent blue-water events, it's held mid-June in even-numbered years and is hosted by the Royal Bermuda Yacht Club. ☏ *441/295–2214* ⊕ *www.bermudarace.com.*

Annapolis Bermuda Ocean Race. First held in 1979, the 753-mile Annapolis Bermuda Ocean Race sets sail in even-numbered years. Hosted by the Royal Hamilton Amateur Dinghy Club, it attracts competitors from all over the world. ⊕ *www.bermudaoceanrace.com.*

Harbour Nights. Harbour Nights, a street festival featuring Bermudian artists, crafts, Gombey dancers, face painting, and the like, takes place every Wednesday night in summer

	on Front, Queen, and Reid Streets in the city of Hamilton. The newly expanded carnival encompasses a larger area in downtown Hamilton and features live entertainers and rides for the kids.
July	**Bermuda Triple Crown.** The island keeps reeling in top-notch anglers with the back-to-back billfish tournaments that make up the Bermuda Triple Crown. First up is the Bermuda Billfish Blast, followed by the Bermuda Big Game Classic, and the Sea Horse Anglers Club Billfish Tournament. As if we needed an excuse to get salty! ☎ *407/571–4680* ⊕ *www.bermudatriplecrown.com.*
July and August	**Cup Match Cricket Festival.** The Cup Match Cricket Festival is a spirited two-day celebration centered on the match between rival Somerset and St. George's cricket clubs. (Locals sport red and navy if they're Somerset fans, dark blue and light blue if they're St. George's fans.) The highlight of Bermuda's events calendar, it's scheduled for the Thursday and Friday before the first Monday in August, in conjunction with two public holidays: Emancipation Day and Somers Day. ☎ *441/234–0327, 441/297–0374.*
August	**Non-Mariners Race.** The very popular Non-Mariners Race is as memorable as it is nonsensical. On the first Sunday after Cup Match, landlubbers hastily cobble together "non-boats" on the beach using cardboard, barrels, and anything else they can get their hands on, then attempt to race them in Mangrove Bay. No paddles, oars, engines, or sails are permitted, and contraptions that manage to float far are disqualified. ☎ *441/234–2248.*
FALL	
September	**International Sand Sculpture Competition.** Bermuda's fine pink sand is put to good use during Horseshoe Bay's one-day International Sand Sculpture Competition, typically held on the Saturday before Labour Day. Teams of up to six people are encouraged to get creative and build the craziest sculptures possible on a 15-by-15-foot patch of beach. Prizes are awarded in seven categories, including Families, Professionals, and Tourists. ☎ *441/505–7822.*
	Bank of Bermuda Foundation Triathlon Race Series. Triathletes cap their calendar with the Bank of Bermuda Foundation Triathlon Race Series. Entrants in the team event swim,

	bike, and run around the historic city of St. George's on the last Sunday in October—expect great fanfare and excitement from spectators! ⊕ *www.bermudatriathlon.com.*
October	**Argo Group Gold Cup.** The weeklong Argo Group Gold Cup sees match-race skippers (America's Cup competitors among them) vie for the titular trophy and a $100,000 purse. Races are in Hamilton Harbour, and the Royal Bermuda Yacht Club opens its doors for the event, making this one especially appealing to spectators. ☎ *441/295–2214* ⊕ *www.argogroupgoldcup.com.*
November	**Reconvening of Parliament.** On the first Friday in November, the Reconvening of Parliament kicks off when the governor, in full regalia, arrives at Hamilton's Cabinet Building in a horse-drawn landau. His Speech from the Throne (detailing new policies and initiatives) usually begins around 11 am, so arrive by 10:15 to secure a good spot. ☎ *441/292–7408* ⊕ *www.parliament.bm.* **World Rugby Classic.** During the World Rugby Classic, former international players from around the globe again represent their respective countries in matches at the National Sports Centre in Devonshire Parish. Afterward, fans can mix with the players in a "tavern tent" behind the touchline. ☎ *441/295–6574* ⊕ *www.worldrugby.bm.*

BERMUDA WITH KIDS

What to See and Do

Bermuda is generally seen as a destination for honeymooners and baby boomers, but it's also a great place for families, with plenty of kid-friendly attractions.

The **Bermuda Aquarium, Museum & Zoo** tops many family itineraries thanks to cute critters and engaging displays that include walk-through enclosures, super-size fish tanks, a tidal touch pool, and a glass-enclosed beehive. BAMZ also offers thrice-daily seal feedings and docent-led weekend activities that are equal parts entertainment and education, plus a fun outdoor play area where little ones can make discoveries at their own pace.

You can introduce your offspring to still more animals at the **Dockyard's Maritime Museum.** Goats graze on the upper grounds (their job is to keep the grass well mowed), and bottlenose dolphins interact with participants in the various Dolphin Quest programs. Marine life awaits next door, too, at the affordable **Snorkel Park.**

Though they're not as tourist oriented, Bermuda's other fortresses attract youngsters as well. **Fort St. Catherine**'s 17th-century ramparts and spooky underground passages set the perfect stage for playing make-believe. There are also some cool bonus features (among them an arsenal of antique weapons and replica crown jewels) that can help keep the gang entertained on those rare rainy days.

Elsewhere, families can go underground at **Crystal Caves,** where guides point out formations that look like familiar skylines and spacecraft; or go underwater at the **Bermuda Underwater Exploration Institute,** where you can experience deep-sea diving in a simulator pod. The upwardly mobile, meanwhile, can climb 185 steps to the top of **Gibbs Hill Lighthouse,** the highest spot in Bermuda.

The **Bermuda National Gallery** is surprisingly family friendly as well. It runs a number of special programs aimed directly at youngsters and provides drawing stations where they can create their own masterpieces.

Where to Eat and Stay

Kids will have to forgo their favorite fast food on Bermuda because the island is essentially a franchise-free zone; however, there are a number of family-friendly options. ⇨ *For a few of our favorites, see the Best Bets for Kids feature box in Chapter 3, Where to Eat.*

There are a few select hotels, among them the **Fairmont Southampton, Elbow Beach,** and **Grotto Bay,** which go the extra mile for families. The Fairmont Southampton has kid-friendly menus and a real year-round kids' club with activities scheduled each day. Elbow Beach has less impressive kids' activities, but it too offers a kids' club. Grotto Bay has facilities designed for families with small children. The enclosed bay, fish-feeding aquarium, two underground caves with supervised exploring, and the kiddie pool beside the larger pool put parents at ease when their children hit the water. **Pompano Beach Club** has an arcade room, table games, and a kids' pool.

Smaller properties (with smaller price tags) are also excellent choices for families with children. Try **Clairfont Apartments,** which offers one bedrooms close to the south-shore beaches and a three-minute walk from a large playground.

WEDDINGS AND HONEYMOONS

Bermuda is a popular wedding destination because of its secluded pink beaches, easy access from the United States, well-established infrastructure, which includes English-speaking wedding personnel, and its remarkably high romance quotient (the island even has an honest-to-goodness Lovers' Lane).

The Big Day

There's a whole host of wedding planners ready and willing to do the hard work for you.

Bermuda Bride. Nikki Begg is internationally renowned for delivering breathtaking Bermuda destination weddings. ☎ 441/295–8697 ⊕ www.bermudabride.com.

The Bridal Suite Bermuda. The knowledgeable wedding consultants at The Bridal Suite Bermuda will work tirelessly to create the most unforgettable day of your life. ☎ 441/292–2025 ⊕ www.bridalsuitebermudaweddings.com.

Most larger resorts have their own wedding planners.

License. Couples must complete and send a Notice of Intended Marriage form to the **Bermuda Registry General** (☎ 441/297–7709 ⊕ www.registrygeneral.gov.bm) within three months of their intended wedding date. A fee of $338 must accompany the form. The notice is then published in the local newspaper. There is a waiting period of 15 days, and if no formal objection is raised, the license will be issued. The license to marry is valid for three months from the date of issue.

The Perfect Backdrop. The obvious choice for a Bermuda destination wedding is right on the beach. Another popular choice is the sunset cliff-top ceremony looking down over the turquoise water. Many hotels will set up gazebos on their beaches or in their gardens. You can also go for the more unusual grounds of historic properties like the World Heritage Centre in St. George's or Fort Hamilton overlooking the capital city.

Local Customs. Bermudians serve two wedding cakes; the groom's cake is plain, often a pound cake, and the multitier bride's cake is a dark fruitcake. Another tradition is for the bride and groom to walk hand in hand beneath a Bermuda moongate—an archway made of limestone and coral usually found at the entrance to gardens. It's said that all who do so are assured everlasting luck.

The Honeymoon

Many resorts offer honeymoon suites and special packages for newlyweds. Here are our top picks.

Cambridge Beaches Resort & Spa. Sunsets, candlelit dinners, and beautiful scenery are all at this adults-only resort, which offers the ultimate pampering experience.

Elbow Beach Resort. This cottage colony set in lush gardens welcomes its honeymooners with a bottle of bubbly. There are beautiful beachfront cottages, and the spa has couples' treatment rooms.

The Loren at Pink Beach. With 45 oceanfront suites set on 8 coastal acres, an escape does not get much more private or luxe than at the island's newest hotel. Book a couples' spa treatment set in rooms overlooking the Atlantic.

The Reefs Resort & Club. This cliff-side luxury resort has breathtaking views. You'll get champagne and chocolate-covered strawberries on your arrival, and you can book a gourmet dinner right on the beach.

EXPLORING
BERMUDA

Visit Fodors.com for advice, updates, and bookings

Updated
by Robyn
Bardgett

Bermuda is justifiably famous for pink-sand beaches, impossibly blue water, and kelly-green golf courses. But that's only the beginning. Thanks to its colorful past, this small sliver of land also has a surprising number of historic sites. In addition to countless quaint old cottages, it's said to have the oldest continually inhabited town of English origin in the Western Hemisphere and—because of its strategic Atlantic location—more forts per square mile than any other place on earth.

Bermuda has a distinctive culture, too: one that combines a reverence for British traditions dating back to colonial days with a more relaxed attitude befitting a subtropical island. You'll most likely see the British influences within the government, legal, and educational systems. In court, for instance, local lawyers may still wear formal flowing robes—yet there's a good chance that they're sporting Bermuda shorts beneath them. You'll also see "bobbies" (policemen) directing traffic, red telephone boxes and postboxes, and hear lots of cricket talk, as it's the island's national sport.

African and Caribbean influences are more subtle, but they can be spotted through the music and dance of calypso and reggae. Look out for the island's Gombey dancers; they may only look like colorful characters wildly jumping up and down, but they actually have a history embedded in African tribal music.

There is certainly no shortage of things to see in Bermuda. St. George's or the Town of St. George, at the island's East End, is the original 1600s settlement and a UNESCO World Heritage site. It has streets full of well-preserved history, as well as a whole host of Bermuda National Trust properties. The city of Hamilton (not to be confused with the parish of the same name farther northeast) is home to Bermuda's principal harbor and most of its shops. It's also the main departure point for sightseeing boats, ferries, and the pink-and-blue buses that ramble all over the island. The Royal Naval Dockyard, at the West End, is a former British shipyard that has been transformed into a stunning tourist attraction. Spend a day there shopping or museum- and art-gallery-hopping.

All three main neighborhoods can be explored easily on foot. The rest of the island, however, is best discovered by taxi, motor scooter, or even bicycle—but only if you're fit, because Bermuda is hilly! Two-person electric rental cars—Renault Twizys—from Current Vehicles (⊕ *www. currentvehicles.com*) are the island's newest form of transportation and a much safer option than mopeds. Less than 4 feet wide, these mini electric cars are the perfect size for Bermuda's narrow roads.

HAMILTON AND CENTRAL PARISHES

With a permanent resident population of 1,500 households, Hamilton doesn't qualify as a major metropolis. Yet it has enough stores, restaurants, and offices to amp up the island's energy level. Moreover, it has a thriving international business community (centered on financial and investment services, insurance, telecommunications, global management of intellectual property, shipping, and aircraft and ship registration), which lends it a degree of sophistication seldom found in so small a center.

The central parishes cover the large area of Paget, Warwick, and Devonshire. These parishes are much sleepier than Hamilton and provide great nature and beach respites when you tire of city life. Convenient buses and ferries connect the parishes, so trips outside Hamilton are easy and a fun way to get off the tourist track.

TIMING

Although it's possible to buzz through Hamilton in a few hours, you should plan to give it a day if you're going to take in some of the museums, Fort Hamilton, and the Bermuda Underwater Exploration Institute. Serious shoppers should set aside another half day to browse around the shops. Set aside one day for some of the nature sites in the central parishes, and another day if you want to relax at the beaches.

TOP ATTRACTIONS

Bermuda National Gallery. Housed on the second floor in the City Hall & Arts Centre, in the East Exhibition Room, the Bermuda National Gallery is home to Bermuda's national art collection. The permanent exhibits include paintings by island artists as well as European masters like Gainsborough and Reynolds; African masks and sculpture; and photographs by internationally known artists, such as Bermudian Richard Saunders (1922–87). The fine and decorative art pieces in the Bermuda Collection reflect the country's multicultural heritage. Temporary exhibits are also a major part of the museum's program, and on any given day you can see a selection of local work along with a traveling exhibit from another museum. For a comprehensive look at the collections, join one of the free docent-led tours offered Thursday at 10:30 (private ones can be arranged on request). Lectures and other special programs are listed in the gallery's online calendar. Parents should note that some of these are targeted specifically at children and there is an interactive education space at the gallery entrance. ⊠ *City Hall & Arts Centre, 17 Church St., 2nd fl., Hamilton* ☎ *441/295–9428* ⊕ *www.bng. bm* ⊠ *$5* ☉ *Closed Sun.*

Bermuda Society of Arts Gallery. On the upper floor of City Hall & Arts Centre, in the West Wing, the Bermuda Society of Arts Gallery displays work by its members. Its frequently changing juried shows attract talented local painters, sculptors, and photographers. Art collectors will be pleased to learn that many pieces may also be purchased. ⊠ *City Hall & Arts Centre, 17 Church St., Hamilton* ☎ *441/292–3824* ⊕ *www.bsoa. bm* ⊠ *Free* ☉ *Closed Sun.*

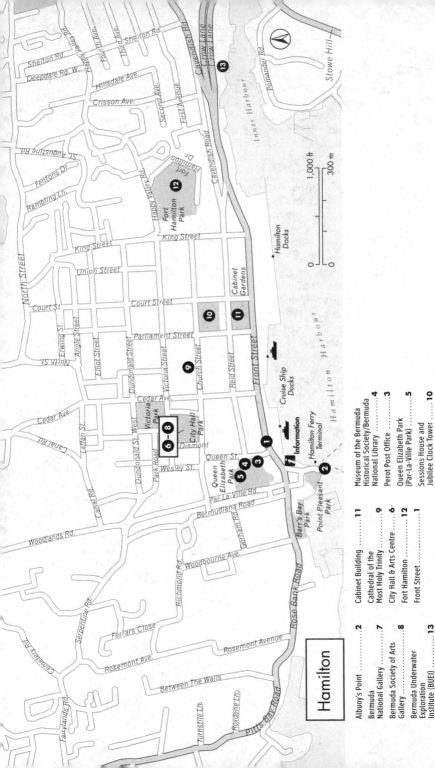

Hamilton

Albuoy's Point 2

Bermuda
National Gallery 7

Bermuda Society of Arts
Gallery 8

Bermuda Underwater
Exploration
Institute (BUEI) 13

Cabinet Building 11

Cathedral of the
Most Holy Trinity 9

City Hall & Arts Centre ... 6

Fort Hamilton 12

Front Street 1

Museum of the Bermuda
Historical Society/Bermuda
National Library 4

Perot Post Office 3

Queen Elizabeth Park
(Par-La-Ville Park) 5

Sessions House and
Jubilee Clock Tower 10

A GOOD WALK IN HAMILTON

Any tour of Hamilton should begin on **Front Street,** a tidy thoroughfare lined with ice cream–color buildings, many with cheery awnings and ornate balconies. The Visitor Information Centre next to the Ferry Terminal at No. 8 Front Street is a good starting point. Continue west and swing down Point Pleasant Road to **Albuoy's Point** for a splendid view of Hamilton Harbour. Afterward, retrace your steps, passing the Ferry Terminal Building where passengers board boats for sightseeing excursions. (You can also depart from here on more affordable round-trip rides to the Dockyard and St. George's via the Sea Express ferry.) Stroll toward the intersection of Front and Queen Streets, where you can see the Birdcage, a much-photographed traffic box named for its designer, Michael "Dickey" Bird.

Turn up Queen Street to see the 19th-century **Perot Post Office.** Just beyond it is the **Museum of the Bermuda Historical Society/ Bermuda National Library.** Follow Queen Street away from the harbor to Church Street to reach the **City Hall & Arts Centre,** which houses the Bermuda National Gallery, the

Bermuda Society of Arts Gallery, and a performing arts venue.

At the City Hall steps, turn east on Church Street and pass the Hamilton Bus Terminal. One block farther, the imposing **Cathedral of the Most Holy Trinity** looms up before you. Next, past the cathedral near the corner of Church and Parliament Streets, you'll come to **Sessions House.** Keep going down Parliament to Front Street for a look at the **Cabinet Building** and, in front of it, the Cenotaph for fallen Bermudian soldiers. From here you might head back to Front Street for a leisurely stroll past (or into) the shops, then linger over lunch in one of the many cafés overlooking the harbor.

If you're up for a longer walk (about 15 minutes east from the Cenotaph) or are traveling by scooter or taxi, head to the **Bermuda Underwater Exploration Institute (BUEI). Fort Hamilton** is another worthwhile destination, though the road to it— north on King Street, then a sharp right on Happy Valley Road—is a bit too steep for casual walkers. The moated fort has gorgeous grounds, underground passageways, and great views of Hamilton and its harbor.

FAMILY **Bermuda Underwater Exploration Institute (BUEI).** The 40,000-square-foot Ocean Discovery Centre showcases local contributions to oceanographic research and undersea discovery. Highlights include the world-class shell collection amassed by resident Jack Lightbourn (three of the 1,000 species were identified by and named for Lightbourn himself) and a gallery honoring native-born archaeologist Teddy Tucker featuring booty retrieved from Bermudian shipwrecks. The equipment that made such discoveries possible are also displayed, including a replica of the bathysphere William Beebe and Otis Barton used in their record-smashing 1934 dive. (Forget the Bermuda Triangle: the real mystery is how they descended a half mile in a metal ball less than 5 feet in diameter!) A more modern "submersible," Nautilus-X2, lets wannabe explorers take a simulated seven-minute trip to the ocean floor. Special events, like lectures, glowworm cruises, and whale-watching trips, are available, too, for an added fee. The on-site Harbourfront restaurant is a lovely choice for lunch. ■TIP➜ **Pedestrians may access the facility by following the sidewalk on the water side of Front Street. Motorists must drive out of town on Front Street, round the traffic circle, and exit at the lane signposted for the BUEI, because it's only accessible to inbound vehicles.** ✉ *40 Crow La., Hamilton* ⚓ *Off E. Broadway* ☎ *441/292–7219* ⊕ *www.buei.bm* 🎟 *$15.*

Cathedral of the Most Holy Trinity. After the original Anglican sanctuary on this site was torched by an arsonist in 1884, Scottish architect William Hay was enlisted to design a replacement. True to his training, he set out to erect a Gothic-style structure in the grand European tradition. Mission accomplished. Inside, the clerestory in the nave is supported by piers of polished Scottish granite; soaring archways are trimmed in stone imported from France; and the choir stalls and bishop's throne are carved out of English oak. The pulpit, meanwhile, is modeled on the one in Hay's hometown cathedral (St. Giles in Edinburgh), and the whole thing is crowned by a copper roof that stands out among Bermuda's typical white-topped buildings. Yet for all the European flourishes, Bermuda Cathedral still has a subtropical flair. After all, the limestone building blocks came from the Par-la-Ville quarry and one of its loveliest stained-glass windows—the Angel Window on the east wall of the north transept—was created by local artist Vivienne Gilmore Gardner. ■TIP➜ **After sauntering around the interior, you can climb the 155 steps of the church tower for a heavenly view of Hamilton and its harbor.** ✉ *29 Church St., Hamilton* ☎ *441/292–4033* ⊕ *www.anglican. bm* 🎟 *Cathedral free; tower $3.*

City Hall & Arts Centre. Set back from the street, City Hall contains Hamilton's administrative offices as well as two art galleries and a performance hall. Instead of a clock, its tower is topped with a bronze wind vane—a prudent choice in a land where the weather is as important as the time. The building itself was designed in 1960 by Bermudian architect Wilfred Onions, a champion of balanced simplicity. Massive cedar doors open onto an impressive lobby notable for its beautiful chandeliers and portraits of mayors past and present. To the left is The Earl Cameron Theatre, a major venue for concerts, plays, and dance performances. To the right are the civic offices. A handsome cedar staircase leads upstairs to two upper-floor art galleries. (An elevator gets you there, too.) ✉ *17 Church St., Hamilton* ☎ *441/292–1234* ⊕ *www.cityhall.bm.*

FAMILY
Fodor's Choice
★

Crystal and Fantasy Caves. As far back as 1623, Captain John Smith (of Pocahontas fame) commented on these "vary strange, darke, and cumbersome" caverns. Nevertheless, it came as a surprise when two boys, attempting to retrieve a lost ball, discovered Crystal Cave in 1907. The hole through which the boys descended is still visible. But, thankfully, you can now view their find without having to make such a dramatic entrance. Inside, tour guides will lead you across a pontoon bridge that spans a 55-foot-deep subterranean lake. Look up to see stalactites dripping from the ceiling or down through the perfectly clear water to see stalagmites rising from the cave floor. Amateur spelunkers can also journey through geologic time at Crystal's smaller sister cave,

Fantasy. After being closed to the public for decades, it reopened in 2001. Set aside 30 minutes to see one cave; 75 minutes if you plan to take in both. ⊠ *8 Crystal Caves Rd., Hamilton ✛ Off Wilkinson Ave., Bailey's Bay* ☎ *441/293–0640* ⊕ *www.caves.bm* ✉ *One cave $22; combination ticket $30.*

NEED A BREAK

Swizzle Inn. If the beauty of Crystal Caves doesn't leave you reeling, a rum swizzle certainly will. Bermuda's potent national drink was supposedly invented at the Swizzle Inn, about five minutes on foot from the caves. ⊠ *3 Blue Hole Hill, Hamilton* ☎ *441/293–1854.*

FAMILY **Fort Hamilton.** This imposing moat-ringed fortress has underground passageways that were cut through solid rock by Royal Engineers in the 1860s. Built to defend the West End's Royal Naval Dockyard from land attacks, it was outdated even before its completion, but remains a fine example of a polygonal Victorian fort. Even if you're not a big fan of military history, the hilltop site's stellar views and stunning gardens make the trip worthwhile. On Monday at noon, from November to March, bagpipes echo through the grounds as the kilt-clad members of the Bermuda Islands Pipe Band perform a traditional skirling ceremony. ■**TIP➔ Due to one-way streets, getting to the fort by scooter can be a bit challenging. From downtown Hamilton head north on Queen Street, turn right on Church Street, then turn left to go up the hill on King Street. Make a sharp (270-degree) right turn onto Happy Valley Road and follow the signs. Pedestrians may walk along Front Street to King Street.** ⊠ *Happy Valley Rd., Hamilton* ☎ *441/292–1234* ✉ *Free.*

Fodor's Choice **Masterworks Museum of Bermuda Art.** Behind Camden House sits the
★ island's first purpose-built state-of-the-art museum: the Masterworks Museum of Bermuda Art. Like its former incarnation (the Masterworks Foundation), the venue's theme is "Bermuda through the Eyes of Artists," and the soaring main gallery is devoted to island-inspired works by internationally renowned figures such as Georgia O'Keeffe, Andrew Wyeth, and Winslow Homer. Two other galleries display (and sell) paintings by native-born artists. ⊠ *Botanical Gardens, 183 South Rd.* ☎ *441/299–4000* ⊕ *www.bermudamasterworks.org* ✉ *$5.*

Museum of the Bermuda Historical Society/Bermuda National Library. Mark Twain admired the giant rubber tree that stands on Queen Street in the front yard of this Georgian house, formerly owned by postmaster William Bennett Perot and his family. Though charmed by the tree, which had been imported from what is now Guyana in the mid-19th century, Twain lamented that it didn't bear rubbery fruit in the form of overshoes and hot-water bottles. The library, about which he made no tongue-in-cheek comment, was established in 1839, and its reference section has virtually every book ever written about Bermuda, as well as a microfilm collection of Bermudian newspapers dating back to 1784.

To the left of the library entrance is the Historical Society's museum. The collection is eclectic, chronicling the island's past through interesting—and in some cases downright quirky—artifacts. One display, for instance, is full of Bermudian silver dating from the 1600s; another focuses on tools and trinkets made by Boer War prisoners who were exiled here in 1901 and 1902. Check out the portraits of Sir George Somers and his wife, painted around 1605, and of William Perot and his wife that hang in the entrance hall. The museum offers limited-edition prints ($60) from its vast photographic archives. You can also pick up a free copy of the letter George Washington wrote in 1775; addressed to the inhabitants of Bermuda, it requests gunpowder for use in the American Revolution. ⊠ *13 Queen St., Hamilton* ✛ *Opposite Reid St.* ☎ *441/299–0029 library, 441/295–2487 museum* ⊕ *www.bnl.bm* ⌨ *Free* ⊗ *Closed Sun.* ☞ *Tours by appointment.*

NEED A BREAK

Bailey's Ice Cream. If you've got kids in tow—or are driving a scooter—you may want to skip the rum and stick to Bailey's—Bailey's Ice Cream, that is. The popular parlor, directly across from the Swizzle Inn, dishes up some two dozen flavors of homemade all-natural ice creams, plus low-fat frozen yogurts and fat-free sorbets. ■ TIP→ This store accepts cash only. ⊠ *2 Blue Hole Hill, Bailey's Bay, Hamilton* ☎ *441/293–8605.*

WORTH NOTING

Albuoy's Point. For a ringside seat to the show of sailboats and passenger ferries zigzagging around the many islands that dot Hamilton Harbour, grab a bench beneath the trees at Albuoy's Point, a small waterside park. Nearby is the Royal Bermuda Yacht Club, founded in 1844 and granted the use of the term *Royal* by Prince Albert in 1845. Today luminaries from the international sailing scene hobnob with local yachtsmen and business executives at the club's 1930s headquarters. If you're around between April and November, you might even catch one of the many club-sponsored racing events. ⊠ *Hamilton* ✛ *Off Front St.*

Bermuda Farmers' Market. One of the best places to mingle with Onions and, yes, buy a few edible ones is the Bermuda Farmers' Market held every Saturday from 8 to noon, mid-November through June. It features up to 30 vendors who sell only Bermuda-grown, -caught, or -made products. Along with organic produce and assorted home-baked items, goodies like handcrafted soaps and honey derived from the pollen of island wildflowers are for sale. ✛ *At the Botanical Gardens inside the Jack King bldg.* ☎ *441/333–6198.*

Botanical Gardens. Established in 1898, the Botanical Gardens are filled with exotic subtropical plants, flowers, and trees. The 36-acre property features a miniature forest, an aviary, a hibiscus garden with more than 150 species, and collections of orchids, cacti, fruits, and ferns. In addition to these must-see sights is an intriguing must-smell one: the Garden for the Sightless. Designed primarily for the blind, it has fragrant plants (like geranium, lemon, lavender, and spices), plus Braille signage. Weather permitting, free 60- to 90-minute guided tours of the Botanical Gardens begin from the Visitor's Information Centre at 10:30 Tuesday, Wednesday, and Friday. ⊠ *18 Berry Hill Rd.* ☎ *441/236–5902* ⌨ *Free.*

Camden House. This gracious white house within the Botanical Gardens is the official residence of Bermuda's premier. Tours of the interior are given Tuesday and Friday noon to 2, except when official functions are scheduled. ⊠ *169 South Rd.* ☎ *441/236–5732.*

Cabinet Building. Bermuda's Senate (the upper house of Parliament) sits in a dignified Cabinet Building completed in 1841 and remodeled almost a century later. The most rewarding time to be here is during the formal opening of Parliament, traditionally held on the first Friday of November. His Excellency the Governor, dressed in a plumed hat and full regalia, arrives on the grounds in a landau drawn by magnificent black horses and accompanied by a police escort. A senior officer, carrying the Black Rod made by the Crown jewelers, next asks the speaker of the House, elected representatives, and members of the Senate chamber to convene. The governor then presents the Throne Speech from a tiny cedar throne dating from 1642. At other times of the year, assuming Parliament is in session, you may visit the Senate chambers on Wednesday from November to July to watch debates that are alternately lively and long-winded. Note that the gallery to the left of the main entrance is intended for public use. ⊠ *105 Front St., Hamilton* ☎ *441/292–5501* ⊕ *www.gov.bm* ⊠ *Free.*

> ## WHAT'S IN A NAME?
>
> Bermudians cultivated onions long before Americans did. In fact, throughout the 19th century they were one of the island's major exports, and its people were so closely identified with the tear-inducing plant that anyone born and bred here came to be known as an "Onion." Though competition eventually put an end to the lucrative trade, this nickname for locals stuck.

Front Street. Running along the harbor, Hamilton's main thoroughfare bustles with small cars, motor scooters, bicycles, buses, the occasional horse-drawn carriage, and sometimes hordes of cruise-ship passengers. The prime attractions here are the high-class low-rise shops that line the street, but don't overlook small offshoots and alleyways like Chancery Lane, Bermuda House Lane, and the Walkway, where you'll stumble upon hidden-away boutiques. The Visitor Information Centre (☎ *441/295–1480*), next to the Ferry Terminal at No. 8 Front Street, is a good place to strike out from when you're ready to explore the rest of Hamilton. Open Monday through Saturday 9–4, it's the place to go for pamphlets, maps, and to have your questions answered. It also has brochures for self-guided city walking tours.

Paget Marsh. Along with some of the last remaining stands of native Bermuda palmetto and cedar, this 25-acre reserve— virtually untouched since presettlement times and jointly owned and preserved by the Bermuda National Trust and the Bermuda Audubon Society—contains a mangrove forest and grassy savanna. These unspoiled habitats can be explored via a boardwalk that features interpretive signs describing the endemic flora and fauna. When lost in the cries of the native and migratory birds that frequent this natural wetland, you can quickly forget that bustling Hamilton is just minutes away. ⊠ *Lovers La.* ☎ *441/236–6483* ⊕ *www.bnt.bm* ⊠ *Free.*

The Bermuda Triangle Demystified

Long before the myth of the Bermuda Triangle became legend, Bermuda had already earned a reputation as an enchanted island. It was nicknamed "The Devil's Island" by early sea travelers, frightened by the calls of cahow birds and the squeals of wild pigs that could be heard onshore. But perhaps the most damning tales were told by sailors terrified of being wrecked on Bermuda's dangerous reefs. The island's mystical reputation is believed to have inspired Shakespeare's *The Tempest*, a tale of shipwreck and sorcery in "the still-vexed Bermoothes."

The early origin of the Triangle myth stretches as far back as Columbus, who noted in his logbook a haywire compass, strange lights, and a burst of flame falling into the sea. Columbus, as well as other seamen after him, also encountered a harrowing stretch of ocean now known as the Sargasso Sea. Ancient tales tell of sailboats stranded forever in a windless expanse of water, surrounded by seaweed and the remnants of other unfortunate vessels. It's true that relics have been found in the Sargasso Sea—an area of ocean between Bermuda and the Caribbean—but the deadly calm waters are more likely the result of circular ocean currents sweeping through the North Atlantic rather than paranormal activity.

In the past 500 years at least 50 ships and 20 aircraft have vanished in the Triangle, most without a trace—no wreckage, no bodies, nothing. Many disappeared in reportedly calm waters, without having sent a distress signal. Among the legends is that of Flight 19. At 2:10 on the afternoon of December 5, 1945, five TBM Avenger Torpedo Bombers took off from Fort Lauderdale, Florida, on a routine two-hour training mission. Their last radio contact was at 4 pm. The planes and 27 men were never seen or heard from again. The official navy report said the planes disappeared "as if they had flown to Mars."

The bizarre disappearances attributed to the Triangle have been linked to everything from alien abduction to sorcery. Although the mystery has not been completely solved, there are scientific explanations for many of the maritime disasters that have occurred in the Triangle. The most obvious answers are linked to extreme weather conditions with which any Bermudian fisherman would be well acquainted. "White squalls"—intense, unexpected storms that arrive without warning on otherwise clear days—are probable culprits, along with waterspouts, the equivalent of sea tornadoes. The most recent scientific theory on the infamous Triangle suggests that the freakish disappearance of ships and aircraft could be the result of large deposits of methane gas spewing up from the ocean floor. Huge eruptions of methane bubbles may push water away from a ship, causing it to sink. If the highly flammable methane then rises into the air, it could ignite in an airplane's engine—causing it to explode and disappear.

Fact or fiction, the Triangle is a part of local lore that won't disappear anytime soon. But don't let it scare you away—this myth isn't the only thing that makes Bermuda seem so magical.

—Kim Dismont Robinson

NEED A
BREAK

Bulli.Social. When you're in the mood for a picnic in the park, pick up supplies at Bulli.Social right beside the Queen Elizabeth Park entrance or pull up a chair in the restaurant's outdoor seating area just inside the park. Come for gourmet burgers, poutine, or the Ultimate Bacon Butty—bacon jam, Bermuda Smokehouse pork belly, candied bacon, and pork cheek confit on a soft, crusty roll. For a taste of Bermuda's social scene, stop by instead for Friday-night happy hour. ⊠ *7 Queen St., Hamilton* ☎ *441/232–2855* ⊕ *www.bullisocial.com* ⊘ *Closed Sun.*

2

Perot Post Office. To some, this rather austere 1840s structure is simply a place to mail a letter. To stamp collectors, on the other hand, the Perot Post Office, named for Hamilton's first postmaster, is a veritable shrine. William Bennett Perot was certainly a genial fellow: he would meet arriving steamers, collect the incoming mail, stash it in his beaver hat, and then stroll around Hamilton to deliver it, greeting each recipient with a tip of his chapeau. But it was his resourcefulness that made him most famous among philatelists. Tired of individually handstamping outgoing letters, Perot began printing stamps in 1848. Of the thousands he produced, only 11 still exist—and several of those are owned by Queen Elizabeth. If you'd like to get your hands on one, be prepared to dig deep. In June 2005 a Perot-era one-penny stamp sold at auction for a record-breaking $244,000. ⊠ *9 Queen St., Hamilton* ☎ *441/292–9052* ⊠ *Free.*

Queen Elizabeth Park (Par-la-Ville Park). Next to the Perot Post Office is the Queen Street entrance to Queen Elizabeth Park (there's another entrance on Par-la-Ville Road), which was officially renamed in 2012 to mark the Diamond Jubilee celebration of Queen Elizabeth II. Once postmaster William Perot's private garden, it has winding paths, luxuriant blooms, plentiful benches, and a photogenic Bermuda moongate. Long popular with people-watchers, it now houses the Bermuda National Library and Bermuda Historical Society Museum, too. Return visitors will notice that the Bermuda National Gallery has created a sculpture garden in the park by installing several major outdoor works. On summer Saturdays you will find Gombey dancers entertaining visitors here. ⊠ *Queen St., Hamilton.*

NEED A
BREAK

City Café. City Café is a New York–inspired deli that serves made-to-order sandwiches (including vegetarian variations) as well as tasty breakfasts. Because of its location next to the bus terminal on Church Street, City Café is a convenient place to grab a bite before catching a bus to other parts of the island. If you have time to fill up before your bus departs, continue walking past the deli (away from the harbor) to Victoria Park, where you can chow down in style amid ornamental shrubbery. ⊠ *4 Washington St., Hamilton* ☎ *441/296–9462* ⊕ *www.citycafe.bm.*

Sessions House and Jubilee Clock Tower. This eye-catching Italianate edifice, erected in 1819, is where the House of Assembly (the lower house of Parliament) and the Supreme Court convene. The Florentine towers and colonnade, decorated with red terra-cotta, were added to the building in 1887 to commemorate Queen Victoria's Golden Jubilee. The Victoria Jubilee Clock Tower made its striking debut—albeit a few years late—at midnight on December 31, 1893. Bermuda's Westminster-style Parliament meets on the second floor, where the speaker rules the roost in a powdered wig and robe. (The island has approximately 14 times as many politicians per capita as Europe or North America, so maintaining order is no small feat.) Sartorial splendor is equally evident downstairs in the Supreme Court, where wigs and robes (red for judges, black for barristers) are again the order of the day.

> **GO FOR GOLD**
>
> To sightsee like a VIP, sign up for a National Trust guided tour. The outing begins at Waterville with a "special access" stroll through the historic house and surrounding gardens. After being served refreshments, groups continue on by taxi to Paget Marsh for an exclusive tour of the reserve. Contact the Bermuda National Trust, as reservations are required in advance, at ☎ *441/236–6483*. You must have at least four people in your group.

■ **TIP→ You're welcome to watch the colorful proceedings: bear in mind, though, that visitors, too, are required to wear appropriate attire.** Call first to find out when parliamentary sessions and court cases are scheduled. ⊠ *21 Parliament St., Hamilton* ☎ *441/292–7408 House of Assembly, 441/292–1350 Supreme Court* ⊕ *www.gov.bm* ☒ *Free.*

Waterville. Bermuda's National Trust (the nonprofit organization that oversees the restoration and preservation of many of the island's gardens, open spaces, and historic buildings) has its offices in Waterville: a rambling estate overlooking Hamilton Harbour. Waterville was home to the Trimingham family for seven generations. In fact, their much-loved (and still dearly missed) department store started out here in 1842. The drawing and dining rooms, both laden with art and antiques donated by the family, are open to the public during business hours. Also worth seeing is a superb showcase garden planted by the Bermuda Rose Society. ⊠ *2 Pomander Rd.* ☎ *441/236–6483* ⊕ *www.bnt.bm* ☒ *Free* ⊙ *Closed weekends.*

ST. GEORGE'S AND EASTERN PARISHES

St. George's and Hamilton are about 10 miles and 200 years apart. The latter wasn't even incorporated as a town until 1792; and by the time Hamilton became capital in 1815, St. George's had already celebrated its bicentennial.

The settlement of Bermuda began in what is now the Town of St. George (or St. George's) when the *Sea Venture*—flagship of an English fleet carrying supplies to Jamestown, Virginia—was wrecked on Bermuda's treacherous reefs in 1609. Four hundred years later, no visit to the island would be complete without a stop in this picturesque and remarkably preserved example of an early New World outpost.

Although St. George's is a living community—not a living-history museum—it retains the patina of authenticity. In fact, in 2000 it was named a UNESCO World Heritage site. That designation puts it on a par with spots like the Great Wall of China and the Taj Mahal in India. But don't expect awe-inspiring edifices here. On the contrary, St. George's chief charm lies in tiny walled cottages, simple colonial churches, and labyrinthine alleys that beg to be explored.

Also over in the east of the island, you will find the parishes of Smith's and Hamilton. This is probably the quietest corner of the island, so it's a great spot to enjoy tranquil nature trails. Tucked away in Hamilton Parish, however, you'll find two of the island's biggest attractions: the Bermuda Aquarium, Museum & Zoo, and Crystal Caves. The East End is also home to some of Bermuda's finest golf courses.

TIMING

Given its small size, St. George's has a disproportionately large number of historic buildings, plus pleasant gardens and enticing shops. They say you can't get lost here—but you can certainly lose track of time. So give yourself a day to explore its nooks and crannies. Allow another day to take in the nearby Bermuda Aquarium, Museum & Zoo and Crystal Caves.

TOP ATTRACTIONS

FAMILY
Fodor's Choice
★

Bermuda Aquarium, Museum & Zoo (*BAMZ*). Established in 1926, the Bermuda Aquarium, Museum & Zoo (BAMZ for short) is one of Bermuda's top attractions, and with harbor seals, flocks of flamingos, exhibits on local animals and marine life, and a coastal walkway with stunning water views, it's no wonder. In the aquarium the big draw is the North Rock Exhibit, a 140,000-gallon tank that gives you a diver's-eye view of the area's living coral reefs (one of the largest living coral collections in the world) and the colorful marine life it sustains. The museum section has multimedia and interactive displays focusing on native habitats and the impact humans have on them. The island-themed zoo displays more than 300 birds, reptiles, and mammals. Don't miss the "Islands of Australasia" exhibit with its lemurs, wallabies, and tree kangaroos, or "Islands of the Caribbean," a huge walk-through enclosure that gets you within arm's length of ibises and golden lion tamarins. Other popular areas include an outdoor seal pool, tidal touch tank, and cool kid-friendly Discovery Room. Take a break at AZU Beastro, the farm-to-table café located on the grounds of the zoo where you can find good food and great views. ⊠ *40 N. Shore Rd., Flatts Village* ☎ *441/293–2727* ⊕ *www.bamz.org* ⊠ *$10.*

Bermuda National Trust Museum at the Globe Hotel. Erected as a governor's mansion around 1700, this building became a hotbed of activity during the American Civil War. From here, Confederate Major Norman Walker coordinated the surreptitious flow of guns, ammunition, and war supplies from England, through Union blockades, into American ports. It saw service as the Globe Hotel during the mid-19th century and became a National Trust property in 1951. A short video, *Bermuda, Centre of the Atlantic,* recounts the history of Bermuda, and a memorabilia-filled exhibit entitled "Rogues & Runners: Bermuda and the American Civil War" describes St. George's when it was a port for Confederate blockade runners. This is also the location of the Trustworthy Gift Shop.

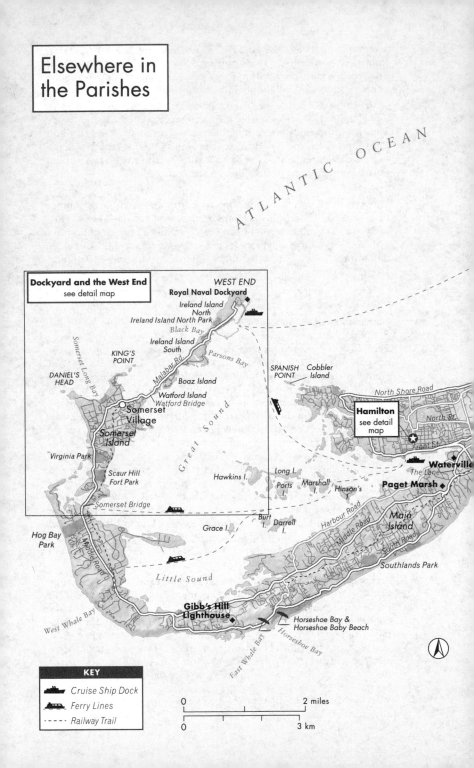

Elsewhere in the Parishes

ATLANTIC OCEAN

Dockyard and the West End
see detail map

WEST END
Royal Naval Dockyard

Ireland Island North
Ireland Island North Park
Black Bay
Ireland Island South

Parsons Bay

SPANISH POINT
Cobbler Island

North Shore Road

Somerset Long Bay
KING'S POINT

DANIEL'S HEAD

Malabar Rd.
Boaz Island
Watford Island
Watford Bridge

Great Sound

North St.

Hamilton
see detail map

Front St.

Somerset Village
Somerset Island

Virginia Park

Hawkins I.

Long I.

Waterville
The Lane
Paget Marsh

Scaur Hill Fort Park

Ports I.
Marshall I.
Hinson's I.

Somerset Bridge

Burt I.
Darrell I.

Harbour Road

Main Island

Hog Bay Park

Grace I.

Middle Road

Southlands Park

Middle Road

South Road

Little Sound

West Whale Bay

Gibb's Hill Lighthouse

Horseshoe Bay & Horseshoe Baby Beach

East Whale Bay

Horseshoe Bay

0   2 miles

0   3 km

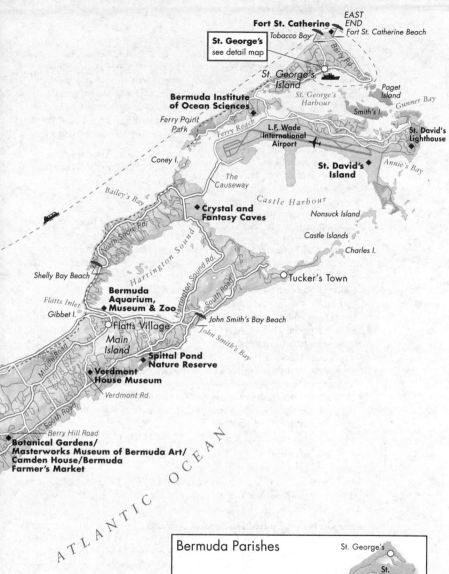

EAST
END

Fort St. Catherine — Fort St. Catherine Beach
Tobacco Bay

St. George's
see detail map

St. George's Island

Barry Rd.

Paget Island

Gunner Bay

Bermuda Institute of Ocean Sciences

St. George's Harbour

Smith's I.

Ferry Point Park

Ferry Reach

L.F. Wade International Airport

St. David's Lighthouse

Coney I.

The Causeway

St. David's Island

Annie's Bay

Bailey's Bay

Castle Harbour

Crystal and Fantasy Caves

Nonsuck Island

Castle Islands

Charles I.

Shelly Bay Beach

North Shore Rd.

Harrington Sound

Harrington Sound Rd.

South Road

Tucker's Town

Flatts Inlet

Gibbet I.

Bermuda Aquarium, Museum & Zoo

Flatts Village

John Smith's Bay Beach

Main Island

Spittal Pond Nature Reserve

John Smith's Bay

Middle Road

Verdmont House Museum

Verdmont Rd.

South Road

Berry Hill Road

Botanical Gardens/ Masterworks Museum of Bermuda Art/ Camden House/Bermuda Farmer's Market

ATLANTIC OCEAN

Bermuda Parishes

St. George's

St. George's

Hamilton

Smiths

Somerset Village

Devonshire

Sandys

Pembroke

HAMILTON

Paget

Warwick

Southampton

A GOOD WALK IN ST. GEORGE'S

Start your tour in **King's Square**, then stroll out onto **Ordnance Island** to see a replica of *Deliverance*: the ship built as a replacement for the *Sea Venture*. Behind you, just up the street, is the **Bermuda National Trust Museum at the Globe Hotel**, and across the square is the **Town Hall**. Venturing up King Street, notice the fine Bermudian architecture of **Bridge House**. At the top of King Street is the **Old State House**, the earliest stone building in Bermuda.

Walk up Princess Street to Duke of York Street and turn right, following the sidewalk to the **Bermudian Heritage Museum**. Across Duke of York Street, you can find **Somers Garden**, where Sir George Somers's heart is reportedly buried. After walking through the garden, climb the steps to Blockade Alley for a view of the **Unfinished Church** on a hill ahead. To your left are Duke of Kent Street, Featherbed Alley, and the **St. George's Historical Society Museum, Printery, and Garden**. Next, cross Clarence Street to Church Lane and turn right on Broad Alley

to reach the **Old Rectory**. Straight ahead (or as straight as you can go among these twisted streets) is Printer's Alley, which in turn links to **Nea's Alley**, where a whiff of 19th-century scandal still lingers.

Return to Church Lane and enter the yard of **St. Peter's Church**, a centuries-old sanctuary that, until the building of the Old State House, did double duty as the colony's only public meeting place. (The main entrance is on Duke of York Street.) From the church, continue down Duke of York Street until you reach Queen Street on your right. A short walk up it brings you to the **Bermuda Perfumery and Garden** at Stewart Hall, which will be on the left. Turn around and walk back to Duke of York Street and go right until you get to Barber's Alley, turning left to reach **Tucker House**, which has been transformed from a prominent merchant's home into a museum. From there continue along Water Street, veering left again on Penno's Drive to visit the new **World Heritage Centre** at Penno's Wharf.

✉ *32 Duke of York St., St. George's* ☎ *441/297–1423* ⊕ *www.bnt.bm* 🎫 *$5; $10 combination ticket includes admission to Tucker House and Verdmont* ⊘ *Closed Thurs., Fri., and Sun.*

Bermuda Perfumery and Garden (Lili Bermuda). In 2005 this perfumery moved from Bailey's Bay in Hamilton Parish, where it had been based since 1928, to historic Stewart Hall. Although the location changed, the techniques it uses did not: the perfumery still manufactures and bottles all its island-inspired scents on-site using more than 3,000 essential oils extracted from frangipani, jasmine, oleander, and passionflower. Guides are available to explain the entire process, and there's a small museum that outlines the company's history. You can also wander around the gardens and stock up on your favorite fragrances in the showroom. ✉ *Stewart Hall, 5 Queen St., St. George's* ☎ *441/293–0627* ⊕ *www. lilibermuda.com* 🎫 *Free* ⊘ *Closed Sun.*

FAMILY **Fort St. Catherine.** Surrounded by a dry moat and accessed by a drawbridge, this restored and formidable hilltop fort has enough tunnels, towers, redoubts, and ramparts to satisfy even the most avid military

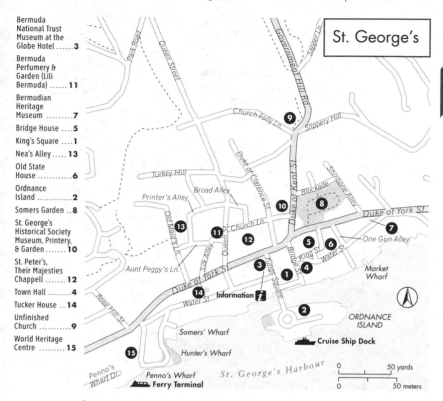

St. George's

historian—or adrenaline-fueled child. The original fort was built around 1614 by Bermuda's first governor, Richard Moore, but it was remodeled and enlarged at least five times. In fact, work continued on it until late in the 19th century. On-site an intriguing collection of antique weapons complements the impressive architecture. Standing out among the pistols and muskets is an 18-ton muzzle-loading cannon, which was capable of firing 400-pound shells a full half mile. ⊠ *15 Coot Pond Rd., St. George's* ☎ *441/297–1920* ⌫ *$7* ☉ *Closed weekends Nov.–May.*

FAMILY
Fodor's Choice
★

Spittal Pond Nature Reserve. This Bermuda National Trust park has 64 acres for roaming, though you're asked to keep to the well-marked walkways that loop through the woods and along the spectacular shoreline. More than 30 species of waterfowl—including herons, egrets, and white-eyed vireos—winter here between November and May, making the reserve a top spot for birders. Get your timing right and you may be able to spy migrating whales as well. History buffs may be more interested in climbing the high bluff to Portuguese Rock. Early settlers found this rock crudely carved with the date 1543 along with other markings that are believed to be the initials "RP" (for *Rex Portugaline,* King of Portugal) and a cross representing the Portuguese Order of Christ. The theory goes that a Portuguese ship was wrecked on the island and that its sailors marked the occasion before departing on a newly built ship. The rock was removed to prevent further damage by erosion, and a bronze cast of the original stands in its place. A plaster-of-paris version is also on display at the Museum of the Bermuda Historical Society in Hamilton. ✉ *South Rd.* ☎ *441/236–6483* ⊕ *www.bnt. bm* ✉ *Free.*

Fodor's Choice

★

St. Peter's, Their Majesties Chappell. Because parts of this whitewashed stone church date back to 1620, it holds the distinction of being the oldest continuously operating Anglican church in the Western Hemisphere. It was not, however, the first house of worship to stand on this site. It replaced a 1612 structure made of wooden posts and palmetto leaves that was destroyed in a storm. The present

ATTEN-SHUN!

The evolution of British military architecture between 1612 and 1956 can be traced through fortifications that dot the coast near St. George's. To get a sense of how diverse they are, follow your visit to Fort St. Catherine with a trip to **Alexandra Battery** (about a mile away along Barry Road) and nearby **Gates Fort**. The former, built in the mid-1800s, features Victorian innovations like cast-iron facings and concrete emplacements. The latter is a reconstruction of a small militia fort from the 1620s that was named for Sir Thomas Gates, the first survivor of the *Sea Venture* to reach dry land.

church was extended in 1713 (the oldest part is the area around the triple-tier pulpit), with the tower and wings added in the 19th century. Befitting its age, St. Peter's has many treasures. The red-cedar altar, carved in 1615 under the supervision of Richard Moore (a shipwright and the colony's first governor), is the oldest piece of woodwork in Bermuda. The late-18th-century bishop's throne is believed to have been salvaged from a shipwreck, and the baptismal font, brought to the island by early settlers, is an estimated 900 years old. There's also a fine collection of Communion silver from the 1600s in the vestry. Nevertheless, it's the building itself that leaves the most lasting impression. With rough-hewn pillars, exposed cedar beams, and candlelit chandeliers, the church is stunning in its simplicity. After viewing the interior, walk into the churchyard to see where prominent Bermudians, including Governor Sir Richard Sharples, who was assassinated in 1973, are buried. A separate graveyard for slaves and free blacks (to the west of the church, behind the wall) is a poignant reminder of Bermuda's segregated past. ✉ *33 Duke of York St., St. George's* ☎ *441/297–2459* ⊕ *www.stpeters.bm* ✉ *Donations appreciated.*

Tucker House. Tucker House is owned and lovingly maintained as a museum by the Bermuda National Trust. It was built in the 1750s for a merchant who stored his wares in the cellar (a space that now holds an archaeological exhibit). But it's been associated with the Tucker family ever since Henry Tucker, president of the Governor's Council and a key participant in the Bermuda Gunpowder Plot, purchased it in 1775. His descendents lived here until 1809, and much of the fine silver and heirloom furniture—which dates primarily from the mid-18th and early-19th centuries—was donated by them. As a result, the house is essentially a tribute to this well-connected clan whose members included a Bermudian governor, a U.S. treasurer, a Confederate navy captain, and an Episcopal bishop.

The kitchen, however, is dedicated to another notable—Joseph Haine Rainey—who is thought to have operated a barber's shop in it during the Civil War. (Barber's Alley, around the corner, is also named in his honor.) As a freed slave from South Carolina, Rainey fled to Bermuda at the outbreak of the war. Afterward he returned to the United States and, in 1870, became the first black man to be elected to the House of Representatives. A short flight of stairs leads down to the kitchen, originally a separate building, and to an enclosed kitchen garden. ⊠ *5 Water St., St. George's* ☎ *441/297–0545* ⊕ *www.bnt.bm* ✉ *$5; $10 combination ticket includes admission* to National Trust Museum in Globe Hotel and Verdmont ⊘ *Closed Tues. and Thurs.–Sun.*

> ### ALL FIRED UP
>
> In 1775 the Continental Congress imposed a ban on exports to colonies not supporting their trade embargo against England. Bermuda depended on the American colonies for grain, so a delegation of Bermudians traveled to Philadelphia offering salt in exchange for the resumption of grain shipments. Congress rejected the salt, but agreed to lift the ban if Bermuda sent gunpowder instead. A group of Bermudians, including two members of the esteemed Tucker family, then broke into the island's arsenal, stole the gunpowder, and shipped it to Boston. The ban was soon lifted.

FAMILY **Verdmont House Museum.** This National Trust property, which opened as a museum in 1956, is notable for its Georgian architecture, but what really sets this place apart is its pristine condition. Though used as a residence until the mid-20th century, virtually no structural changes were made to Verdmont since it was erected around 1710. Former owners never even added electricity or plumbing (so the "powder room" was strictly used for powdering wigs). The house is also known for its enviable collection of antiques. Some pieces—such as the early-19th-century piano—were imported from England. Most are 18th-century cedar, however, crafted by Bermudian cabinetmakers. Among the most interesting artifacts are the pint-size furnishings and period toys that fill Verdmont's upstairs nursery. A china coffee service, said to have been a gift from Napoléon to U.S. President James Madison, is also on display. The president never received it, though, since the ship bearing it across the Atlantic was seized by a privateer and brought to Bermuda. Verdmont also has its share of resident ghosts: among them, an adolescent girl who died of typhoid there in 1844. ⊠ *6 Verdmont La.* ✛ *Off Collector's Hill* ☎ *441/236–7369* ⊕ *www.bnt.bm* ✉ *$5; $10 combination ticket with Bermuda National Trust Museum in Globe Hotel and Tucker House* ⊘ *Closed Thurs. and Sat.–Tues.*

WORTH NOTING

Bermuda Institute of Ocean Sciences. In 1903—long before environmental issues earned top-of-mind awareness—scientists began studying marine life at this mid-Atlantic facility formerly known as the Bermuda Biological Station for Research. Now researchers from around the world come here to work on projects dealing with hot topics like global warming, marine ecology, and acid rain. You can learn all about them on a free 90-minute tour that starts at 10 am the first Wednesday of the month, in the reception building. Tours cover the grounds and laboratory. You might also see the station's 168-foot research vessel, R/V *HSBC Atlantic Explorer,* if it happens to be docked that day. ✉ *17 Biological Station, Ferry Reach, St. George's* ☎ *441/297–1880* ⊕ *www.bios.edu* ✉ *Donations accepted.*

Bermudian Heritage Museum. The history, trials, and accomplishments of black Bermudians are highlighted in this converted 1840s warehouse. Photographs of early black residents including slaves, freedom fighters, and professionals line the walls, and the works of black artisans are proudly exhibited. Look, in particular, for the display about the *Enterprise,* a slave ship that was blown off course to Bermuda while sailing from Virginia to South Carolina in 1835. Since slavery had already been abolished on the island, the 78 slaves on board were technically free—and the Local Friendly Societies (grassroots organizations devoted to liberating and supporting slaves) worked to keep it that way. Society members obtained an injunction to bring the slaves' case into court and escorted the "human cargo" to their hearing in Hamilton, where many spoke in their own defense. All except one woman and her four children accepted the offer of freedom. Today countless Bermudians trace their ancestry back to those who arrived on the *Enterprise.* Appropriately enough, the museum building was once home to one of the Friendly Societies. ✉ *Water and Duke of York Sts., St. George's* ☎ *441/297–4126* ⊕ *bermudianheritagemuseum.com* ✉ *$3.*

Bridge House. This 17th-century building, owned by the National Trust, was previously home to several of Bermuda's governors—and at least one ghost. Mistress Christian Stevenson, who was condemned as a witch in 1653, proclaimed her innocence at this spot, and now seems reluctant to leave it. Other National Trust properties also qualify as "favorite haunts." For instance, the Old Rectory on Broad Alley is said to have a spirit who plays the spinet in the wee hours of the morning. ✉ *1 Bridge St., St. George's* ⊕ *www.bnt.bm.*

King's Square. In a town where age is relative, King's Square is comparatively new. The square was only created in the 19th century after a marshy part of the harbor was filled in. Today it still looks rather inauspicious, more a patch of pavement than a leafy common, yet the square is St. George's undisputed center. Locals frequently congregate here for civic celebrations. Visitors, meanwhile, come to see the replica stocks and pillory. Formerly used to punish petty crimes, these grisly gizmos—together with a replica ducking stool—are now popular props for photo ops. Reenactments of historical incidents, overseen by a town crier in full colonial costume, are staged in the square April through

CLOSE UP

Slavery in Bermuda

2

Within a few years of the colony's founding, slavery had become a fact of life in Bermuda. As early as 1616, slaves—most of whom were "imported" as household servants and tradespeople rather than field workers—began arriving, first from Africa and then from the Caribbean. In the mid-1600s they were joined by Native American captives (among them, the wife of a Pequod chief). The practice flourished to such an extent that by the time British legislation finally abolished it in 1834, slaves made up more than half of the island's population.

The date the abolition decree was issued, August 1, continues to be marked island-wide. Known as Emancipation Day, it's a time for cricket matches, concerts, and, of course, Gombey dancing: a colorful form of self-expression, rooted in African tradition, which slave owners had banned. If you can't time your trip to coincide with the festivities, you can still bone up on the backstory by following the African Diaspora Heritage Trail. Affiliated with UNESCO's international Slave Route Project, it highlights sites related to the Bermudian slave trade.

Some of the trail's 11 stops are already tourist staples. For instance, in St. George's the slave graveyard at St. Peter's Church is a designated site; as is Tucker House, where Joseph Rainey (the first black man to be elected to the U.S. House of Representatives) sat out the Civil War. Also on the list is the Commissioner's House at the Royal Naval Dockyard, which has an exhibit that vividly evokes the age of slavery through artifacts like iron shackles and glass trade beads.

Other sites are obscure, but nonetheless illuminating. Take Cobb's Hill Methodist Church in Warwick Parish. Dedicated in 1827, seven years before Emancipation, it was the first sanctuary in Bermuda built by and for blacks. Because they struggled to complete it in their rare off-hours (often working by candlelight!), the church is both a religious monument and a symbol of human resilience. For further details on the African Diaspora Heritage Trail, pick up a brochure at any Visitor Information Centre.

—Susan MacCallum-Whitcomb

November, Monday to Thursday and Saturday at noon, and December through March on Wednesday and Saturday at noon. ⊠ *Water St., St. George's* ⊕ *www.stgeorgesfoundation.org.*

Nea's Alley. While roaming the back streets, look for Nea's Alley. Nineteenth-century Irish poet Thomas Moore, who lived in St. George's during his tenure as registrar of the admiralty court, waxed poetic about both this "lime-covered alley" and a lovely woman he first encountered here: his boss's teenaged bride, Nea Tucker. Though arguably the most amorous, Moore wasn't the only writer to be inspired by Bermuda. Mark Twain wrote about it in *The Innocents Abroad,* and his exclamation "you go to heaven if you want to; I'd druther stay in Bermuda" remains something of a motto in these parts. Two 20th-century playwrights, Eugene O'Neill and Noel Coward, also wintered—and worked—on the island. More recently, Bermuda resident Peter Benchley took the idea for his novel *The Deep* from the ships lost offshore. ✉ *Between Printer's Alley and Old Maid's La., St. George's.*

Old State House. A curious ritual takes place every April in King's Square as one peppercorn, regally placed upon a velvet pillow, is presented to the mayor of St. George's amid much pomp and circumstance. The paltry peppercorn is the rent paid annually for the Old State House by the Masonic Lodge St. George No. 200 of the Grand Lodge of Scotland. This fraternal organization has occupied the building since Bermuda's Parliament—the third oldest in the world after Iceland's and England's—vacated it in 1815 when the capital moved to Hamilton. The Old State House was erected in 1620 in what Governor Nathaniel Butler believed was the Italian style, so it's one of the few structures in Bermuda to feature a flat roof. Builders used a mixture of turtle oil and lime as mortar, setting the style for future Bermudian buildings. ✉ *4 Princess St., St. George's* ☎ *441/297–8043* 🖳 *Free.*

FAMILY **Ordnance Island.** Ordnance Island, directly across from King's Square, is dominated by a splendid bronze statue of Sir George Somers, commander of the *Sea Venture*. Somers looks surprised that he made it safely to shore—and you may be surprised that he ever chose to set sail again when you spy the nearby *Deliverance*. It's a full-scale replica of one of two ships—the other was the *Patience*—built under Somers's supervision to carry survivors from the 1609 wreck onward to Jamestown. But considering her size (just 57 feet from bow to stern) *Deliverance* hardly seems seaworthy by modern standards. ✉ *Across from King's Sq., St. George's.*

Somers Garden. After sailing to Jamestown and back in 1610, Sir George Somers—the British admiral charged with developing the Bermudian colony—fell ill and died. According to local lore, he instructed his nephew Matthew Somers to bury his heart in Bermuda, where it belonged. Matthew sailed for England soon afterward, sneaking the body aboard in a cedar chest so as not to attract attention from superstitious sailors, and eventually buried it near Somers's birthplace in Dorset. Although it can't be proven that Matthew actually carried out his uncle's wishes, it's generally believed that Admiral Somers's heart was indeed left behind in a modest tomb at the southwest corner of the park. When the tomb was opened many years later, only a few bones, a pebble, and some bottle fragments were found. Nonetheless, ceremonies were held at the empty grave in 1920, when the Prince of Wales christened this pleasant, tree-shrouded park Somers Garden. ✉ *Bordered by Shinbone and Blockade Alleys, Duke of Kent and Duke of York Sts., St. George's* 🖳 *Free.*

St. David's Island. In a place famous for manicured lawns and well-tended gardens, St. David's Island feels comparatively wild. Nevertheless, the real highlight is—quite literally—St. David's Lighthouse. Built in 1879 of Bermuda stone and occupying the tallest point on the East End, this red-and-white-striped lighthouse rises 208 feet above the sea, providing jaw-dropping views of St. George's, Castle Harbour, and the reef-rimmed south shore. This is also a great place to spot humpback whales passing through Bermuda's waters in April and May. ✉ *Lighthouse Hill, St. George's* ☎ *441/236–5902* 🖳 *Free.*

St. George's Historical Society Museum, Printery, and Garden. Furnished to resemble its former incarnation as a private home, this typical Bermudian building reveals what life was like in the early 1700s. Along with period furnishings, such as a 1620 statehouse table, it has assorted documents and artifacts pertaining to the colonial days. But it's the re-created kitchen—complete with palmetto baskets and calabash dipping gourds—that really takes the cake. Downstairs the printery features a working replica of a Gutenberg-style press, as well as early editions of island newspapers. The beautiful cottage gardens behind the museum are also worth a visit. ⊠ *3 Featherbed Alley, St. George's* ⊹ *Near Duke of Kent St.* ☎ *441/297–8013* ☞ *$5* ☉ *Closed Sun. year-round and Mon., Tues., Thurs., and Fri. in Jan.–Apr.*

Town Hall. St. George's administrative offices are housed in a putty-color two-story structure that dates back to 1808. Inside the cedar-paneled hall—where the civic government still meets—you can see portraits of past mayors. Better yet, you can get some face time with the current one. Midday on Wednesday, November through March, the mayor greets visitors and gives a brief talk. ⊠ *5 King's Sq., St. George's* ☎ *441/297–1532* ☞ *Free.*

Unfinished Church. Work began on this intended replacement for St. Peter's Church in 1874. But, just as it neared completion, construction was halted by storm damage and disagreements within the church community. Hence the massive Gothic Revival pile sat—unfinished and crumbling—until the Bermuda National Trust stepped in to stabilize the structure in 1992. With soaring stone walls, a grassy floor, and only the sky for a roof, it's the sort of atmospheric ruin that poets and painters so admire. ⊠ *Duke of Kent St., St. George's* ☎ *441/236–6483* ⊕ *www.bnt.bm.*

FAMILY **World Heritage Centre.** Housed in an 1860 customs warehouse next to the Penno's Wharf Cruise Ship Terminal, the World Heritage Centre was developed under the auspices of the St. George's Foundation, and includes an exhibits gallery, an education center, retail galleries, and regular talks, tours, and historical reenactments. You can view an introductory film (*A Stroll Through St. George's*) and visit the ground-floor Orientation Exhibits Gallery, which showcases several hundred years of civic history. In an effort to make the past palatable—even to very young guests—this gallery has engaging models, ranging from a miniaturized version of St. George's (circa 1620) to a full-scale mock-up of the deck of the *Sea Venture*. It also contains a costume corner where kids can dress up in period outfits. ⊠ *19 Penno's Wharf, St. George's* ☎ *441/297–5791* ⊕ *www.stgeorgesfoundation.org* ☞ *$5.*

DOCKYARD AND WESTERN PARISHES

Bermuda is denser than you might imagine. But in contrast to Hamilton and St. George's, the island's West End seems positively pastoral. Many of the top sites here are natural ones: namely the wildlife reserves, wooded areas, and beautiful waterways of Sandys Parish. The notable exception is Bermuda's single largest tourist attraction—the Royal Naval Dockyard.

Its story begins in the aftermath of the American Revolution, when Britain suddenly found itself with neither an anchorage nor a major ship-repair yard in the western Atlantic. Around 1809, just as Napoléon was surfacing as a serious threat and the empire's ships were becoming increasingly vulnerable to pirate attack, Britain decided to construct a stronghold in Bermuda. Dubbed the "Gibraltar of the West," the Dockyard operated as a shipyard for nearly 150 years. The facility was closed in 1951, although the Royal Navy maintained a small presence here until 1976 and held title to the land until 1995.

Today the redeveloped Dockyard now has trees and shrubs where once there were vast stretches of concrete; private yachts calmly float where naval vessels once anchored and cruise ships dock at the terminal; and historic structures—like the Clocktower and Cooperage buildings—house restaurants, galleries, shops, even a movie theater. A strip of beach has been turned into a snorkel park. And at the center of it all are the National Museum of Bermuda and Dolphin Quest: two popular facilities that share a fortified 6-acre site.

Outside the Dockyard, Sandys and Southampton are just a short bus ride away. You'll notice that Sandys (pronounced Sands) is made up of several islands, all connected by bridges, including the smallest draw-bridge in the world. It's in this parish that you'll also find Somerset Village, which is a popular spot for swimming and fishing. Southampton is the place to head if you want to soak up some rays; don't miss Horseshoe Bay.

TIMING

Allow a full day for exploring this area. Before setting out, check public transit schedules carefully (you'll find them online at ⊕ *www.gov.bm*). By water, the trip can take anywhere from 30 minutes to more than an hour depending on which ferry you choose. On land, Buses 7 and 8 depart from Hamilton about every 15 minutes and take an hour to reach the Dockyard via South or Middle Road.

TOURS

Segway Tours of Bermuda. In a land where cars are limited to one per household, alternate means of transportation matter—which explains why Bermuda's efficient public transit system is so revered. Now Segway Tours of Bermuda adds a higher-tech option: 90-minute Dockyard tours conducted year-round on übercool, two-wheeled Segway human transporters. The tours, which combine Bermuda's history and present day, depart daily from the yellow double-decker bus at 10, noon, 2, and 4. ⊠ *Dockyard* ☎ *441/236–1300* ⊕ *www.segway.bm*.

TOP ATTRACTIONS

FAMILY   **Dolphin Quest.** After immersing yourself in maritime history at the National Museum of Bermuda, you can immerse yourself—literally—in the wonderful world of dolphins. Dolphin Quest offers a range of in-water programs that allow adults and children ages five or older to pet, play with, and swim alongside its eight Atlantic bottlenose dolphins in the historic Keep Pond. There are even specially designed

A TOUR OF DOCKYARD AND THE WEST END

To make the most of your visit to the West End, plan to combine sea and land transportation. Transit tokens, tickets, and passes work on both ferries and buses, allowing you to hop on and off wherever you please. If you have a bicycle or scooter, you can bring it on the ferry; however, you'll be charged an extra adult fare to take the latter. Once you arrive, the Dockyard itself can be covered easily on foot. But other sights are rather far apart. So plan to take a taxi, bus, or ferry if you're continuing on to Somerset or elsewhere.

The logical place to begin a tour is the Royal Naval Dockyard. Start your day by visiting the **National Museum of Bermuda** and **Dolphin Quest,** which are housed together in a stone fortress built between 1837 and 1852. To the left of the entrance is the **Snorkel Park,** a small protected reef where you can get up close to marine life. Across from the museum entrance, the tempting art gallery and permanent art-and-crafts market in the **Old Cooperage** also warrant a visit. To the west are a pottery shop, glassblowing center, and other businesses that occupy attractive old military warehouses; just south is the **Clocktower Mall,** where you can find still more shops. The new Visitor Information Centre is close to the ferry stop. Finish your tour here, or continue via ferry to Somerset Island.

For an interesting change of pace, opt for the slow boat (not the one heading directly to Hamilton) out of the Dockyard. You'll pass by Boaz and Watford islands on your way to Somerset Island, fringed on both sides with beautiful secluded coves, inlets, and bays. Getting off the ferry at Watford Bridge, you can make a quick jaunt into **Somerset Village,** which consistently ranks among Bermuda's prettiest communities.

The next sights, reached via Somerset Road, are best visited by bus or scooter. About 2 miles east of Somerset Village, opposite the Willowbank Hotel, is the entrance to the **Heydon Trust Property,** which boasts a tiny 1616 chapel. Around the bend on your left is **Fort Scaur,** a serene spot with sweeping views of the Great Sound. Linking Somerset Island with the rest of Bermuda is **Somerset Bridge.** Across the bridge, Somerset Road becomes Middle Road, which leads into Southampton Parish.

sessions, conducted from a submersible bench, for younger kids. Since entry to the Dolphin Quest area is free with museum admission, anyone can watch the action. Participation in the actual programs, however, range in price, and advance booking is recommended. For $700 you can be a dolphin trainer for the day. ⊠ *The Keep, Maritime La., Old Royal Naval Dockyard, Dockyard* ☎ *441/234–4464* ⊕ *www. dolphinquest.com.*

Fort Scaur. The British chose the highest hill in Somerset for the site of this fort, built in the late 1860s and early 1870s to defend the flank of the Dockyard from possible American attacks. British troops were garrisoned here until World War I; and American forces were, ironically, stationed at the fort during World War II. Today its stone walls are surrounded by 22 acres of pretty gardens, and the view of the

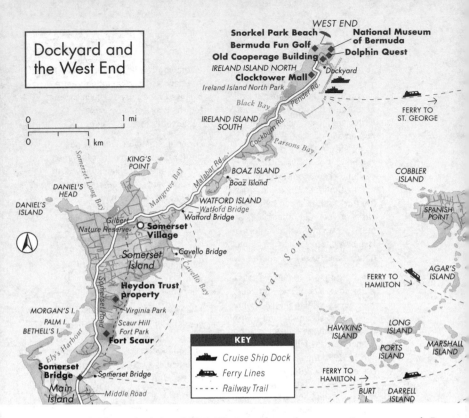

Great Sound and Ely's Harbour from the parapet is unsurpassed. Be sure to check out the early-Bermuda Weather Stone, which is billed as a "perfect weather indicator." A sign posted nearby solemnly explains all. There is also access to the Railway Trail. ⊠ *107 Somerset Rd., Dockyard* ☎ *441/236–5902* ⊠ *Free.*

TEA TIME

The Dining Room. After Gibbs Hill Lighthouse was automated in 1969, the keeper's cottage at its base was converted into an eatery. Whether you're looking for a filling meal or just a refreshing drink to quench your thirst, this quaint little restaurant serves dinner Tuesday to Sunday and lunch from Friday to Sunday. Seafood and pizzas are the specialties on the menu. ⊠ *68 St. Anne's Rd., Southampton* ☎ *441/238–8679* ⊕ *www.bermuda-dining.com* ☺ *Closed Mon.*

FAMILY

Gibbs Hill Lighthouse. Designed in London and opened in 1846, this cast-iron lighthouse soars above Southampton Parish and stands 117 feet high and 362 feet above the sea. The light was originally produced by a concentrated burner of four large, circular wicks. Today the beam from the 1,000-watt bulb can be seen by ships 40 miles out to sea and by planes 120 miles away at 10,000 feet. The haul up the 185 spiral stairs is an arduous one—particularly if you dislike heights or

CLOSE UP

The Bermuda Railway

The history of the Bermuda Railway—which operated on the island from 1931 to 1948—is as brief as the track is short. Bermuda's Public Works Department considered proposals for a railroad as early as 1899, and Parliament finally granted permission in 1922 for a line to run from Somerset to St. George's. But laying tracks was a daunting task, requiring the costly and time-consuming construction of long tunnels and swing bridges. By the time it was finished, the railway had cost investors $1 million, making it, per mile, the most expensive railway ever built.

"Old Rattle and Shake," as it was nicknamed, began to decline during World War II. Soldiers put the train to hard use, and it proved impossible to obtain the necessary maintenance equipment. At the end of the war the government acquired the distressed railway for $115,000. Automobiles arrived in Bermuda in 1946, and

train service ended in 1948, when the railway was sold in its entirety to British Guiana (now Guyana). Then, in the 1980s, the government gave new life to the ground it had covered by converting the tracks into trails.

Today the secluded 18-mile recreational Bermuda Railway Trail runs the length of the island, offering fabulous coastal views along the way. Restricted to pedestrians, horseback riders, and cyclists, the trail is a delightful way to see the island away from the traffic and noise of main roads. You might want to rent a bike if you plan to cover the entire trail, as many enthusiastic travelers do. Do note, though, that many portions of the trail are isolated—so you should avoid setting out alone after dark. Regardless of when you go, it's wise to first pick up a free copy of the Bermuda Railway Trail Guide available at Visitor Information Centres.

2

---

tight spaces. But en route to the top you can stop to catch your breath on eight landings, where photographs and drawings of the lighthouse help divert attention from your aching appendages. Once on the balcony, you'll be rewarded by panoramic island views. ⊠ *68 St. Anne's Rd., Southampton* ☎ *441/238–8069* ⊕ *www.bermudalighthouse.com* ✉ *$2.50* ☉ *Closed Feb.*

FAMILY

Fodor's Choice

★

National Museum of Bermuda. The Maritime Museum, ensconced in Bermuda's largest fort, displays its collections in a series of old munitions warehouses that surround the parade grounds and Keep Pond. Insulated from the rest of the Dockyard by a moat and massive stone ramparts, it is entered by way of a drawbridge. At the Shifting House, right inside the entrance, you can wander through rooms filled with relics from some of the 350-odd ships wrecked on the island's reefs. Other buildings are devoted to seafaring pursuits such as whaling, shipbuilding, and yacht racing. More displays are in the 19th-century Commissioner's House, on the museum's upper grounds. Built as both home and headquarters for the Dockyard commissioner, the house later served as a barracks during World War I and was used for military intelligence during World War II. Today, after an award-winning restoration, it contains exhibits on Bermuda's social and military history. A must-see is the Hall of History, a mural of Bermuda's history covering 1,000 square feet. It took local artist Graham Foster more than 3½ years to paint. You'll also likely want to snap some photos of the sheep that graze outside the building: their job is to keep the grass well mowed. ⊠ *The Keep, Maritime La., Old Royal Naval Dockyard, Dockyard* ☎ *441/234–1418* ⊕ *www.nmb.bm* ☒ *$15.*

FAMILY **Snorkel Park Beach.** Evidence of the Dockyard's naval legacy can be viewed at this protected inlet, accessed through a stone tunnel adjacent to the National Museum of Bermuda. Beneath the water's surface lie cast-iron cannons dating from 1550 to 1800, plus an

> ### SOME ASSEMBLY REQUIRED
>
> Though it may appear to be yet another stalwart stone building, the Commissioner's House is actually an engineering landmark. Designed by a naval architect, it was the world's first prefabricated residence. The component parts—made of cast iron rather than standard wood—were constructed in England between 1823 and 1827, then shipped to Bermuda, where they were assembled and sheathed in local limestone.

antique anchor and gun-carriage wheel. The true attractions, however, are colorful fish (you might see more than 50 varieties) and other sea creatures including anemones, sea cucumbers, and assorted species of coral. Thanks to amenities like floating rest stations, snorkeling and scuba diving couldn't be easier. Everything is available to rent, including kayaks, pedalos, Jet Skis, and underwater scooters. This is a family beach by day, catering mainly to cruise ship passengers, and a nightclub by night with beach parties and island barbecues. ⊠ *7 Maritime La., Dockyard* ☎ *441/234–6989* ⊕ *www.snorkelparkbeach.com* ☒ *$5.*

WORTH NOTING

Bermuda Fun Golf. The design team had a bit of fun with these minilinks: featuring 18 holes representing the best golf courses from around the world—including Augusta National and St. Andrews—it'll challenge even the most experienced minigolfers. ■TIP➜ **Surprisingly, Bermuda Fun Golf is one of the best places to watch the sunset with uninterrupted views.** There's also a bar serving cold drinks and snacks. ⊠ *7 Maritime La., Dockyard* ☎ *441/400–7888* ⊕ *www.fungolf.bm.*

Clocktower Mall. A pair of 100-foot towers makes it impossible to miss the Clocktower Mall. (Observant folks will note that one of them features a standard clock, the other a tide indicator.) Inside this 19th-century building, the Royal Navy's administrative offices have been replaced by distinctly Bermudian boutiques—including specialty shops and branches of Front Street favorites. These are particularly popular on Sunday because most stores outside the Dockyard area are closed. ⊠ *Dockyard* ☎ *441/234–1709* ⊕ *www.dockyardbermuda.com* ☒ *Free.*

Heydon Trust Property. A reminder of what the island was like in its early days, this blissfully peaceful 44-acre preserve remains an unspoiled open space, except for a few flower gardens. Pathways with well-positioned park benches wind through it, affording some wonderful water views. If you continue along the main path, you'll reach rustic Heydon Chapel.

CLOSE UP

Bermudian Architecture

The typical Bermudian building is built of limestone block, usually painted white or a pastel shade, with a prominent chimney and a tiered, white roof that Mark Twain likened to "icing on the cake." More than just picturesque, these features are proof that "necessity" really is "the mother of invention." Limestone, for instance, was a widely available building material—and far better able to withstand hurricane-force winds than the old English-style wattle and daub.

The distinctive roof, similarly, was not developed for aesthetic reasons. It's part of a system that allows Bermudians to collect rainwater and store it in large tanks beneath their houses. The special white roof paint even contains a purifying agent. If your visit includes some rainy days, you may hear the expression, "Good day for the tank!" This is rooted in the fact that Bermuda has no freshwater. It relies on rain for drinking, bathing, and cooking water, as well as golf-course and farmland irrigation. So residents are careful not to waste the precious liquid. The island has never run out of water, though the supply was stretched during World

War II, when thousands of U.S. soldiers were stationed in Bermuda.

Moongates are another interesting Bermudian structural feature, usually found in gardens and walkways around the island. These Chinese-inspired freestanding stone arches, popular since the late 18th century, are still often incorporated into new construction. Thought to bring luck, the ring-shaped gates are favored as backdrops for wedding photos.

Other architectural details you may notice are "welcoming arms" stairways, with banisters that seem to reach out to embrace you as you approach the first step, and "eyebrows" over window openings. Also look for butteries: tiny, steep-roofed cupboards, separate from the house, and originally built to keep dairy products cool in summer. If you wonder why, in this warm climate, so many houses have fireplaces in addition to air conditioners, come in January, when the dampness makes it warmer outside than in.

—Revised by Susan MacCallum-Whitcomb

Built in the early 1600s, it's Bermuda's smallest church. Weddings can be arranged by prior appointment. The chapel is open Monday through Saturday from 8 to 4. ⊠ *16 Heydon Dr., Dockyard* ⊹ *Off Somerset Rd.* ☏ *441/234–1831* ⊠ *Free.*

Old Cooperage Building. Inside this former barrel-making factory, you can find the Bermuda Craft Market and the Bermuda Arts Centre. The former—arguably the island's largest and best-priced crafts outlet—showcases the wares of more than 60 craftspeople, including quilters, candle makers, and wood carvers. The latter is a member-run art gallery that displays innovative high-end work. Exhibits change every month and may include watercolors, oils, sculpture, and photography—much of which is for sale. ■ **TIP→ A half-dozen artists also maintain studios on the premises, so leave some time to watch them at work.** ⊠ *4 Maritime La., Dockyard* ☏ *441/234–3208 Craft Market, 441/234–2809 Arts Centre* ⊕ *www.artbermuda.com* ⊠ *Free.*

Frog & Onion Pub. The supersize fireplace in which coopers used to forge their barrel bands is the focal point of the Frog & Onion Pub. Architectural interest aside, this naval-theme pub makes a great place for a lunch break, an afternoon libation, or even a quick game of pool. The menu has traditional fare (think Cornish pasty and fish-and-chips) as well as thirst-quenching ales made on-site by the Dockyard Brewing Company. ⊠ *The Old Cooperage, Dockyard* ☎ *441/234–2900* ⊕ *www.frogandonion.bm.*

Somerset Bridge. The West End is connected to the rest of Bermuda by Somerset Bridge, and once you have crossed over it you're no longer, according to local lingo, "up the country." More than marking a boundary, Somerset Bridge is something of an attraction in its own right because it's reputed to be the world's smallest drawbridge. It opens a mere 18 inches, just wide enough to accommodate the mast of a passing sailboat. ⊠ *Between Somerset and Middle Rds., Dockyard.*

Somerset Village. Its position on Mangrove Bay once made it a popular hideout for pirates. But judging by Somerset Village's bucolic appearance, you'd never guess that now. The shady past has been erased by shady trees, quiet streets, and charming cottages. As far as actual attractions go, this quaint one-road retreat has only a few eateries and shops—most of them offshoots of Hamilton stores. Nevertheless, it provides easy access to Springfield and the Gilbert Nature Reserve, a 5-acre woodland with paths that connect to some of the most scenic portions of Bermuda's Railway Trail. ⊠ *Gilbert Nature Reserve, 29 Somerset Rd., Dockyard* ⊹ *At Springfield* ⊕ *www.bnt.bm.*

WHERE TO EAT

Updated by
Amy Peniston

What's incredible about the Bermuda restaurant scene isn't so much the number or quality of restaurants, but the sheer variety of cuisines represented on the menus, especially considering that Bermuda is such a tiny island. It hosts a medley of global cuisines—British, French, Italian, Portuguese, American, Caribbean, Indian, Chinese, and Thai—palatable reminders of Bermuda's history as a colony.

Many superior independent and resort restaurants attract a constant and steady stream of internationally acclaimed chefs, assuring that the latest techniques and trends are menu regulars. At the same time, virtually all restaurant menus list traditional Bermudian dishes and drinks, so you have the opportunity to taste local specialties at almost any meal.

As you might expect, methods are not all that's imported. Roughly 80% of Bermuda's food is flown or shipped in, most of it from the United States. This explains why restaurant prices are often higher here than on the mainland.

Nevertheless, there are a number of delicious local ingredients that you should look for. At the top of the list is extraordinary seafood, like lobster (best during September through March), crab, oysters, mussels, clams, red snapper, rockfish, tuna, and wahoo. Additionally, many chefs work with local growers to serve fresh seasonal fruits and vegetables, such as potatoes, carrots, leeks, tomatoes, corn, broccoli, and Bermuda onions (one of the island's earliest exports); and in the fruit department, strawberries, cherries, bananas, and *loquats* (small yellow fruit used for preserves). Imports notwithstanding, Bermudian cuisine really begins and ends with local ingredients and traditional preparations, and therein lies the island's culinary identity.

While in Bermuda, try to eat like a local and put a couple of traditional dishes to the test. Bermuda is a seafood lover's paradise, with favorite dishes including mussel pie, shark hash, and codfish and bananas. As for soups, you can go for fish chowder, conch chowder, or traditional Portuguese black-eyed bean soup. Don't forget to kick back and relax after your meal with a rum swizzle, a Black and Coke, or a Dark 'n' Stormy. Ginger beer—which is quite different from ginger ale—remains the island's most popular soda for the kids.

BERMUDA DINING PLANNER

RESERVATIONS

Reservations are always a good idea. We mention them only when they're essential or not accepted. Book as far ahead as you can and reconfirm when you arrive, especially in high season. Many restaurants close—or curtail hours or days of service—in the off-season, so call ahead before setting out for lunch or dinner.

TOP 5 DINING

For Sunday brunch, feast on codfish and potatoes and cassava pie at the Fairmont Southampton Resort's Windows on the Sound restaurant (otherwise only open to guests).

Enjoy a lazy afternoon at the Swizzle Inn with a huge plate of nachos and a pitcher of rum swizzle.

Grab some jerk chicken and rice 'n' peas from the Jamaican Grill, and picnic at Horseshoe Bay.

Have a loaded fish sandwich with plenty of tartar sauce from Keith's Kitchen. The blue-and-white food truck is located in the BAA car park, a (very worthwhile!) 10-minute walk from Front Street.

Savor fresh rockfish served with stunning sunsets and sea views at the Beach House overlooking Achilles Bay.

WHAT TO WEAR

Bermuda has had a reputation for strict sartorial standards, but most of the midprice restaurants are much more casual these days. In many of the pubs and bars in town you would not be out of place in shorts and a T-shirt. It's a different story in more upscale restaurants, often attached to hotels. Even when not required, a jacket for men is rarely out of place. In our restaurant reviews we mention dress only when men are required to wear either a jacket or a jacket and tie.

MENU INFORMATION

Restaurant and menu guides are available at any Visitor Information Centre. The island's telephone directory also publishes a good selection of restaurant menus.

PRICES

Much harder to swallow than a delicious Bermuda fish chowder are the prices of dining out. Bermuda has never sought a reputation for affordability, and restaurants are no exception. A few greasy spoons serve standard North American fare (and a few local favorites) at a decent price, but by and large you should prepare for a bit of sticker shock. Don't be surprised if dinner for two with wine at one of the very top places—Tom Moore's Tavern, for example—puts a $200–$300 dent in your pocket. A 17% service charge is almost always added to the bill "for your convenience."

OUR REVIEWS

Reviews are listed alphabetically within region. Prices in the restaurant reviews are the average cost of a main course at dinner or, if dinner is not served, at lunch. Taxes and service charges are generally included.

WHAT IT COSTS IN U.S. DOLLARS			
$	$$	$$$	$$$$
Restaurants	under $21	$21–$30	$31–$40	over $40

Prices are per person for a main course at dinner. The bill usually includes a 17% service charge.

3

HAMILTON AND CENTRAL PARISHES

HAMILTON

The capital city has the largest concentration of eateries within a stone's throw from one another. It's best to explore the food options on foot, as most are based in and around Front Street, and it won't take long to find something to satisfy your craving. Don't forget to stroll down the side streets and alleyways, as some of the best restaurants are tucked away out of sight. Many restaurants have balconies overlooking picturesque Hamilton Harbour, which makes this area a great spot for alfresco dining. Don't be surprised to see restaurant staff clearing away their tables and chairs around 10 pm, when the restaurants are transformed into clubs and the fun really begins.

$$
ITALIAN
✗ **Angelo's Bistro.** Located in a busy alleyway between Reid Street and Front Street, this unassuming eatery is a well-kept secret for great Italian food. The menu features island-inspired meat and seafood dishes, handmade pastas and warm focaccia, as well as a number of vegan and gluten-free options. **Known for:** authentic Italian cuisine; alfresco courtyard dining; attentive owner and staff. ⑤ *Average main: $25* ✉ *Walker Arcade, 12 Reid St., Hamilton* ☎ *441/232–1000* ⊕ *www.angelosbistro. bm* ⊘ *Closed Sun.*

$$$
EUROPEAN
Fodor's Choice
★
✗ **Ascots.** Housed in an elegant former mansion just outside downtown Hamilton and run under the exacting standards of owners Angelo Armano and Edmund Smith, Ascots' creative and seasonal menu offerings incorporate fresh ingredients from local farmers and fishermen. For something different, start off with the Bermuda fish cakes or the chilled banana soup with black rum—it's unusual but very popular. **Known for:** exquisite food presentation; relaxed patio overlooking lush gardens; award-winning wine list. ⑤ *Average main: $40* ✉ *Royal Palms Hotel, 24 Rosemont Ave.* ☎ *441/295–9644* ⊕ *www.ascots.bm* ⊘ *Closed Sun. No lunch Sat.*

$$$
SEAFOOD
✗ **Barracuda Grill.** The tastefully decorated contemporary dining room—mahogany-framed chairs and banquettes, soft-gold lights over the tables—is reminiscent of sophisticated big-city restaurants, and the food that comes to the table is created by a culinary team dedicated to excellence. Polish off an expertly shaken martini at the bar before easing into your meal with a bowl of island-style fish chowder. **Known for:** daily locally caught fish; lively martini bar; creatively plated dishes. ⑤ *Average main: $36* ✉ *5 Burnaby Hill, Hamilton* ☎ *441/292–1609* ⊕ *www.barracuda-grill.com* ⊘ *No lunch weekends.*

$
CARIBBEAN
✗ **Bermuda Bistro at the Beach.** Despite what the name suggests, this restaurant is right in the heart of Hamilton. Savor the day's fresh fish special while enjoying an afternoon filled with people-watching and happy hour drink specials on the open-air patio. **Known for:** easygoing patio dining; weekend party atmosphere; affordable eats. ⑤ *Average main: $19* ✉ *103 Front St., Hamilton* ☎ *441/292–0219* ⊕ *www. thebeachbermuda.com.*

$$ ✕**Bistro J.** Delivering prompt,
BISTRO impeccable service and outstanding value, this quiet spot offers fixed-price two- and three-course meals at lunch and dinner. Fresh pasta, seafood, and local produce are combined in an imaginative daily menu that's written on a large blackboard hanging on the wall. **Known for:** daily fixed-price menus; unbeatable value; warm, relaxed atmosphere. ⑤ *Average main: $29* ✉ *Chancery La., Hamilton* ✛ *Off Front St.* ☎ *441/296–8546* ⊕ *www.bistroj. bm* ☰ *No credit cards* ⊗ *No lunch weekends. No dinner Sun.*

$$$ ✕**Bolero Brasserie.** The smartly
BRASSERIE dressed waitstaff, bustling atmosphere, and art-filled walls lend an authentic European feel to this beloved Front Street bistro. Owner and chef Johnny Roberts takes great pride in Bolero's frequently updated brasserie menu, featuring snails, ballotine of foie gras, roast rack of lamb, and even black pudding. **Known for:** seasonally inspired bistro menu; harbor-view balcony; lively atmosphere. ⑤ *Average main: $33* ✉ *95 Front St., Hamilton* ✛ *Entrance on Bermuda House La.* ☎ *441/292–4507* ⊕ *www.bolerobrasserie.com* ⊗ *Closed Sun. No lunch Sat.*

$$ ✕**Bouchée.** It's worth the walk west out of Hamilton to see why this
FRENCH charming French restaurant is a firm favorite with locals and tourists alike. Rise and shine with the extensive breakfast fare while enjoying the sophisticated-casual atmosphere and a morning pick-me-up cocktail. **Known for:** reasonably priced breakfast fare; leisurely weekend brunch; French café atmosphere. ⑤ *Average main: $26* ✉ *75 Pitts Bay Rd., Hamilton* ✛ *Near Woodburne Ave.* ☎ *441/295–5759* ⊕ *www.bouchee. bm* ⊗ *No dinner Sun. or Mon.*

$ ✕**Bulli.Social.** Bermuda's only gourmet burger restaurant is spicing up
AMERICAN Hamilton's lunchtime scene with an array of creatively topped patties, poutines, and hot dogs. Enjoy the social buzz out back on the patio, which overlooks Queen Elizabeth Park and transforms into a lively happy hour hot spot on Fridays and Saturdays. **Known for:** gourmet burgers; full bar and patio seating; lively happy hour. ⑤ *Average main: $16* ✉ *7 Queen St., Hamilton* ☎ *441/232–2855* ⊕ *www.bullisocial.com* ⊗ *Closed Sun.*

$ ✕**Buzz.** With more than 10 venues across the island, Buzz is a cheap
CAFÉ and cheerful café with a variety of made-to-order breakfast and lunch options. Inexpensive and convenient snacks, cold drinks, and plenty of healthy choices make this an essential spot to refuel. **Known for:** variety of sandwiches and wraps; convenient grab-and-go snacks; coffee and smoothies. ⑤ *Average main: $10* ✉ *Washington Mall, 7 Reid St., Upper Level, Hamilton* ☎ *441/295–1979* ⊕ *www.buzzcafe.bm* ☰ *No credit cards.*

GOOD TO GO

Miles Market. Miles is the Balducci's of Bermuda, with a large selection of upscale or hard-to-find specialty food items. The deli encompasses the finest imported and local meats and fish. There's also a mouthwatering range of pastries, cakes, and Godiva chocolates. Many items are on the expensive side, but the quality and selection are without rival. The supermarket delivers anywhere on the island. ✉ *96 Pitts Bay Rd., Hamilton* ✛ *Near Fairmont Hamilton Princess* ☎ *441/295–1234* ⊕ *www.miles.bm.*

3

$ ✕ **Café Cairo.** Experience authentic Middle Eastern cuisine and the ambi-
MIDDLE EASTERN ence of North Africa at this relaxed restaurant and nightclub. With
a menu of exotic flavors, this popular eatery showcases Bermuda's
adventurous culinary streak, satisfying the palates of well-traveled
islanders and visitors. **Known for:** party vibe; hookah on the balcony;
live DJs on weekends. $ *Average main: $16* ✉ *93 Front St., Hamilton*
☎ *441/295–5155* ◷ *Closed Sun.*

$ ✕ **Chopsticks.** Locals and visitors alike come here for an extensive menu
ASIAN that includes Szechuan, Hunan, Cantonese, and Mandarin favorites.
FAMILY Top Chinese choices include the sesame chicken and the house specialty,
Peking duck. **Known for:** diverse Asian-fusion menu; convenient take-
out; indoor waterfall. $ *Average main: $19* ✉ *88 Reid St., Hamilton*
☎ *441/292–0791* ⊕ *www.chopsticks.bm* ◷ *No lunch weekends.*

$$ ✕ **Coconut Rock and Yashi Sushi Bar.** Whether you're in the mood for
ECLECTIC shrimp tempura and sashimi served in a quiet room with black-lacquer
tables and paper lanterns, or you're hankering for a salad and a steak
surrounded by loud music videos, these adjoining restaurants can
satisfy. Well hidden beneath Hamilton's main shopping street, the
venue transforms into a lively cocktail destination at night, especially
on weekends. **Known for:** eclectic international cuisine; after-work
hangout for locals; cocktail spot at night. $ *Average main: $21* ✉ *Wil-
liams House, downstairs, 20 Reid St., Hamilton* ☎ *441/292–1043,
441/296–6226* ◷ *No lunch Sun.*

$$ ✕ **Crown & Anchor.** Light and airy, with an upscale hotel feel, Crown
ECLECTIC & Anchor offers everything from quiet afternoon tea service to lively
happy hour specials. Businesspeople, hotel guests, couples, and families
will enjoy the attentive service and new outdoor seating area. **Known
for:** traditional afternoon tea; breakfast buffet; outdoor seating. $ *Aver-
age main: $23* ✉ *Hamilton Princess Hotel, 76 Pitts Bay Rd., Hamilton*
☎ *441/295–3000.*

$ ✕ **The Docksider Pub & Restaurant.** Whether it's high noon, happy hour,
BRITISH or late Saturday night, locals love to mingle at this sprawling Front
Street sports bar. Classic pub fare with a Bermudian twist—think
nachos with homemade chili, Dark 'n' Stormy pork ribs, and fish-and-
chips—pairs perfectly with the impressive variety of beers, ciders, and
spirits. Join the English Premier League Football fans that gather en
masse to watch their favorite teams or sip your dessert—a Dark 'n'
Stormy—out on the porch as you watch Bermuda stroll by. **Known
for:** Bermuda-style pub food; passionate sports fans; crowded nightlife
scene. $ *Average main: $16* ✉ *121 Front St., Hamilton* ☎ *441/296–
3333* ⊕ *www.docksider.bm.*

$$ ✕ **Flanagan's Irish Pub & Restaurant.** Bermuda's only Irish pub is a din-
IRISH ing, music, and sports hot spot with a balcony overlooking Hamilton
Harbour. Choose from an extensive list of homemade comfort-food
classics such as beer-battered fish-and-chips and shepherd's pie, while
sipping a handcrafted island cocktail. **Known for:** tasty pub food; color-
ful island cocktails; harbor-view balcony. $ *Average main: $24* ✉ *69
Front St., 2nd fl., Emporium Bldg., Hamilton* ☎ *441/295–8299* ⊕ *www.
flanagans.bm* ▭ *No credit cards.*

$$$
INTERNATIONAL

✕Harbourfront. Whether you dine inside beside the enormous floor-to-ceiling windows or outside on the dock, every seat in the house has beautiful views of the ocean. Expertly prepared fresh sushi shines alongside international specialties and locally caught fish. **Known for:** expertly prepared sushi; picturesque harbor views; waterfront dining. $ *Average main: $37 ✉ 40 Crow La., Hamilton ✛ Next to Bermuda Underwater Exploration Institute (BUEI) ☎ 441/295–4207 ⊕ www.harbourfront.bm ⊘ No lunch Sun.*

> **OK, RACHAEL RAY!**
>
> If you've an eye for bargains, the Hog Penny in Hamilton has been showcased on the Food Network's "$40 a Day." Rachael Ray said it was the place to go in Bermuda for a value-priced meal.

3

$$$
AMERICAN

✕Harry's. A sleek bar and sophisticated decor provide an elegant backdrop for intimate dinners and classy power lunches. The steak-house classics, which feature flavorful aged beef and a variety of gourmet sides, are highly regarded. **Known for:** classic steak-house entrées; lively happy hour on the patio; elegant dining room. $ *Average main: $39 ✉ The Waterfront, 96 Pitts Bay Rd., Hamilton ☎ 441/292–5533 ⊕ www.harrys.bm ⊟ No credit cards ⊘ Closed Sun.*

$$
BRITISH

✕Hog Penny Pub and Restaurant. Veterans of London pub crawls may feel nostalgic at this dark, wood-filled watering hole off Front Street where you can enjoy old-style British comfort food and the ambience of Hamilton's oldest licensed establishment, opened in 1957. Imported ales as well as local craft beers from Dockyard Brewing Company are on offer to pair with your homemade shepherd's pie, fish-and-chips, or bangers and mash. **Known for:** nostalgic feel; old-style British pub fare; delicious fish chowder. $ *Average main: $25 ✉ 5 Burnaby St., Hamilton ☎ 441/292–2534 ⊕ www.hogpennypub.com.*

$
INDIAN
Fodor's Choice
★

✕House of India. Slightly off the beaten track, this authentic Indian restaurant is well worth the 10-minute walk or short cab ride from the town center. Outstanding chicken tikka masala, beef curry, and plenty of vegetarian options can be perfectly spiced to your liking. **Known for:** authentic Indian cuisine; fresh naan bread; eclectic lunch buffet. $ *Average main: $18 ✉ 58 North St., Hamilton ☎ 441/295–6450 ⊕ www. houseofindia.biz ⊘ No lunch weekends.*

$
JAMAICAN

✕Jamaican Grill. Journey outside the familiar city limits to Court Street and you'll find Jamaican food at its best. The Thomas family is proud of their Jamaican heritage and want everyone to taste Caribbean classics like jerk and curry chicken, fried dumplings, and beans and rice. **Known for:** authentic Jamaican specialties; convenient takeout; genuinely friendly staff. $ *Average main: $15 ✉ 32 Court St., Hamilton ☎ 441/296–6577 ⊘ Closed Sun.*

$$
ITALIAN
FAMILY
Fodor's Choice
★

✕La Trattoria. Tucked away in a narrow Hamilton alley, this family-favorite restaurant has a warm, yellow and brick interior and a crew of friendly Italian waiters. Without a doubt the king of the menu is pizza—La Trattoria's pies are cooked in Bermuda's only brick, wood-burning pizza oven and are garnished with over 20 inventive toppings. **Known for:** Bermuda's only wood-burning pizza oven; Italian waitstaff;

family-friendly charm. $ *Average main: $25* ✉ *23 Washington La., Hamilton* ☎ *441/295–1877* ⊕ *www.latrattoria.bm* ☾ *No lunch Sun.*

$$$
ITALIAN

✕ **Little Venice.** Little Venice is a little pricey, but it also sets the bar with its attentive, old-world hospitality, flavorful Italian dishes, and freshly made pasta. Bermuda's business elite gather for drinks and appetizers after work, making their way through a wine list that boasts 1,000 different wines from around the world. **Known for:** top-notch Italian food worthy of the price tag; exceptional service; homemade pasta. $ *Average main: $37* ✉ *32 Bermudiana Rd., Hamilton* ☎ *441/295–3503* ⊕ *www.littlevenice.bm* ☾ *No lunch Sat. Closed Sun.*

$$
SEAFOOD
FAMILY

✕ **Lobster Pot.** Bermudians swear by this spot, where a maritime-themed dining room is filled with brass nautical gear, lobster traps, and sun-bleached rope. The fresh local lobster, available September through March, is most requested next to rockfish, snapper, wahoo, and mahimahi with fried bananas and almonds, all local favorites. **Known for:** fresh seasonal lobster; Bermuda fish chowder; laid-back, nautical-themed atmosphere. $ *Average main: $27* ✉ *6 Bermudiana Rd., Hamilton* ☎ *441/292–6898* ⊕ *www.lobsterpot.bm* ☾ *No lunch weekends.*

$$
ASIAN

✕ **L'Oriental.** Above its sister restaurant, Little Venice, this Asian hot spot is a favorite among locals for its fresh sushi bar. Take the footbridge—over an indoor stream—to the raised seating at the lively teppanyaki table, where trained chefs stylishly slice, stir, and season your steak and veggies onto your plate. **Known for:** teppanyaki bar; fresh sushi; Asian-themed decor. $ *Average main: $29* ✉ *32 Bermudiana Rd., Hamilton* ☎ *441/296–4477* ⊕ *www.loriental.bm* ☾ *No lunch weekends.*

$$$
BISTRO

✕ **Muse.** Across the street from the ferry terminal, this spot is a lunch-time favorite among locals. Dine and people-watch from the patio lounge chairs on street level or sip rum swizzle while enjoying a view of Hamilton Harbour on the Rooftop Skybar. **Known for:** happy hour specials; rooftop lounge; Friday night DJs. $ *Average main: $35* ✉ *17 Front St., Hamilton* ☎ *441/296–8788* ⊕ *www.muse.bm* ▭ *No credit cards* ☾ *No lunch weekends. No dinner Sun.*

$$
CARIBBEAN
FAMILY

✕ **The Pickled Onion.** This former whiskey warehouse is now a lively restaurant serving crowd-pleasing Bermudian cuisine, as well as a handful of Latin- and Asian-flavored dishes. If you get there early enough, grab a table on the veranda overlooking the harbor and be sure to stick around—this is a fabulous spot to hang out and enjoy live music. **Known for:** balcony overlooking Front Street; Sunday brunch; live entertainment. $ *Average main: $26* ✉ *53 Front St., Hamilton* ☎ *441/295–2263* ⊕ *www.thepickledonion.com.*

$$$
SEAFOOD
Fodor's Choice
★

✕ **Port O' Call.** A two-level restaurant and sushi bar with a modern look and elegant feel, Port O'Call is one of the few ground-entry dining spots on Front Street, with an outdoor dining area reminiscent of a European sidewalk café. The fresh local fish—such as wahoo, tuna, grouper, and snapper—is cooked perfectly, and the preparations are creative. **Known for:** sophisticated patio dining; sceney happy hour; delicious cheese-cake. $ *Average main: $39* ✉ *87 Front St., Hamilton* ☎ *441/295–5373* ⊕ *www.portocall.bm* ☾ *No lunch weekends. Closed Sun.*

QUICK BITES

Chatterbox Café. Sip a delicious fruit smoothie and enjoy a healthy breakfast or lunch at this popular spot at the entrance of Washington Mall on Reid Street. The salad bar selection is well worth the trip. **Known for:** salad bar; sandwiches and paninis; to-go pastries. ⊠ *Washington Mall, 7 Reid St., Hamilton* ☎ *441/295–3263* ▤ *No credit cards* ☾ *Closed Sun.*

City Café. Conveniently located across from the bus station in Hamilton, this tiny spot is the perfect place for a quick bite before a long day of exploring. Omelets, home fries, and chocolate chip pancakes are just a few of the options available between 7 am and 11 am. **Known for:** build-your-own sandwiches and paninis; salad bar; Bermuda codfish breakfast. ⊠ *4 Washington St., Hamilton* ☎ *411/296–9462* ⊕ *www.citycafe. bm* ▤ *No credit cards* ☾ *Closed Sun.*

Common Ground. Hidden along Chancery Lane off Front Street, this popular lunch spot offers fresh sandwiches, wraps, salads, and baked goods. It also serves one of the best cups of coffee and a Saturday-morning crepe breakfast the kids will love. **Known for:** coffee drinks; healthy lunch options; light breakfast. ⊠ *11 Chancery La., Hamilton* ⊹ *Off Front St.* ☎ *441/292–2353* ⊕ *www.commonground.bm* ▤ *No credit cards* ☾ *Closed Sun.*

Dangelini's Cafe & Bakery. Watch Hamilton come alive from the shade of a harbor-view table at this little spot located right next to the ferry terminal. You'll find hot and cold caffeinated concoctions as well as homemade pastries, scones, and muffins, often still warm from the oven. **Known for:** fresh baked goods; convenient location; delicious coffee. ⊠ *8 Front St., Hamilton* ☎ *441/295–5272* ☾ *Closed Sun.*

Delicious. Downstairs in the Washington Mall's new food court, this spot lives up to its name with delicious sandwiches and other tasty offerings. The venue is home to a number of other small cafés offering everything from build-your-own burrito bowls to buffet-style international cuisine. **Known for:** fish sandwich; hold and cold lunch options; quick, friendly service. ⊠ *20 Church St., lower level, Washington Mall, Hamilton* ☎ *441/295–5890* ▤ *No credit cards* ☾ *Closed Sun.*

$$
ITALIAN
FAMILY
✕ **Portofino.** With its shuttered windows and brick walls covered in art, photos, and antiques, this well-worn spot, with an Italian owner and staff, has all the charm of a unassuming-but-good eatery in a small Italian village. On balmy evenings, share the calamari or garlic bread—two starters for which the restaurant is renowned—outside on the dining area patio. **Known for:** outstanding pizza; tasty starters; speedy takeout. ⑤ *Average main: $21* ⊠ *20 Bermudiana Rd., Hamilton* ⊹ *Off Front St.* ☎ *441/292–2375, 441/295–6090 takeout* ⊕ *www.portofino.bm* ☾ *No lunch weekends.*

$$$
EUROPEAN
✕ **The Red Carpet.** Old-fashioned charm and consistently attentive service are two reasons why this tried-and-true restaurant is a favorite among local politicians and businesspeople. Located in the old Armoury

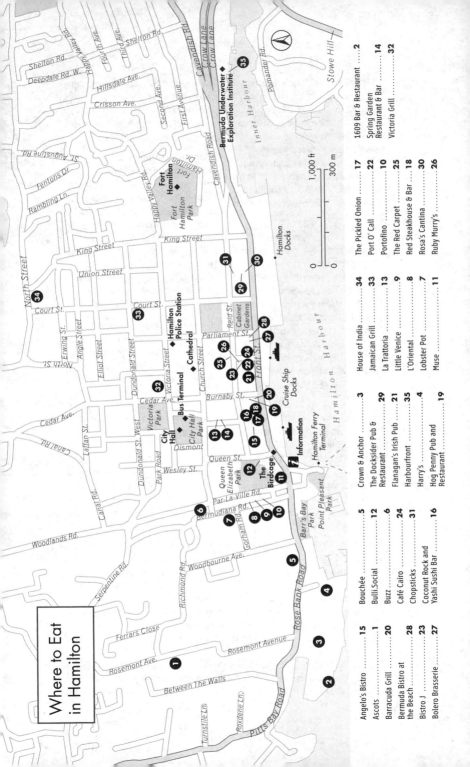

Where to Eat in Hamilton

Picnic Perfect

Ditch your proper place settings for a little sea breeze with that sandwich.

With verdant open spaces sprinkled with shady poinciana trees, the **Botanical Gardens,** on Middle Road in Paget, make a peaceful inland setting for a picnic. The gardens have a few picnic tables and plenty of benches, plus spacious lawns where you can spread a blanket. Bring your own supplies, or pick up lunch at Homer's Café, located just inside the Masterworks Museum of Bermuda Art, also on the premises.

Clearwater Beach in St. David's is one of Bermuda's nicest picnic spots, with tables near to and on the beach. You can pick up picnic supplies at the grocery store about ¼ mile away or order lunch to go from one of St. David's casual eateries.

Just west of popular Warwick Long Bay, tiny, tranquil **Jobson Cove**

beach is backed by the dramatic cliffs and greenery of South Shore Park. There are no tables and no snack bars, and often no people—perfect for a private picnic on the sand.

If you want a tried-and-tested picnic spot, head to **John Smith's Bay** in Smith's Parish. The wooden picnic tables beneath the trees make it a popular spot for locals. Get there early if you want a good spot overlooking the beach.

Adjacent to a Bermuda Audubon Society nature reserve, **Somerset Long Bay Park** in Sandys has a semicircular beach, fluffy spruce trees, and shallow water. It's also a terrific place for birding: it borders on an Audubon Society sanctuary. You can find tables under the trees near the beach and a grocery store less than ½ mile away.

building, it's a very popular lunch spot, serving plenty of fresh seafood and local favorites like fish chowder. **Known for:** excellent seafood selection; fish chowder; loyal crew of lunchtime regulars. $ *Average main: $38* ✉ *Armoury Bldg., 37 Reid St., Hamilton* ☎ *441/292–6195* ⊗ *Closed Sun.*

$$$
STEAKHOUSE

✗ **Red Steakhouse & Bar.** Sleek and modern, with a dining room, lounge, VIP balcony, and outdoor patio area, Red is so much more than a typical steak house. Meat lovers swoon for the signature certified Angus beef cuts, paired with a one or two creative sides—the Parmesan truffle fries are a must. **Known for:** harbor-view patio seating; certified Angus prime steaks; Friday happy hour. $ *Average main: $40* ✉ *55 Front St., Hamilton* ☎ *441/292–7331* ⊕ *www.redbermuda.com* ▬ *No credit cards* ⊗ *No lunch Sat.–Mon.*

$$
MEXICAN
FAMILY

✗ **Rosa's Cantina.** Just a three-minute stroll from the ferry terminal to the opposite end of Front Street is Bermuda's own taste of Mexico. Rosa's offers easygoing, friendly service, balcony seating, and a comprehensive menu of Tex-Mex favorites. **Known for:** sizzling fajitas; award-winning fish sandwich; balcony seating. $ *Average main: $22* ✉ *121 Front St., Hamilton* ☎ *441/295–1912* ⊕ *www.rosas.bm.*

$
INDIAN

✕ **Ruby Murrys.** Serving authentic, affordable Indian cuisine, this relaxed eatery located on a quiet, cobblestoned alley off Front Street is a particularly popular lunchtime destination for its à la carte and buffet-style fare. The quality and variety of dishes will suit any palate—just be sure to sample one of the fresh breads from the tandoor. **Known for:** traditional Indian food; lunch buffet; great value. ⑤ *Average main: $19* ✉ *Chancery La., Hamilton* ☎ *441/295–5058* ⊕ *www.rubymurrys.bm* ⊙ *No lunch weekends.*

$$
CARIBBEAN

✕ **1609 Bar & Restaurant.** Ascend a short flight of stairs at the end of the Hamilton Princess pier and enjoy the chic island vibe at this harbor-view restaurant. Stylish and modern, the 1609 is the perfect spot for a romantic rendezvous, complete with a tasteful assortment of wines by the bottle and specialty cocktails by the pitcher served with tasty salads and fish chowder to start, followed by a goat cheese pizza or fresh fish tacos. **Known for:** bird's-eye harbor view; social buzz; specialty cocktails. ⑤ *Average main: $29* ✉ *76 Pitts Bay Rd., Hamilton* ☎ *441/295–3000* ⊕ *www.thehamiltonprincess.com/dining/1609-restaurant* ▭ *No credit cards.*

$
CARIBBEAN

✕ **Spring Garden Restaurant & Bar.** If you've never had Barbadian, or as Barbados natives like to call it, "Bajan" food, grab a seat in the shade of a palm tree and try panfried flying fish—a delicacy in the islands. Another good choice is the broiled mahimahi served in creole sauce, or, in season, steamed, broiled, or curried lobster. **Known for:** Caribbean cuisine; relaxed island hospitality; Friday-night DJs playing soca and reggae music. ⑤ *Average main: $18* ✉ *19 Washington La., Hamilton* ✛ *Off Reid St.* ☎ *441/295–7416* ⊙ *Closed Sun.*

$
CARIBBEAN
FAMILY
Fodor'sChoice
★

✕ **Swizzle Inn.** Swizzle Inn created one of Bermuda's most hallowed drinks—the rum swizzle: gold and black rum, triple sec, orange and pineapple juices, and bitters. This place is a local landmark, with a warm and welcoming atmosphere, friendly staff, and plenty of affordable pub fare. **Known for:** pitchers of rum swizzle; decent pub fare; quiz nights. ⑤ *Average main: $20* ✉ *87 Blue Hole Hill, Bailey's Bay, Hamilton* ☎ *441/293–1854* ⊕ *www.swizzleinn.com.*

$$$
CARIBBEAN
Fodor'sChoice
★

✕ **Tom Moore's Tavern.** In a house that dates from 1652, Tom Moore's Tavern has a colorful past and a charming, historical feel. Though not inexpensive, the impeccably prepared cuisine is fresh, light, and innovative, perfect for a special occasion or romantic date. **Known for:** special-occasion dining; decadent soufflés; over-the-top service. ⑤ *Average main: $38* ✉ *7 Walsingham La., Bailey's Bay, Hamilton* ☎ *441/293–8020* ⊕ *www.tommoores.com* ⊙ *No lunch.*

$$
SOUTHERN

✕ **Victoria Grill.** American bistro-style comfort food is served in the chic dining room, outside on the breezy veranda, and downstairs in the courtyard where you can enjoy both the rum bar and the alfresco setting. Highlights here include the guacamole (prepared tableside), fresh grilled fish, and authentic Spanish paella. **Known for:** alfresco dining; tableside fresh guacamole; popular happy hour. ⑤ *Average main: $29* ✉ *29 Victoria St., Hamilton* ☎ *441/296–5050* ⊕ *www.victoria-grill.com* ▭ *No credit cards* ⊙ *No lunch Sat. Closed Sun.*

CENTRAL PARISHES

Right in the middle of the island, you'll find some of the finest dining opportunities available in Bermuda. The Central Parishes cover the large area of Paget, Warwick, and Devonshire. Many of the best restaurants are in luxury hotels and resorts. The only downside is if you're not staying in one of these resorts, the area is not easily reachable by public transport. Taking a cab is your best option.

> ### NOT-SO-FAST FOOD
>
> If you think something may be missing from the horizon of Bermuda eateries, you are quite right. Apart from a lone KFC (which snuck in sometime during the 1970s), you won't find any fast-food chains on the island. The majority of Bermuda's residents strongly believe that allowing American franchises onto the island would dilute Bermuda's distinctive foreign (and rather upscale) appeal, eventually leading to the island's resembling Anyplace, USA. Adjust your eyes (and belly) to the absence of big golden double arches!

$$$ ✗ **Beau Rivage.** This upscale, water-
FRENCH front eatery with an alfresco patio, a vast selection of wines, and extensive menu adds a little ooh-la-la to Bermuda's restaurant scene. Specialties include crispy duck breast, herb risotto, and beef Wellington. **Known for:** delicious French cooking; panoramic views of Hamilton Harbour; Sunday brunch. Ⓢ *Average main: $39* ✉ *Newstead Belmont Hills Resort, 27 Harbour Rd.* ☎ *441/232–8686* ⊕ *www.newsteadbelmonthills.com.*

$$$ ✗ **Blu Bar & Grill.** An expansive vista of aquamarine waters, white roofs,
ECLECTIC and green palm trees—not to mention the view across the manicured golf course—makes Blu Bar & Grill one of the island's prettiest spots for dinner, especially at sunset. The cuisine, which is loosely American with bold flavors and lots of exotic herbs and spices, encompasses not only steaks and ribs but also tempuras. **Known for:** sunset views from the patio; fresh sushi; eclectic menu. Ⓢ *Average main: $35* ✉ *Newstead Belmont Hills Golf Course, 97 Middle Rd.* ☎ *441/232–2323* ⊕ *www. blu.bm* ☾ *No lunch.*

$$$ ✗ **Café Coco.** Part of the Coco Reef Resort, this warm, ocean-side restau-
CARIBBEAN rant has a real European feel to it. Enjoy a candlelit dinner in the dining room, which looks like a white Mediterranean villa, complete with archways and art depicting typical street scenes, or enjoy your meal on the outside terrace overlooking the swimming pool and coastline. **Known for:** spectacular views; intimate dining room; summer barbecue buffets. Ⓢ *Average main: $33* ✉ *Coco Reef Resort, 3 Stonington Circle* ⊕ *Off South Shore Rd.* ☎ *441/236–5416* ⊕ *www.cocoreefbermuda.com.*

$$$ ✗ **Fourways Inn.** Fourways has risen to preeminence as much for its
EUROPEAN lovely 17th-century surroundings as for its award-winning cuisine and
Fodor's Choice famous Sunday brunch. The elegant yet charming interior, with mahog-
★ any banisters, burgundy carpeting, impressionist prints, and silver-and-crystal table settings, evokes the image of a fine French manor. **Known for:** popular Sunday brunch; historic ambience; decadent dessert soufflés. Ⓢ *Average main: $39* ✉ *1 Middle Rd.* ☎ *441/236–6517* ⊕ *www. fourways.bm* ☾ *No lunch. No dinner Sun.*

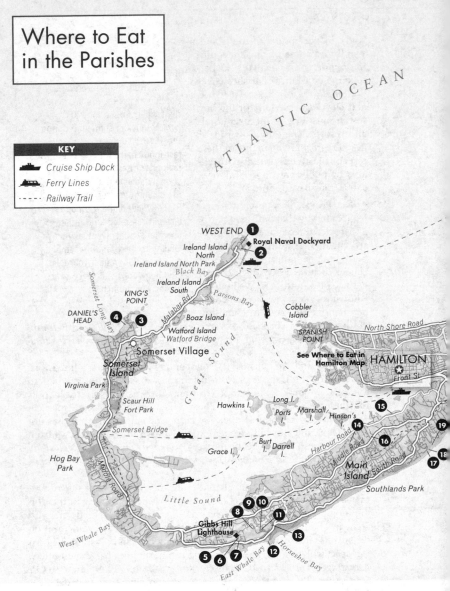

Where to Eat in the Parishes

KEY

- Cruise Ship Dock
- Ferry Lines
- - - - Railway Trail

ATLANTIC OCEAN

WEST END **1**

◆ **Royal Naval Dockyard**

2

Ireland Island North

Ireland Island North Park

Black Bay

Ireland Island South

Parsons Bay

Cobbler Island

Somerset Long Bay

KING'S POINT

DANIEL'S HEAD

4 **3**

Boaz Island

Watford Island

Watford Bridge

SPANISH POINT

North Shore Road

See Where to Eat in Hamilton Map

HAMILTON

Front St.

Somerset Village

Somerset Island

Virginia Park

Great Sound

Hawkins I.

Long I.

Marshall I.

Hinson's

15

Ports I.

14

19

Scaur Hill Fort Park

Somerset Bridge

Grace I.

Burt I. *Darrell I.*

Harbour Road

16

Middle Road

Main Island

South Road

17

18

Hog Bay Park

Little Sound

Southlands Park

Gibbs Hill Lighthouse

8 **9** **10**

11

West Whale Bay

5 **6** **7**

12

13

East Whale Bay *Horseshoe Bay*

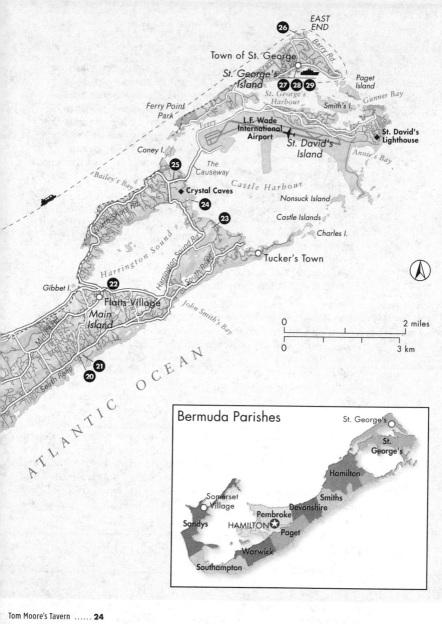

EAST END

Town of St. George
St. George's Island

Paget Island

26

27 28 29

St. George's Harbour

Gunner Bay

Smith's I.

Ferry Point Park

Ferry

L.F. Wade International Airport

St. David's Lighthouse

St. David's Island

Annie's Bay

Coney I.

25

The Causeway

Castle Harbour

Crystal Caves

24

Nonsuck Island

23

Castle Islands

North Shore Rd.

Charles I.

Harrington Sound Rd.

Harrington Sound

Tucker's Town

Gibbet I.

22

South Road

Flatts Village

Main Island

John Smith's Bay

Midland Rd.

21

South Road

20

ATLANTIC OCEAN

0 ———————— 2 miles

0 ———————— 3 km

Bermuda Parishes

St. George's

St. George's

Hamilton

Somerset Village

Smiths

Devonshire

Pembroke

Sandys

HAMILTON

Paget

Warwick

Southampton

SWEET TREATS

Bailey's Ice Cream. This remains a firm favorite with locals. Try the rum raisin or banana flavor! ⊠ *6 Blue Hole Hill, Bailey's Bay, Hamilton* ☎ *441/293–8605* ▭ *No credit cards* ⊙ *Closed in winter.*

Double Dip Express. Mix and match every flavor of ice cream imaginable—well worth the trek! ⊠ *1 Kindley Field Rd., St. George's* ☎ *441/293–5959* ▭ *No credit cards.*

Nannini's. Cool off with smooth and creamy Häagen-Dazs ice cream, sorbet, and frozen yogurt. ⊠ *Clock Tower Shopping Mall, Dockyard* ☎ *441/234–2474* ▭ *No credit cards.*

Rock Island Coffee. What's the perfect afternoon pick-me-up? In Bermuda, we'd venture that it's something in the order of an iced chai latte, a handmade scone, and a seat in the shade at Rock Island Coffee. ⊠ *48 Reid St., Hamilton* ☎ *441/296–5241* ⊕ *www.rockisland. bm* ▭ *No credit cards* ⊙ *Closed Sun.*

Temptations Cafe. Enjoy a sticky pastry, hazelnut coffee, or delicious frozen treat. ⊠ *31 York St., St. George's* ☎ *441/297–1368* ▭ *No credit cards* ⊙ *Closed Sun.*

$$$
MEDITERRANEAN

✕**Lido Restaurant.** In the beachfront dining room at the Elbow Beach Resort, with waves breaking just below, the Lido Restaurant is regarded as one of the island's most romantic settings. Reserve a table near the window and choose from an excellent seafood selection—which includes a delicious octopus salad and stuffed Bermuda lobster—for a truly memorable dining experience. **Known for:** romantic dining; expansive beach views; lively nightlife scene on the terrace. ⑤ *Average main: $37* ⊠ *Elbow Beach Resort, 60 South Shore Rd.* ☎ *441/236–9884* ⊕ *www.lido.bm* ⊙ *No lunch.*

$$$
MEDITERRANEAN

✕**Mickey's Beach Bistro.** Mickey's is hands-down the place to go for an unforgettable alfresco meal on the beach. Enjoy the view while you savor a tropical cocktail and peruse an extensive list of Continental and local specialties. **Known for:** on-the-beach dining; relaxed, island atmosphere; family-friendly lunch. ⑤ *Average main: $35* ⊠ *Elbow Beach Resort, 60 South Shore Rd.* ☎ *441/236–9107* ⊕ *www.lido.bm* ⊙ *Closed Nov.–Apr.*

ST. GEORGE'S AND EASTERN PARISHES

ST. GEORGE'S

St. George's is a lovely dining spot, with many restaurants right by the water's edge. You can sit back and relax as you watch life at sea and even dip your toes to cool down. It's the perfect place to stop for dinner after you've built up an appetite walking around the Old Town's museums and historic buildings. The restaurants here are less crowded and more relaxed than those in Hamilton and Dockyard. You'll probably find yourself dining with some of the country's politicians without even realizing it.

CLOSE UP

Best Bets for Kids

Harbour Nights. Harbour Nights festival in Hamilton (Wednesday evenings, May through September) lets kids eat on their feet. Choose fish sandwiches, patties, wraps, sweets, and more from booths and kiosks along Front, Reid, and Queen Streets. ⊠ Hamilton ▭ No credit cards.

Paraquet. This American-style diner's low counter with stools is ideal for little ones to watch what's going on in the kitchen. The large selection of kids' food, milk shakes, and the well-priced menu make this a great spot for families. ⊠ 68 South Shore Rd. ☎ 441/236–5842 ▭ No credit cards.

Pizza House. Youngsters love being creative and eating with their hands, so let them have the best of both worlds by creating their own pizza;

head here to see who can come up with the tastiest combination of toppings. Especially hungry kids will love the double cheeseburger or jumbo hot dog. ☎ 441/293–5700 ▭ No credit cards.

Shelly Bay. Bermuda has the ideal picnic venue to keep the younger set entertained all day long. Shelly Bay in Hamilton Parish has a huge children's play area right next to its sandy beach, so little ones won't have time to be bored. ⊠ Hamilton ▭ No credit cards.

Warwick Lanes. Let the kids knock 'em down with a family bowling challenge at Warwick Lanes. Between games, pick off the menu at the on-site Last Pin restaurant. ⊠ Hill View, 47 Middle Rd. ☎ 441/236–5290 ▭ No credit cards.

$$$
CARIBBEAN
Fodor's Choice
★

✕ **The Beach House.** Well off the beaten path, overlooking Achilles Bay next to the historic Fort St. Catherine, the Beach House offers a dining experience unlike anywhere else on the island. Elegant balcony seating, a chilled glass of wine, and a vibrant sunset set the scene for a memorable evening. **Known for:** sunset dining; tranquil beachfront location; seafood selection. ⑤ *Average main: $35* ⊠ *The St. George's Club, 6 Rose Hill, St. George's* ⊹ *Overlooking Achilles Bay* ☎ *441/297–1400* ⊕ *www.stgeorgesclub.bm* ▭ *No credit cards* ⊘ *Closed Nov.–Apr.*

$$
BISTRO

✕ **Tempest Bistro.** Located a short stroll from King's Square down Water Street, Tempest Bistro boasts a quiet, secluded entrance, an inspired menu, and a stunning view of the harbor. A relatively nondescript facade opens into a rustic brick-and-tile interior, lending to the restaurant's laid-back, old-fashioned allure. **Known for:** inventive daily specials; curated wine list; quiet, romantic dining. ⑤ *Average main: $26* ⊠ *22 Water St., St. George's* ☎ *441/297–0861* ⊘ *No dinner Sun. Closed Tues* ▭ *No credit cards.*

$$
SEAFOOD
FAMILY

✕ **Wahoo's Bistro & Patio.** With a name like Wahoo's, it's no surprise that this restaurant's menu features a wide variety of fresh, local seafood. Though often crowded, the patio offers an unbeatable view of the water; kids will love throwing scraps to schools of fish near the dock. **Known for:** fresh local seafood; fish-feeding from the patio; wahoo nuggets. ⑤ *Average main: $29* ⊠ *36 Water St., St. George's* ☎ *441/297–1307* ⊕ *www.wahoos.bm* ▭ *No credit cards* ⊘ *Closed Mon. during winter.*

$$ ✕**White Horse Pub & Restaurant.**
CARIBBEAN Located in the former Merchant's
Hall, which dates back to the
1600s, this rustic harborside res-
taurant is overflowing with history.
The menu features a variety of pub
favorites as well as fresh seafood
and pizza. **Known for:** breezy patio
dining; generous portions; historic
setting. $ *Average main: $28* ⌷ *8
King's Sq., St. George's* ☎ *441/297–
1838* ⊕ *www.whitehorsebermuda.com.*

> **DID YOU KNOW?**
>
> An 80-foot harbor mural by
> Eurasian artist Gerard Henderson
> winds around The Point restaurant.
> Originally hung in the Pan Am
> offices in Manhattan, the impres-
> sive artwork brings a little piece
> of history to Bermuda.

EASTERN PARISHES

The east of the island is best known for the Swizzle Inn, and it's proba-
bly the one place that most people have heard of before they even arrive.
Its reputation is legendary, and it doesn't disappoint. Other restaurants
are quite spread out from Flatts Village to St. David's, but they will be
well worth the trek. Your efforts will be rewarded with the freshest of
ingredients (there's an abundance of fishermen at this end of the island)
away from the crowds.

$$ ✕**North Rock Brewing Company.** The copper and mahogany tones of
BRITISH the handcrafted beers and ales are reflected in the warm interior of
this casual bar and restaurant, Bermuda's only brewpub. North Rock
offers an extensive selection of seafood and pub favorites, plus locally
made ales from Dockyard Brewing Company to accompany your meal.
Known for: traditional pub fare; Bermuda-made beers from Dockyard
Brewing Co.; crowd-pleasing menu. $ *Average main: $28* ⌷ *10 South
Shore Rd.* ✛ *Near Collector's Hill* ☎ *441/236–6633.*

$$$ ✕**The Point.** If you can have just one splurge in Bermuda, let it be for the
CARIBBEAN creative and flawlessly crafted entrées on offer at The Point. Tradition
Fodor's Choice and innovation commingle in a menu that highlights local produce, like
★ Tucker's Farm goat cheese and Bermuda rockfish. **Known for:** multi-
course dining experience; international cuisine; beautiful plating. $ *Av-
erage main: $39* ⌷ *Rosewood Tucker's Point, 60 Tucker's Point Dr.,
Tucker's Town, Ferniegair* ☎ *441/298–4077* ⊕ *www.rosewoodhotels.
com* ⌂ *Jacket required.*

$$ ✕**Rustico Restaurant & Pizzeria.** At Rustico, you can dine on colorful Ital-
ITALIAN ian specialties and appreciate the beauty of the quaint village of Flatts,
across from the Bermuda Museum, Aquarium & Zoo. Start with stylish
cocktails at the bar before settling in for some of Bermuda's best thin-
crust pizza. **Known for:** thin-crust pizza; alfresco dining on the patio;
homemade pastas. $ *Average main: $30* ⌷ *8 North Shore Rd., Flatts
Village* ☎ *441/295–5212* ⊕ *www.bermuda-dining.com.*

$ ✕**Speciality Inn.** You may have to wait a few minutes for a table, but you
CARIBBEAN can't beat Specialty Inn for satisfying, reasonably priced meals. A favor-
FAMILY ite of locals and families, this South Shore restaurant is cheerful and
clean, with a large, no-frills menu that features everything from pizza to

CLOSE UP

The Dish on Local Dishes

Shark hash, made of minced shark meat sautéed with spices, may not sound too appetizing, but it's a popular Bermudian appetizer, usually served on toast.

Bermudians love **codfish cakes**— made of salted cod mashed with cooked potatoes and fresh thyme and parsley, then shaped into patties and panfried. They taste great topped with a zesty fruit salsa and a side of mesclun salad.

The island's traditional weekend brunch is a huge plate of **boiled or steamed salt cod** with boiled potatoes, onions, and sliced bananas, all topped with a hard-boiled egg or tomato sauce, and, sometimes, avocado slices.

Cassava pie—a savory blend of cassava, eggs, sugar, and either pork or chicken—is a rich, flavorful dish (formerly reserved for Christmas dinner) often offered as a special side. More common is **mussel pie,** made of shelled mussels, potatoes, and onions, baked and seasoned with thyme, parsley, and curry.

As for Bermudian desserts, **bananas** baked in rum and brown sugar are to die for, and **loquat or banana crumble** is sweet and rich.

sushi. **Known for:** home-style family cooking; good value food; codfish and potato breakfast. ⑤ *Average main: $18* ✉ *Collectors Hill, 4 South Shore Rd.* ☎ *441/236–3133* ⊕ *www.specialityinn.bm* ⊘ *Closed Sun.*

DOCKYARD AND WESTERN PARISHES

$$$ ✕ **Bacci.** A winning combination of authentic Italian cuisine, fine dining,
ITALIAN and gracious service is what you can find at Bacci, which translates as "quick and friendly kisses." Perched atop Turtle Hill Golf Course, the restaurant is decorated in bright and bold colors with impressive panoramic views. Bacci celebrates all that is great about Italy, and the chefs are not afraid to experiment with whatever is freshest at market. **Known for:** fresh house-made pasta; sweeping golf course views; delicious bread and appetizers. ⑤ *Average main: $35* ✉ *Fairmont Southampton Resort, 101 South Shore Rd.* ☎ *441/238–8000* ⊕ *www.fairmont.com/southampton-bermuda* ⊘ *No lunch.*

$$ ✕ **Bone Fish.** Though service isn't exactly speedy, the happy, social vibe
CARIBBEAN and huge patio make Bone Fish a local and tourist favorite. Choose from Bermuda-style catch of the day, fish-and-chips, rib-eye steaks, and homemade pasta, and chat with Italian owner Livio Ferigo who loves to mingle with diners. **Known for:** social patio seating; live music; colorful cocktails. ⑤ *Average main: $29* ✉ *6 Dockyard Terr., Dockyard, Somerset* ☎ *441/234–5151* ⊕ *www.bonefishbermuda.com.*

$$$ ✕ **Breezes.** Breezes offers a flavorful, island-inspired menu and a location
CARIBBEAN that is simply perfect—these beachfront views and ocean breezes are exactly what a Bermudian vacation is all about. Time your dinner for sunset to truly take advantage of the locale and, for out-of-this-world romance, reserve a table right on the beach. **Known for:** spectacular

sunsets; on-the-beach dining; live music. ⑤ *Average main: $35* ⊠ *Cambridge Beaches Resort, 30 Kings Point Rd., Somerset* ☎ *441/234–0331* ⊕ *www.cambridgebeaches.com* ⊘ *Closed Oct.–May.*

$$$
CARIBBEAN
Fodor's Choice
★

✗ **Coconuts.** Nestled between high cliff rocks and a pristine private beach on the southern coast, this outdoor restaurant is one of the best places to nab that table overlooking the ocean. The menu changes often, but you can always be sure of fresh, local produce, and fish prepared with customary Bermudian flair. **Known for:** dramatic views from the cliff-side terrace; romantic tables on the beach; fresh local fish. ⑤ *Average main: $34* ⊠ *The Reefs, 56 South Shore Rd.* ☎ *441/238–0222* ⊕ *www.thereefs.com* ⊘ *Closed Nov.–Apr.*

$$
EUROPEAN

✗ **The Dining Room.** At the base of Gibbs Hill Lighthouse, in the old Lighthouse Tea Room, this adorable little restaurant is the perfect place to rest after the climb up and down the tower's 185 spiraling steps. Eclectic lunch and dinner menus include everything from traditional fish and chicken dishes to salads and homemade lasagna. **Known for:** bird's-eye views; fresh seafood; cozy, intimate dining. ⑤ *Average main: $27* ⊠ *68 St. Anne's Rd., Southampton* ☎ *441/238–8679* ⊕ *www.bermuda-dining.com* ⊘ *Closed Mon.; no lunch Tues.–Thurs.*

$$
BRITISH
FAMILY

✗ **Frog & Onion Pub.** Housed in the former Royal Naval Dockyard warehouse, this nautical-themed restaurant is loved locally for its good food, craft beers, and lively atmosphere. The menu caters to every palate and includes juicy burgers, hearty house-made pub pies, and a selection of fresh local fish plates. **Known for:** lively spot; flights of local Bermuda beers; satisfying pub grub. ⑤ *Average main: $25* ⊠ *The Cooperage, 4 Freeport Rd., Dockyard* ☎ *441/234–2900* ⊕ *www.frogandonion.bm.*

$$
SEAFOOD

✗ **Gulfstream.** Located opposite the entrance to one of Bermuda's most popular beaches, Horseshoe Bay, this restaurant offers a selection of surf-and-turf dishes plus plenty of options for vegetarians and picky eaters. Guests rave about the thin-crust pizzas and the market-fresh fish. **Known for:** fresh local fish; crispy thin-crust pizza; friendly staff. ⑤ *Average main: $26* ⊠ *117 South Rd., Southampton* ☎ *441/238–1897* ⊕ *www.bermuda-dining.com* ⊟ *No credit cards.*

$$$
BRITISH
FAMILY

✗ **Henry VIII.** As popular with locals as it is with vacationers from nearby Southampton resorts, the lively Henry VIII exudes an Old English charm that stops just short of "wench" waitresses and Tudor styling. It's a bit pricey for what you get, but you can find a mix of English and Bermudian menu favorites, including steak-and-mushroom pie, rack of lamb, and fish chowder. **Known for:** Sunday brunch; sushi bar; live jazz music. ⑤ *Average main: $33* ⊠ *69 South Shore Rd., Southampton* ☎ *441/238–1977* ⊕ *www.henrys.bm.*

$$
BRITISH
Fodor's Choice
★

✗ **Newport, a Gastropub.** Named after the biennial Newport to Bermuda sailing race, this nautical-themed restaurant is located in the lobby level of the Fairmont Southampton hotel. It proudly offers Bermuda's only true gastropub experience, complete with a charcuterie station and fresh raw bar. **Known for:** fish-and-chips; shared platters; nautical theme. ⑤ *Average main: $25* ⊠ *Fairmont Southampton Resort, 101 South Shore Rd.* ☎ *441/238–8000* ⊕ *www.fairmont.com/southampton-bermuda* ⊘ *No lunch.*

CLOSE UP

Where to Take Tea

When afternoon arrives, Bermuda, like Britain, pauses for tea. Usually, tea is served between 3 and 5, but teatime can mean anything from an urn or thermos and cookies sitting on a sideboard to the more formal stiff-pinkie presentation of brewed-to-order tea in a porcelain or silver teapot, served with cream and sugar on a tray, and accompanied by finger sandwiches and scones with clotted cream and jam.

Fairmont Hamilton Princess. The Crown & Anchor restaurant in the Fairmont Hamilton Princess serves a posh afternoon tea on Saturdays and Sundays from 3 to 5. For $48, plus gratuities, you'll enjoy a refined selection of teas, sweets, and finger sandwiches. ⊠ 76 Pitts Bay Rd., Hamilton ☎ 441/295–3000 ⊕ www. thehamiltonprincess.com/dining.

Jasmine Lounge. Located in the Fairmont Southampton hotel, this quiet, elegant venue is perfectly suited to traditional afternoon tea, homemade scones, and adorable finger sandwiches. Tea is served daily from 3 to 5, for $29 plus gratuities. ⊠ The Fairmont Southampton, 101 South Shore Rd., Southampton ⊕ www.fairmont.com/southampton-bermuda ▭ No credit cards.

Sweet P. Located in the same building as the Bermuda Perfumery in St. George's, Sweet P offers high tea on Wednesday and Saturday from 1 to 5. For $30 (plus gratuities) you'll enjoy an array of sticky and sinful cakes, tarts, and pastries. ⊠ Stewart Hall, 5 Queen St., St. George's ☎ 441/293–0627 ▭ No credit cards.

$$$ ✕**Ocean Club.** Sample the catch of the day and watch the sun set while
SEAFOOD enjoying the relaxed yet intimate atmosphere on the terrace of Ocean
Fodor's Choice Club, one of the top seafood restaurants on the island. Because it
★ serves only the freshest of fish delivered daily by local fishermen, you
simply must have fish. **Known for:** fresh seafood; ocean-view terrace;
incredible sunsets. ⑤ *Average main: $33* ⊠ *Fairmont Southampton
Resort, 101 South Shore Rd., Southampton* ☎ *441/238–8000* ⊕ *www.
fairmont.com/southampton-bermuda* ⊘ *Subject to seasonal closure
after Oct. 31.*

$$ ✕**Somerset Country Squire.** Overlooking Mangrove Bay, this well-worn
CARIBBEAN tavern is all dark wood and good cheer, with a great deal of malt
FAMILY and hops in between. The food is simple, but a few items stand out:
the Bermuda fish chowder, panfried rockfish, and steak sandwich are
all delicious. **Known for:** scenic beach and bay views; covered patio
seating; summertime barbecues. ⑤ *Average main: $22* ⊠ *10 Mangrove
Bay Rd., Somerset* ☎ *441/234–0105.*

$$$$ ✕**Waterlot Inn.** This graceful, two-story manor house, which dates
AMERICAN from 1670 and once functioned as a bed-and-breakfast, now holds
Fodor's Choice one of Bermuda's most elegant and elaborate steak restaurants. Arrive
★ early to enjoy cocktails, live music, and spectacular sunsets from the
chic outdoor lounge, The Dock. **Known for:** first-class steaks and
seafood; excellent service and setting; magical sunset views on The
Dock. ⑤ *Average main: $51* ⊠ *Jew's Bay, Middle Rd., Southampton*

☎ *441/238–8000* ⊕ *www.fairmont.com/southampton-bermuda* ☽ *No lunch. Closed Mon in winter.*

$ ✕ **Wickets.** Simple yet satisfying American fare and prompt service make
AMERICAN this social restaurant a great spot for families. Swim up an appetite in
FAMILY the pool, then build your own beef, chicken, wahoo, or veggie burger
and retire to the shade with a Dark 'n' Stormy milk shake. **Known
for:** build-your-own burgers; outdoor dining and pool; on-site coffee bar. ⑤ *Average main: $19* ⊠ *Fairmont Southampton Resort, 101
South Shore Rd., Southampton* ☎ *441/238–8000* ⊕ *www.fairmont.
com/southampton-bermuda* ☽ *Closed Nov.–May.*

WHERE TO STAY

Updated by
Amy Peniston

Few places in the world boast the charm of Bermuda's curvaceous, colorful shoreline. It's a boon, then, that the lagoons, coves, and coasts, as well as its inland sanctuaries, are filled with equally colorful, alluring places to stay. But wherever you opt to stay, you are never far away from picture-perfect water views.

The quintessential accommodation on the island is a pink cottage amid manicured gardens and coral-stone pathways. Terraced whitewashed roofs (designed to capture rainwater) sit atop walls of pinks, peaches, and pastels, looking like cakes of ice cream in pink-wafer sand. Add a waterfront setting, and voilà—the lure of Bermuda.

Hamilton has many sophisticated lodging choices, but vacationers looking for beachfront relaxation will be disappointed in the beachless capital city. In fact, all noteworthy beaches are on the southern side of the island. With only a couple of exceptions, beachfront lodging choices are along a 7-mile stretch of coast that runs along the central to western tail of the island, west from Paget to Warwick, Southampton, and Sandys. Lodging choices on the north coast of the island often are on glittering Hamilton Harbour or have deepwater access to the Atlantic, but not beaches.

Bermuda is a land of cottage colonies, cliff-top apartments, and beachfront resort hotels. Hidden along small parish roads, however, you can also find family-run, flower-filled guesthouses and simple, inexpensive efficiencies. In fact, with the exception of the Fairmont Southampton, and the tall but unobtrusive larger main building at Elbow Beach, there are no high-rises in Bermuda. And nowhere do neon signs sully the landscape. Indeed, many of Bermuda's lodging properties are guesthouses, identifiable only by small, inconspicuous signs or plaques. Those who prefer bed-and-breakfasts will have no problem finding quaint retreats with local attention.

BERMUDA LODGING PLANNER

FACILITIES AND SERVICES

The number and quality of facilities vary greatly according to the size and rates of the property. Resort hotels are the best equipped, with restaurants, pools, beach clubs, gyms, and (in the case of Fairmont Southampton and Rosewood Tucker's Point) a golf course. Cottage colonies also typically have a clubhouse with a restaurant and bar, plus a pool or private beach, and perhaps a golf course. Each cottage has a kitchen, and housekeeping services are provided. Small hotels usually have a pool, and some have a restaurant or guest-only dining room, but few have fitness facilities or in-room extras like minibars. Efficiencies or housekeeping apartments almost always come with a kitchen or kitchenette. Some properties have pools, but you may have to take the bus or a scooter to get to the beach. Even the smallest property can arrange sailing, snorkeling, scuba, and deep-sea fishing excursions, as well as sightseeing.

PRICES

Rates at Bermuda's luxury resorts are comparable to those at posh hotels in New York, London, and Paris. An 11.75% government occupancy tax plus a tourism fee is tacked on to all hotel bills, and a service charge is levied. Some hotels calculate the service charge as 10% of the bill, whereas others charge a per-diem amount. There's a mandatory 17% service charge for food and beverage bills and some resorts add a resort fee. The only way to be sure of your final hotel bill is to call ahead to confirm rates. Virtually every hotel on the island offers at least one vacation package—frequently some kind of honeymoon special—and many of these are extraordinarily good deals.

You can shave about 40% off your hotel bill by visiting Bermuda in low or shoulder seasons. Because temperatures rarely dip below 60°F in winter, the low season (November through March) is ideal for tennis, golf, and shopping.

When pricing accommodations, always ask what's included. Most lodgings offer a choice of meal plans, several with "dine-around" privileges at other island restaurants.

WHAT IT COSTS IN U.S. DOLLARS				
	$	$$	$$$	$$$$
Hotels	under $201	$201–$300	$301–$400	over $400

Prices are for two people in a standard double room in high season, excluding 9.75% tax and 10% service charge.

OUR REVIEWS

Reviews are listed alphabetically within region. All lodgings listed are equipped with private bathrooms and air-conditioning. Prices in the hotel reviews are the lowest cost of a standard double room in high season, excluding taxes, service charges, and meal plans. Prices for rentals are the lowest per-night cost for a one-bedroom unit in high season. Reviews have been condensed for this book. For expanded lodging reviews and current deals, visit Fodors.com.

HAMILTON AND CENTRAL PARISHES

HAMILTON

Stay in the heart of the city for added convenience. You won't need to worry about paying for a rental bike because everything you could need, such as stores, restaurants, and attractions, is right on your doorstep. This location will prove particularly useful to the business travelers who need to be close to Hamilton's financial sector. It's not the best of locations, however, for families or beach bums.

$$$
B&B/INN

Edgehill Manor. Quaint rooms and light continental breakfasts will make you feel right at home at this comfortable colonial-style 20th-century guesthouse within walking distance of the restaurants, stores, and attractions of Hamilton. **Pros:** quiet pool; well maintained; all rooms have private balconies. **Cons:** no in-house dining; isolated from beaches. ⑤ *Rooms from: $350* ✉ *36 Rosemont Ave., Hamilton* ☎ *441/295–7124* ⊕ *www.edgehillmanorguesthouse.com* ⇗ *14 rooms* �◎ *Breakfast.*

$$$$
RESORT
FAMILY

Grotto Bay Beach Resort. The ocean is never far from sight at this popular resort best known for its two on-site caves; you can treat yourself to a spa treatment in one, then go for a relaxing swim in the other. **Pros:** kids' program in summer; on-site aquatic activities; caves. **Cons:** small beach; can get crowded with package tour groups; airport noise. ⑤ *Rooms from: $429* ✉ *11 Blue Hole Hill, Bailey's Bay, Hamilton* ☎ *441/293–8333, 855/447–6886* ⊕ *www.grottobay.com* ⇗ *212 rooms* �◎ *No meals.*

$$$$
HOTEL
Fodor's Choice
★

The Hamilton Princess & Beach Club. The only full-service resort in Hamilton and located right on the harbor, just steps away from the liveliness of Front Street, the pastel-pink Princess is the reigning royalty of Bermuda lodging, boasting some of the most comfortable rooms on the island and catering to its mainly business guests like no one else. **Pros:** luxurious pool and amenities; only full-service resort in Hamilton; beautiful harbor-front locale. **Cons:** mainly corporate guests; ferry or cab necessary to reach beaches. ⑤ *Rooms from: $575* ✉ *76 Pitts Bay Rd., Hamilton* ☎ *441/295–3000, 800/441–1414* ⊕ *www.thehamilton-princess.com* ⇗ *458 rooms* �◎ *No meals.*

$$
B&B/INN

The Oxford House. The Oxford House is the only true bed-and-breakfast in Hamilton, and one imagines that even if this elegant beige two-story town house, just two blocks from the capital's shops, ferries, and buses had competition, it would still be the best. **Pros:** friendly and attentive service; clean and nicely furnished rooms; right in Hamilton. **Cons:** no pool; isolated from beaches. ⑤ *Rooms from: $270* ✉ *20 Woodbourne Ave., Hamilton* ☎ *441/295–0503* ⊕ *www.oxfordhouse. bm* ⇗ *12 rooms* �◎ *Breakfast.*

$$$
HOTEL

Rosedon Hotel. Expect a tranquil, refined environment and friendly service from longtime staff at this bright, blue-shuttered, white manor house in the center of Hamilton. **Pros:** free shuttle to beach; nice gardens and pool; complimentary afternoon tea. **Cons:** no beach; old-fashioned decor. ⑤ *Rooms from: $348* ✉ *61 Pitts Bay Rd., Hamilton* ☎ *441/295–1640, 800/742–5008 in U.S. and Canada* ⊕ *www.rosedon. com* ⇗ *39 rooms* �◎ *No meals.*

$$$$
RESORT
Fodor's Choice
★

Rosewood Tucker's Point. Dramatically perched above Castle Harbour, the immaculately furnished and spacious rooms at this luxurious escape from it all have picture-perfect water views. **Pros:** amazing ocean views; excellent amenities on-site; tastefully modern rooms. **Cons:** hotel is a substantial distance from its own beach club; in secluded area of the island; expensive. ⑤ *Rooms from: $895* ✉ *60 Tucker's Point Dr., Hamilton* ☎ *441/298–4000, 888/767–3966* ⊕ *www.rosewoodtuckerspoint. com* ⇗ *88 rooms* �◎ *No meals.*

CENTRAL PARISHES

If you can't decide whether to opt for the city or the beach, your best bet is to position yourself between the two. In the Central Parishes you are close enough to enjoy the south shore beaches by day and Hamilton by night. Paget, Warwick, and Devonshire parishes have plenty of hotels to choose from, as this is one of the most picturesque areas of the island.

> ### BERMUDA RESORTS
>
> Americans accustomed to resorts with big private beaches steps from guest rooms will find their expectations best met at Elbow Beach. The Fairmont Southampton is the island's other large-scale beach resort, but its sand is a five-minute walk across the huge property and the street. Cambridge Beaches, Pompano, and The Reefs offer smaller resorts but equally nice beaches.

$
RENTAL
Fodor's Choice
★

Clairfont Apartments. Probably the island's best buy if you're on a budget; although it's not exactly fancy, it's spotlessly clean and the beach is just a five-minute stroll away. **Pros:** affordable; very clean and well maintained; large units. **Cons:** basic furnishings; not beachfront. ⑤ *Rooms from: $160* ⊠ *6 Warwickshire Rd.* ☎ *441/238–3577* ⊕ *www.clairfontapartments.bm* ⬋ *8 rooms* ⧖ *No meals.*

$$$
HOTEL

Coco Reef Resort. In the prime location of the highly desirable Elbow Beach, this hotel's decor may be dated, but you'll probably be too busy admiring the gorgeous views to let it bother you. **Pros:** close to the beach; impressive pool; steps from restaurants at Elbow Beach Resort. **Cons:** accommodations are outdated; prices steep for what you get; limited attractions within walking distance. ⑤ *Rooms from: $399* ⊠ *3 Stonington Circle* ✚ *Off South Shore Rd.* ☎ *441/236–5416* ⊕ *www. cocoreefbermuda.com* ⬋ *64 rooms* ⧖ *No meals.*

$$$$
RESORT
FAMILY

Elbow Beach. It may be pricey, but the intimate hideaway at Elbow Beach with simple and elegant rooms tucked away in cottages dotted through 50 acres of lush gardens and tennis courts is well worth a stay. **Pros:** great beach; luxurious spa; many restaurants to entertain. **Cons:** expensive; huge property can mean a lot of walking. ⑤ *Rooms from: $725* ⊠ *60 South Shore Rd.* ☎ *441/236–3535, 855/463–5269 in U.S. and Canada* ⊕ *www.elbowbeachbermuda.com* ⬋ *98 rooms* ⧖ *No meals.*

$$
B&B/INN
Fodor's Choice
★

Fourways Inn. With a top-notch restaurant on-site, this pleasant cottage colony comes to life at meal times; for the rest of the day, lose yourself in Fourways' quiet solitude and endless hospitality. **Pros:** great dining; excellent old-fashioned service; breakfast delivered daily. **Cons:** little in the immediate area; no activities for kids. ⑤ *Rooms from: $245* ⊠ *1 Middle Rd.* ☎ *441/236–6517, 800/962–7654 in U.S.* ⊕ *www.fourways.bm* ⬋ *11 rooms* ⧖ *Breakfast.*

$$
B&B/INN
Fodor's Choice
★

Granaway Guest House. A 1734 manor house with villa-like lawn and gardens, Granaway is an affordable accommodation option for those who do not need to be on the beach. **Pros:** gardened terrace; relaxing lawn and pool area; historic property. **Cons:** not waterfront or easy walk to beaches; no on-site restaurant. ⑤ *Rooms from: $225* ⊠ *1 Longford Rd.* ✚ *Off Harbour Rd.* ☎ *441/236–3747* ⊕ *www.granaway. com* ⬋ *5 rooms* ⧖ *Breakfast.*

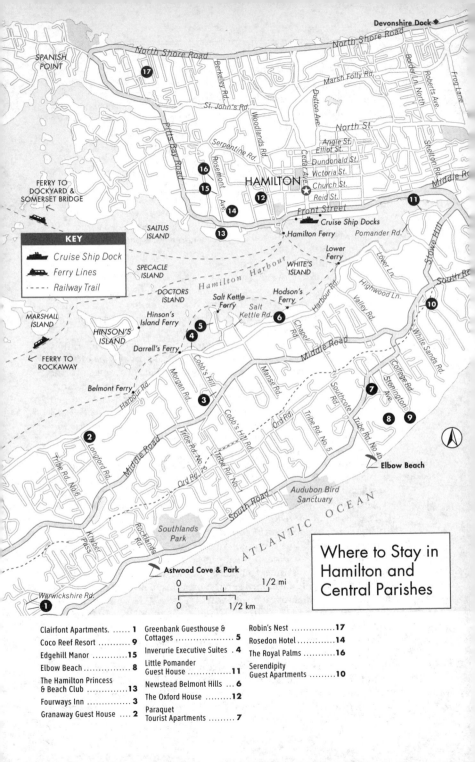

Where to Stay in Hamilton and Central Parishes

CLOSE UP

A Look Ahead at Bermuda Lodgings

Traveling to Bermuda in the near future? Be sure to keep an eye on a few of the highly anticipated headlines within the island's local resort scene.

Excitement surrounds the latest announcements from Morgan's Point developers about the construction of Caroline Bay, a luxurious hotel, golf course, and marina resort to rival the famous Atlantis getaway in the Bahamas. Located in Southampton, this groundbreaking venture will be developed in phases, with the first to be completed by end of 2018. A buzz also surrounds the site of the former Sonesta Beach resort, which was closed and later demolished following hurricane damage. Although the property was recently purchased by the Green family of Bermuda, no firm plans for future development have been released.

In addition to the construction of several new hotels across the island, many existing resorts are receiving major face-lifts. Rosewood Tucker's Point is set to benefit from significant upgrades following its 2017 sale to a Miami-based investment group. In summer 2017, the Hamilton Princess & Beach Club made an application to become the island's first integrated casino resort. Several hearings will determine if the hotel is granted a casino license.

4

$
B&B/INN
Greenbank Guesthouse & Cottages. Greenbank has been family run for close to 60 years, and this is what Bermuda vacations were like back then: by way of entertainment you had a due-west pier with chairs to watch the sunset and a private dock for deepwater swimming. **Pros:** close to ferry; secluded area; relaxed place. **Cons:** no pool or beach. $ *Rooms from: $200* ⊠ *17 Salt Kettle Rd.* ☎ *441–236–3615* ⊕ *www. greenbankbermuda.com* ⟿ *11 rooms* ⟦◎⟧ *Breakfast.*

$$
HOTEL
Inverurie Executive Suites. This recently overhauled harbor-front hotel was designed with the corporate client in mind, outfitted with sleek, modern amenities including galley kitchens and offering private balconies overlooking Hamilton Harbour. **Pros:** balconies over the harbor; next to ferry service. **Cons:** no leisure activities; feels a little impersonal. $ *Rooms from: $285* ⊠ *1 Harbour Rd.* ☎ *441–232–5700* ⊕ *www.inverurie.bm* ⟿ *15 rooms* ⟦◎⟧ *No meals.*

$
B&B/INN
Little Pomander Guest House. The circa-1600 house—one of the island's oldest—is on a quiet one-way residential street that edges along a narrow inlet of Hamilton Harbour. **Pros:** affordable option; nice waterfront views of Hamilton; 10-minute walk to Hamilton or beaches. **Cons:** no beach; dated rooms; linens clean but not contemporary. $ *Rooms from: $150* ⊠ *16 Pomander Rd.* ☎ *441–236–7635* ⟿ *5 rooms* ⟦◎⟧ *Breakfast.*

$$$$
HOTEL
Newstead Belmont Hills. This hotel, linked to a private golf course, has perhaps the ritziest and most contemporary design aesthetic in Bermuda, with some of the sleekest rooms and a gorgeous infinity pool right on the edge of the harbor. **Pros:** harbor views; amazing pool; stylish contemporary amenities. **Cons:** golf course not on premises; no beach. $ *Rooms from: $470* ⊠ *27 Harbour Rd.* ☎ *441–236–6060* ⊕ *www.newsteadbelmonthills.com* ⟿ *45 rooms* ⟦◎⟧ *No meals.*

LODGING ALTERNATIVES

APARTMENT AND VILLA RENTALS

If you want a home base that's roomy enough for a family, consider renting a private house or apartment. Furnished rentals can save you money, especially if you're traveling with a group.

Bermuda Rentals. Bermuda Rentals maintains an up-to-the-minute listing of available properties all over the island *and* makes reservations. The website has photos and good descriptions of what you can expect to find. ⊕ www.bermudarentals.com.

BermudaGetaway. BermudaGetaway lists a selection of high-standard properties but does not accept reservations. For that, you can contact the property owner directly. ⊕ www.bermudagetaway.com.

Coldwell Banker JW Bermuda Realty. Coldwell Banker JW Bermuda Realty requires you to register with the company before an agent will help you find a property that meets your requirements. Its Vacation Rental website, *www.vacationhomesbermuda.*

com, is another helpful source for short- and long-term rental listings. ☎ 441/292–1793 ⊕ www.bermudarealty.com.

BED-AND-BREAKFASTS

Bed-and-breakfasts in Bermuda range from grand, converted Victorians to a couple of rooms with shared bath in a small home. Breakfasts, too, run the gamut, though light continental breakfasts with fresh fruit are more common than hearty bacon-and-eggs meals. Sometimes there is a pool on the property, but to get to the beach you usually have to travel by bus or scooter.

AIRBNB

Airbnb (⊕ www.airbnb.com) has really taken off on the island and it's by far the cheapest way to stay in Bermuda. There are rooms and entire homes for rent all across the island, with a decent number of centrally located places, which is great because there aren't *that* many hotel options near Hamilton. And, of course, you can save money by cooking and eating in.

$
HOTEL

Paraquet Tourist Apartments. For those not picky about room furnishings, Paraquet (pronounced "parakeet") provides a centrally located, motel-like, no-frills stay. **Pros:** convenient diner; affordable; close to the beach. **Cons:** no views; no pool; no amenities. ⑤ *Rooms from: $180* ✉ *72 South Shore Rd.* ☎ *441/236–5842* ⊕ *www.paraquetapartments. com* ⌁ *18 rooms* ⑩ *No meals.*

$$
RENTAL

Robin's Nest. This well-maintained valley property is a tad off the beaten path, in a quiet residential neighborhood about a mile north of Hamilton and within walking distance to a secluded beach cove. **Pros:** well-kept rooms and grounds; pool. **Cons:** out-of-the-way location. ⑤ *Rooms from: $280* ✉ *37 Mount View* ☎ *441/292–4347* ⊕ *www. robinsnestbda.com* ⌁ *8 rooms* ⑩ *No meals.*

$$$$
HOTEL
Fodor's Choice
★

The Royal Palms. The Royal Palms is a winner for having high standards, great service, and a welcoming touch with fresh-from-the-garden flowers to celebrate your arrival. **Pros:** beautiful gardens; wonderful breakfast; top-notch service. **Cons:** no beach; pricey. $ *Rooms from: $460 ⊠ 24 Rosemont Ave. ☎ 441/292–1854, 800/678–0783 in U.S. and Canada ⊕ www.royalpalms.bm ⌨ 32 rooms ⦿ Breakfast.*

$
RENTAL

Serendipity Guest Apartments. The family of the owner of these two budget-friendly studio apartments in residential Paget has been on the island since 1612, and return guests are welcomed as part of that extended family. **Pros:** clean and well maintained; private; near Railway Trail and Paget Nature Reserve. **Cons:** have to walk to beach; no hotel-style services; just two apartments. $ *Rooms from: $160 ⊠ 6 Rural Dr. ☎ 441/236–1192 ⊟ No credit cards ⌨ 2 rooms ⦿ No meals.*

4

ST. GEORGE'S AND EASTERN PARISHES

ST. GEORGE'S

Staying in the heart of this UNESCO World Heritage site is a great opportunity to get to know Bermuda's rich history. You'll be surrounded by some of the prettiest streets on the island, with colorful cottages and scores of little alleyways. St. George's is also right on the water's edge with a handful of beaches within walking distance. There's a warm and welcoming feel to St. George's, so stay a couple of days and you will make friends with the locals.

$
B&B/INN

Aunt Nea's Inn. Stroll down a narrow winding alley to this grand 18th-century home and you'll be treated to the best of St. George's, combining a quaint setting with home comforts. **Pros:** peaceful, pleasant St. George's setting; great service; within walking distance of King's Square. **Cons:** no pool; far from other island destinations. $ *Rooms from: $150 ⊠ 1 Nea's Alley, St. George's ✛ Off Old Maid's La. ☎ 441/296–2868 ⊕ www.auntneasinn.com ⌨ 9 rooms ⦿ Breakfast.*

EASTERN PARISHES

This is the perfect hideaway spot that's off the beaten track. One of the sparsest areas of the island, it really isn't geared toward tourists, but the hotels are in the lovely Castle Harbour area, which offers great water views and water sports opportunities. If you opt for this location, you're in for a peaceful and relaxing getaway.

$$$$
HOTEL
Fodor's Choice
★

The Loren at Pink Beach. Bermuda's newest luxury hotel blends the beauty of a spectacular oceanfront setting with elegant European-inspired architecture, modern and high-end finishes, and an intimate vibe. **Pros:** amazing ocean views; elegant and private; near Mid Ocean and Tucker's Point golf courses. **Cons:** isolated from populated parts of island; limited dining options. $ *Rooms from: $800 ⊠ 116 South Shore Rd., Tucker's Town ☎ 441/293–1666, 844/384–3103 in U.S. ⊕ www. thelorenhotel.com ⌨ 45 rooms ⦿ No meals.*

Where to Stay in the East and West Ends

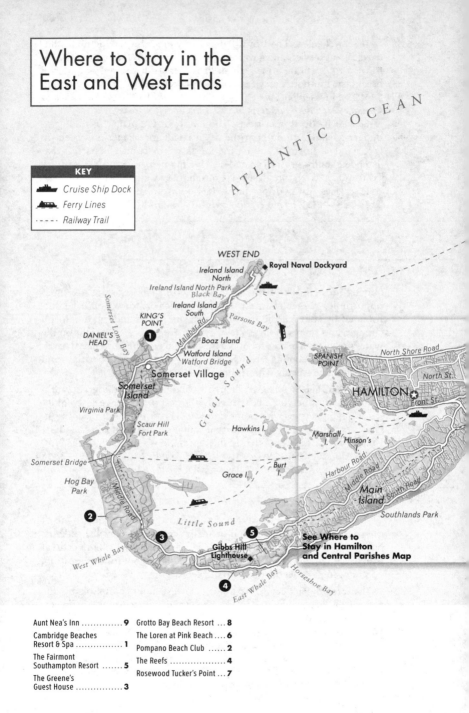

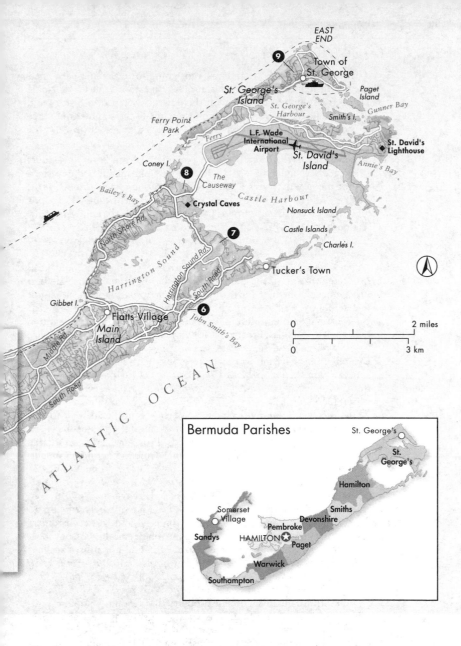

EAST END

9 Town of St. George

St. George's Island

St. George's Harbour

Paget Island

Smith's I.

Gunner Bay

Ferry Point Park

Ferry

L.F. Wade International Airport

St. David's Island

St. David's Lighthouse

Coney I.

8

The Causeway

◆ **Crystal Caves**

Castle Harbour

Annie's Bay

Bailey's Bay

North Shore Rd.

Nonsuck Island

Castle Islands

Charles I.

7

Tucker's Town

Harrington Sound

Harrington Sound Rd.

South Road

Gibbet I.

6

Flatts Village

John Smith's Bay

Main Island

Middle Rd.

South Road

A T L A N T I C   O C E A N

0   2 miles

0   3 km

Bermuda Parishes

St. George's

St. George's

Hamilton

Somerset Village

Smiths

Devonshire

Pembroke

HAMILTON ✪

Paget

Sandys

Warwick

Southampton

DOCKYARD AND WESTERN PARISHES

The western tip of the island has a lot going for it, having been energized with an increase in bars, restaurants, and stores. The Royal Naval Dockyard combines the old with the new; it's steeped in history and also plays home to two cruise-ship terminals. In the summer this place is packed with cruise-ship passengers. This is a nice spot, just not for peace and quiet.

$$$$
RESORT
Fodor's Choice
★

⊡ Cambridge Beaches Resort & Spa. No other Bermuda resort uses its privileged setting better—its 30 acres on a peninsula near the western end of the island creates a sense of meandering expansiveness. **Pros:** private and refined; wide range of room options; beautiful grounds and beaches. **Cons:** far removed from rest of island; not family-friendly. ⑤ *Rooms from: $455* ⊠ *30 King's Point Rd., Somerset* ☎ *441/234–0331, 800/468–7300 in U.S.* ⊕ *www.cambridgebeaches.com* ↘ *94 rooms* ⦿ *Breakfast.*

$$$$
RESORT
FAMILY

⊡ The Fairmont Southampton Resort. With everything you could need on-site and many of the island's bests—the best restaurants, the best private beach, the best kids' club, the biggest spa, the best hotel golf course, lobby, shops, and so on—it is easy to overlook the fact that the Fairmont Southampton is also a clunky, high-rise chain hotel often overrun with families. **Pros:** all-year kids' camp with arcade; full-service resort with golf course; private beach. **Cons:** not much to do outside the hotel; bit of a walk to beach; very busy with families in high season. ⑤ *Rooms from: $467* ⊠ *101 South Shore Rd.* ☎ *441/238–8000, 866/540–4497* ⊕ *www.fairmont.com/southampton-bermuda* ↘ *630 rooms* ⦿ *No meals.*

$
B&B/INN

⊡ The Greene's Guest House. Avoid the crowds and head west to this spacious home where you'll be treated to beautiful views of the Great Sound from the huge front and backyards. **Pros:** airy views; affordable option; use of kitchen for lunch and dinner. **Cons:** aging rooms, amenities, and decor; away from island action. ⑤ *Rooms from: $185* ⊠ *71 Middle Rd., Jennings Bay* ☎ *441/238–0834* ⊕ *www.thegreenesguesthouse.com* ▭ *No credit cards* ↘ *6 rooms* ⦿ *Breakfast.*

$$$$
RESORT
FAMILY

⊡ Pompano Beach Club. Pompano, which is passionately run by an American family, understands its customers—and those customers return year after year for the casual atmosphere and beachfront location. **Pros:** private and intimate resort; cliff-side hot tubs; excellent dining options. **Cons:** expensive; older rooms. ⑤ *Rooms from: $570* ⊠ *36 Pompano Beach Rd.* ☎ *441/234–0222, 800/343–4155 in U.S. and Canada* ⊕ *www.pompanobeachclub.com* ↘ *75 rooms* ⦿ *Breakfast.*

$$$$
RESORT

⊡ The Reefs. An upscale cliff-side property that remains a popular wedding, honeymoon, and luxurious vacation getaway, the Reefs offers serenity and old-world charm as well as a private beach, excellent dining options, and top-notch service. **Pros:** romantic feel; small but beautiful beach; highly rated spa. **Cons:** too serious for families seeking fun; newer additions are very upscale and formal. ⑤ *Rooms from: $549* ⊠ *56 South Shore Rd.* ☎ *441/238–0222, 800/742–2008 in U.S. and Canada* ⊕ *www.thereefs.com* ↘ *81 rooms* ⦿ *Breakfast.*

5

NIGHTLIFE AND THE ARTS

Updated by
Amy Peniston

Bermudians love to drink. That's the title of a popular local song, and it hits the nail right on the head. Yes, the island that gave the world the Dark 'n' Stormy and the rum swizzle might not have the largest selection of hot spots in which to party the night away, but what Bermuda lacks in venues it makes up for in attitude.

Tourists, expats, and locals all mix together to create a melting-pot social scene, especially on Friday night—the unofficial party day for just about everyone living on the Rock. The vibe is civilized but still fun and friendly, and if you're not sure where you want to go, just ask around; people will be more than happy to give you their thoughts—they might even buy you a drink!

If you prefer culture with your rum concoctions, there's plenty to do. City Hall provides a venue for visiting artists on an ad hoc basis. Dramatic productions take place across a variety of venues—anywhere from a hotel auditorium to the back of a Front Street pub.

For a rundown of what's hot and happening in Bermuda, pick up the Bermuda Calendar of Events brochure at any Visitor Information Centre. The free monthly *Bermuda.com* guide also lists upcoming island events and can be accessed online at ⊕ *www.bermuda.com*. *Bermuda*, another free magazine, describes arts, nightlife venues, and dining info and can be found in tourist shops and at the ferry terminal; it's also available digitally at ⊕ *issuu.com/bermudaexploreparadise*. It's also a good idea to check ⊕ *www.bdatix.com* or ⊕ *www.premierticketsglobal.com* for upcoming show information. And to prove there's plenty to do in Bermuda (if you know where to look), the Nothing To Do In Bermuda website is updated regularly (⊕ *www.nothingtodoinbermuda.com*).

Because the arts scene in Bermuda is so casual, many events and performers operate on a seasonal or part-time basis. Your best bet is to check with your hotel or City Hall for current offerings. Old-school bulletin boards in coffee shops are also good places to check for upcoming events.

NIGHTLIFE

Hamilton is the island's central nightlife hub, with a smattering of decent bars and clubs featuring live music and drink promotions. Outside the city there's a thriving nightlife scene within the hotels. In summer, weekly cruises and beach bashes add to the party scene.

Bermuda has a long tradition of producing superb jazz artists (among other genres) so be sure to check event listings when you arrive to see if you can catch some local musicians. As a general rule, both men and women tend to dress smart-casual for clubs. That said, only a few clubs in Hamilton have an actual dress code of no flip-flops or tank tops (and it's not always enforced). Pubs and clubs begin to fill up around 10 or 11.

HAMILTON AND CENTRAL PARISHES

Follow the crowd and enjoy a night out in Hamilton. This is where you'll find most of the island's bars and clubs—and all the people to go with them. You can find a good mix of wine bars, sports bars, dance clubs, and live-music venues to suit your mood. Most of the music is reggae, hip-hop, R&B, and chart hits. Most bars serve light pub fare to keep you going through the night. The busiest night of the week in Hamilton is typically Friday, when everyone heads to the happy hours straight from work. Entrance fees are rare, especially for women, but you can expect to wait in line outside venues for up to 10 minutes.

BARS AND LOUNGES

Bermuda Bistro at the Beach. The Bermuda Bistro at the Beach, aka The Beach, is a cross between an outdoor café and a sports bar. It's clean and relatively cheap, with large television screens showing live sports during the day. At night it operates somewhere between a bar and a nightclub, attracting a mixed (and often rowdy) collection of tourists and locals. The outdoor seating area gets especially crowded into the wee hours of the morning. There's usually a DJ, and sometimes bands; if you're walking down Front Street and you hear loud music, it's probably coming from The Beach. ✉ *103 Front St., Hamilton* ☎ *441/292–0219* ⊕ *www. thebeachbermuda.com.*

Fodor's Choice **Cafe Cairo.** Egyptian-themed Cafe Cairo is without question one of the
★ most popular Hamilton nightspots. Decorated with North African furnishings, it's a great place for an early-evening meal and a view of Front Street. Eating later may lead to indigestion, as after 10 pm it transforms into a jumping nightclub that's almost always packed with both locals and tourists. Food and drink are served until 3 am, and there's a covered balcony where the adventurous can try smoking fruit tobacco pipes called hookahs. Multiple DJs play mostly R&B, soca, and Top 40 hits. After 11 pm on weekends expect to wait in line at the door, as this is where everyone ends up at the end of the night. ✉ *93 Front St., Hamilton* ☎ *441/295–5155.*

Coconut Rock. With a trendy Bermudian restaurant in front and an even trendier sushi bar called Yashi in the back, Coconut Rock has a relaxed and friendly buzz. This is more of a locals' hangout, probably because it's hard to find, tucked away underneath Hamilton's main shopping street. Huge TV screens show music videos and sports. Watch out— the friendly bar staff are more than happy to help you get tipsy or, as Bermudians say, "tapped"! Don't confuse this place with Coconuts, the upscale restaurant at the Reefs resort in Southampton. ✉ *Williams House, downstairs, 20 Reid St., Hamilton* ☎ *441/292–1043.*

Cosmopolitan Ultra Lounge & Nightclub. Cosmo is a chic addition to Hamilton's eclectic party scene. Whether it's Mid-Week Madness or Full Moon Saturday, this spot attracts a crowd that likes to dance. Ascend a red-carpeted flight of stairs into a modern lounge and order a drink from the sleek bar. ✉ *95 Front St., Hamilton* ☎ *441/705–2582.*

The Docksider Pub & Restaurant. Commonly known as Dockies, this bar attracts a loud and fun-loving crowd. Sports fanatics and competitive drinkers gather en masse to support their favorite teams, face off in weekly beer pong tournaments, and play a couple of rounds of darts. The no-frills bar at the entrance always offers a lively party atmosphere and reasonably priced pub food. On weekends, the large back room is opened to make space for hundreds of partiers and a live DJ. There's sometimes a cover charge for theme parties, bands, and tie-ins with local sporting events. Docksider is open until 3 am; the kitchen closes at 10 pm. ⊠ *121 Front St., Hamilton* ☎ *441/296–3333* ⊕ *www.docksider.bm.*

Flanagan's Irish Pub. With live music or a DJ on weekends, all the expected beverages as well as a host of fun drinks like frozen mudslides, homey Flanagan's Irish Pub is a firm favorite for folks who like to dance and talk over drinks. Adjoining the Irish pub is its sister bar, Outback Sports Bar, at the same address. Giant screens show live sports and walls are plastered with photographs of Bermuda's sporting heroes. Both are open until 1 am. ⊠ *Emporium Building, 69 Front St., 2nd fl., Hamilton* ☎ *441/295–8299* ⊕ *www.flanagans.bm.*

The Hamilton Princess & Beach Club. During the high season from May through October, the hotel's Marina Nights happy hour is the place to be seen on Friday from 5 to 10 pm. Enjoy special drink prices, tasty cocktails, live bands, and appetizers from the adjoining 1609 Bar & Restaurant. The views of elegant yachts in the harbor draw a lively crowd of locals and visitors alike to the magnificent lawns of the famous hotel. The vibe is trendy, so don your stylish duds for this night. ⊠ *76 Pitts Bay Rd., Hamilton* ☎ *441/295–3000* ⊕ *www.thehamiltonprincess.com.*

Hog Penny. Small, cozy Hog Penny, aka the *Cheers* bar, was the inspiration for the Bull & Finch Pub in Boston. With dark-wood paneling and hearty, comforting fare like steak-and-kidney pie and bangers and mash, the Hog Penny will likely remind you more of an English country pub than a Boston hangout. Popular musician Will Black plays most nights in the summer, and the floor is cleared for dancing. It's open nightly until 1 am, and it can be very busy. ⊠ *5 Burnaby St., Hamilton* ☎ *441/292–2534* ⊕ *www.hogpennypub.com.*

Pickled Onion. With a cosmopolitan feel and a harbor-view terrace, the Pickled Onion's restaurant and bar caters to a well-heeled crowd of locals and visitors. Live music, usually pop, plays from about 10 pm to 1 am on Tuesday through Saturday in the summer. Open mic nights are extremely popular, as is the dance floor—expect it to be packed! ⊠ *53 Front St., Hamilton* ☎ *441/295–2263* ⊕ *www.thepickledonion.com.*

Robin Hood. Casual, friendly Robin Hood is popular for inexpensive pub fare, pizza, and beer served on the patio under the stars. There's almost always something sports related on the TV, and a late-night snack menu is served until 11 pm. There's a quiz competition on Tuesday nights with general knowledge and entertainment themes; the ever-popular beer pong tournaments and live music are also worth the short walk from Front Street. ⊠ *25 Richmond Rd., Hamilton* ☎ *441/295–3314* ⊕ *www.robinhood.bm.*

Seabreeze. With intimate dining areas and expansive bars, both Seabreeze and downstairs (right on the sand) Mickey's Beach Bar overlook the cool blue waters just beyond the south shore's Elbow Beach.

On weeknights, this complex is simply perfect for a quiet evening for two; on Friday and Saturday things heat up with tapas, cocktails, and live music. ⊠ *Elbow Beach Hotel, 60 South Shore Rd.* ☎ *441/236–9884* ⊕ *www.lido.bm.*

Fodor's Choice
★

Swizzle Inn. Proudly bearing the motto "Swizzle Inn, swagger out," this busy and unique spot is a must-see for visitors. Business cards, exotic money, and even love notes completely cover the walls, ceilings, and doors. Even the tables are scratched with messages and signatures. As the name suggests, it's the best place on the island for a jug of rum swizzle. Entertainment in the summer includes live bands, pub quizzes, and barbecues. The Bailey's Bay venue proved so successful that the owners have set up an equally popular sister bar close to the south-shore beaches in Warwick. ⊠ *3 Blue Hole Hill, Bailey's Bay, Hamilton* ☎ *441/293–1854* ⊕ *www.swizzleinn.com.*

MUSIC AND DANCE CLUBS

Bermuda Folk Club. Known for its monthly get-togethers and open mic nights, the Bermuda Folk Club also has unpublicized gigs and events, so it's worth checking the website before you visit. Drinks are often served at happy hour prices, and the cover is $10, but can rise to more than $20 for off-island acts. Note that musicians might perform any number of musical styles besides folk, including blues and acoustic. ⊠ *Spanish Point Boat Club, 1 Spanish Point Rd.* ⊕ *www.bermudafolkclub.com.*

ST. GEORGE'S AND EASTERN PARISHES

The East End is the quietest corner of the island, but that isn't to say you won't find anything going on. You may just have to look a little harder. The bars in St. George's can get lively in the summer, with offerings such as quiz nights, live bands, and themed nights. But your best bet is to head to the Swizzle Inn for a rowdy night of singing with strangers. The nightly entertainers are more than happy to welcome people to the stage.

BARS AND LOUNGES

North Rock Brewing Company. As well as being a relaxed and traditional pub and restaurant, the North Rock Brewing Company is one of only a few places on the island to get a genuine Bermuda-brewed ale. Try a sampler for a taste of all six of North Rock's famous beers—ranging from the sharp St. David's Light Ale to the head-spinning Whale of Wheat. The relaxed outdoor seating area is the perfect place for a breather if the pub gets too noisy. ⊠ *10 South Shore Rd.* ☎ *441/236–6633.*

The Wharf Restaurant & Bar. The yachting crowd gathers at The Wharf for rum swizzles, moderately priced pub fare, and nautical talk. Waterfront tables, relaxed atmosphere, and quick service make this spot worth the journey to the far northeastern tip of the island. ⊠ *14 Water St., St. George's* ☎ *441/297–3305* ⊕ *www.wharf.bm.*

White Horse. White Horse is great for an afternoon pint on the wooden terrace overlooking the water, where swarms of fish fight for scraps thrown from the tables. There are large-screen TVs for sports fans; sometimes there's nighttime entertainment for everyone else. Finger-licking appetizers, colorful blended drinks, and a view of the water—what more do you need? ✉ *8 King Sq., St. George's* ☎ *441/297–1838* ⊕ *www. whitehorsebermuda.com.*

DOCKYARD AND WESTERN PARISHES

There are a handful of nightspots—most are bars with live entertainment—to keep you entertained in Dockyard. You should head to Snorkel Park Beach if you want to party until the early hours. Some of the island's best nightlife takes place at hotel bars in the Western Parishes. Bermuda's musicians are often found in the less obvious places, so check the live music listings. The Jasmine Lounge at the Fairmont Southampton Resort is a popular late-night venue for locals and hotel guests.

BARS AND LOUNGES

Frog & Onion Pub. Frog & Onion Pub serves a splendid variety of down-to-earth pub fare in a dark-wood, barnlike setting. If you're spending the day at Dockyard, it's a great place to get out of the sun and try a Bermudian rum swizzle or sample a flight of Bermuda-brewed beers. There's a weekly quiz night as well as live performances by Will Black and Tony Brannon every Monday starting at 9 pm. ✉ *The Cooperage, Dockyard, Somerset* ☎ *441/234–2900* ⊕ *www.frogandonion.bm.*

Henry VIII. Henry VIII is a popular restaurant and bar with rich oak paneling, polished brass, and reliably decent live entertainment, especially on weekends. There's a grand piano in the bar, and local entertainers often perform sing-along sessions. A chill, Sunday-night jazz session is a great way to recharge your batteries; afterward, follow the locals as the crowds head from Henry VIII to the nearby Fairmont Southampton. ✉ *69 South Shore Rd.* ☎ *441/238–1977* ⊕ *www.henrys.bm.*

Jasmine Lounge. At night, Jasmine Lounge draws the smartly dressed to its lounge and dance floor. Definitely check out the live entertainment, jazz in particular. A variety of craft cocktails like the exotic Coconut Froth martini and the classic Bermuda old-fashioned will quickly take the edge off. ✉ *Fairmont Southampton Resort, 101 South Shore Rd.* ☎ *441/238–8000.*

Somerset Country Squire. Somerset Country Squire is an unpretentious bar with down-to-earth bar staff and great views of the water. It's a decent spot for a quiet pint in the West End thanks to its outdoor terrace. Pull up a chair and appreciate a true Bermudian watering hole at one of the summertime barbecues. ✉ *10 Mangrove Bay, Somerset* ☎ *441/234–0105.*

MUSIC AND DANCE CLUBS

Club Aqua—Snorkel Park Beach. Up your vacation vibes at this popular club right on the beach. Monday, Wednesday, and Thursday are particularly lively, with barbecue beach bashes, Dark 'n' Stormy nights, rocking DJ sets, and even foam parties. The party often goes strong until 3 am, but if you're a cruise passenger, you won't be far from your bed, as the ship pier at Dockyard is just a stone's throw away. Admission is usually $10, more if there's a special event. ✉ *7 Maritime La., Dockyard, Somerset* ☎ *441/234–6989* ⊕ *www.snorkelparkbeach.com.*

Gombey Dancers

The Gombey dancer is one of the island's most enduring and uniquely Bermudian cultural icons. The Gombey (pronounced *gum*-bay) tradition here dates from at least the mid-18th century, when enslaved Africans and Native Americans covertly practiced a unique form of dance incorporating West Indian, British, and biblical influences. Nowadays, Gombeys mainly perform on major holidays. The Gombey name originates from a West African word, which means rustic drum. The masked, exclusively male dancers move to the accompaniment of Congolese-style drums and the shrill, whistle-blown commands of the troupe's captain. The dancers' colorful costumes include tall headdresses decorated with peacock feathers and capes covered with intricate embroidery, ribbons, and tiny mirrors.

The Gombey tradition is passed from father to son (some of the dancers are as young as 10 years old), and many of the same families have been involved in Bermuda's troupes for generations. Bermudians are extremely proud of their musical heritage, and the sight of the colorful Gombey troupe's ducking and twirling to the mesmerizing rhythm of the rapid drumbeat is one of the most enchanting spectacles on the island. The Gombeys appear at all major events on the island and are the central element of the Bermuda Day parade. It's traditional for crowds to toss money at the dancers' feet. Gombeys are also regularly on display at the Bermuda Harbour Nights event on Front Street in Hamilton. Consult the Visitor Information Centre for other locations.

PERFORMING ARTS

Bermuda's arts scene is concentrated in a number of art galleries—Masterworks in the Botanical Gardens, City Hall in Hamilton, and the Arts Centre in Dockyard are the best known—a handful of performance venues, and a few gathering spots, like Rock Island Coffee on Reid Street. For dramatic and musical performances, the The Earl Cameron Theatre, the Mid-Ocean Amphitheatre at the Fairmont Southampton Resort, and the Ruth Seaton James Auditorium at CedarBridge Academy host the country's best, including Bermuda Festival events.

DANCE

Bermuda School of Russian Ballet. The Bermuda School of Russian Ballet has been around for half a century and presents unique ballet and modern-dance performances. The company's most important performances of the year are during the summer months, when internationally known artists sometimes appear as guests. Showtimes and venues vary, so call for details. ⊠ *127 St. John's Rd., Hamilton* ☎ *441/293-4147* ⊕ *www. balletbermuda.com.*

National Dance Foundation of Bermuda. The National Dance Foundation of Bermuda funds workshops and develops local dance talent. The organization attracts both local and international students as well as support from Bermuda's most famous resident, Catherine Zeta-Jones.

Check local events listings for information on upcoming performances. ☎ *441/236–3319*.

Sabor Dance School. Feel the Latin beat with group classes in salsa, cha-cha, Argentine tango, and merengue. Bermuda has a thriving salsa scene with classes open to all levels; no experience is necessary. Dancers also show off their fancy footwork at a series of social dancing events across the island; check the website for more info. ⊠ *Old Berkeley School, Corner of Berkeley and St. John's Rd., Hamilton* ☎ *441/337–2267* ⊕ *www.bermudasalsa.com.*

United Dance Productions. Every style of dance is taught to adults and children at this popular dance school. Performances are held at various venues throughout the year, including annual recitals in June. Shows include ballet, modern, hip-hop, and also musical theater. ⊠ *Alexandrina Hall, 75 Court St., Hamilton* ☎ *441/232–9933* ⊕ *www.danceudp.com.*

FILM

Bermuda International Film Festival. This top-notch festival is a celebration of independent films from all over the world. A full week of springtime screenings takes place at City Hall in Hamilton. Tickets are sold for individual films as well as for workshops and seminars. Festival parties are also popular, as Hamilton mimics—for a few days at least—the glamour of Sundance, minus the fancy cars. ☎ *441/293–3456* ⊕ *www.biff.bm.*

Neptune Cinema. Neptune Cinema is a 118-seat cinema that typically shows feature films twice a day. Get there early for popular movies, as this small cinema often sells out. ⊠ *The Cooperage, Dockyard* ☎ *441/292–7296* ⊕ *www.libertytheatre.bm.*

Specialty Cinema & Grill. Across the street from City Hall, the Specialty Cinema is Bermuda's most popular two-screen theater. There are usually three showtimes per day per movie. This cinema has a great café out front selling hot food, snacks, and baked goods that you can eat during the movie. Lots of 3-D movies are shown here. ⊠ *11 Church St., Hamilton* ☎ *441/292–2135* ⊕ *www.specialitycinema.bm.*

FINE ARTS FESTIVALS

Bermuda Festival of the Performing Arts. For over 40 years, the Bermuda Festival has featured internationally renowned artists and performers. The two-month program, which begins in mid-January, includes theater, as well as classical and jazz concerts. Most shows take place in City Hall and Fairmont Southampton; tickets are approximately $75 for adults and $35 for students. ☎ *441/295–1291* ⊕ *www.bermudafestival.org.*

FAMILY **Harbour Nights.** Every Wednesday night in summer Front Street hosts a free street festival featuring Bermudian artists, crafts, Gombey dancers, and face painting. Harbour Nights encompasses most of Hamilton: Front Street and Queen Street are closed to traffic, stores stay open later, and throngs of locals and visitors alike sample local art stalls, bouncy castles and rides, food vendors, and live music. It's a great time to try local cuisine like fish cakes, fresh fish, fried chicken, meat pies, and Portuguese deep-fried doughnuts. ■TIP➔ **Make dinner reservations at a restaurant with a balcony overlooking Front Street for a bird's-eye view of the action (Red Steakhouse & Bar and The Pickled Onion are very popular).** ✉ *Front St., Hamilton* 🎫 *Free.*

MUSIC

Bermuda School of Music. The Bermuda School of Music hosts a number of popular events including free lunchtime concerts (check the website for locations) and the well-attended annual Some Enchanted Evening fund-raising event. Check the website for upcoming performances. ☎ *441/296–5100* ⊕ *www.musicschool.bm.*

READINGS AND TALKS

Bermuda National Gallery. The Bermuda National Gallery often hosts a series of lunchtime lectures on art and film in addition to its revolving exhibits. Stop by or call the gallery for a schedule. ✉ *City Hall, 17 Church St., Hamilton* ☎ *441/295–9428* ⊕ *www.bermudanationalgallery.com.*

THEATER

Bermuda Musical & Dramatic Society. The Bermuda Musical & Dramatic Society has some good amateur actors on its roster. Formed in 1944, this active theater society stages performances year-round at its Daylesford headquarters, one block north of City Hall. The Christmas pantomime is always a sellout, as are most other performances, especially the Shakespearean classics. Visit or call the box office at Daylesford, on Dundonald Street, for reservations and information. Tickets are about $30. ✉ *Daylesford Theatre, 11 Washington St., Hamilton* ☎ *441/292–0848 box office, 441/295–5584 bar telephone* ⊕ *www.bmds.bm.*

Gilbert & Sullivan Society. The "G & S" holds big-name theater shows and musicals once or twice a year at City Hall. Bermuda may be a small island, but the talent is amazing with past productions including *South Pacific, The Full Monty, Jesus Christ Superstar, Oliver!,* and *Animal Farm.* Check out what's on the calendar during March and October. ☎ *441/735–1547* ⊕ *www.gands.bm.*

Hasty Pudding Theatricals. Bermuda is the only place outside the United States where Harvard University's Hasty Pudding Theatricals perform. For more than 50 years this satirical troupe has entertained the island during March or April. Each of these Bermuda-based shows incorporates political and social issues of the past year and is staged at The Earl Cameron Theatre in Hamilton. Tickets are about $30. ✉ *City Hall, 17 Church St., Hamilton* ☎ *441/292–1234* ⊕ *www.hastypudding.org.*

VENUES AND SOCIETIES

Bermuda Society of Arts. The Bermuda Society of Arts has an outstanding gallery space upstairs in City Hall. Meet and support local artists at various show openings throughout the year. ⊠ *City Hall, 17 Church St., Hamilton* ☎ *441/292–3824* ⊕ *www.bsoa.bm.*

The Earl Cameron Theatre. The major venue for quality cultural events in Bermuda, The Earl Cameron Theatre hosts fashion shows, comedic acts, and live music—all hugely popular with locals. ⊠ *City Hall, 17 Church St., Hamilton* ☎ *441/292–1234* ⊕ *www.cityhall.bm.*

Rock Island Coffee. Not only is Rock Island Coffee the unofficial watering hole for Bermuda's eclectic group of artists, but also it doubles as an informal art space. Stop by to find out where all the hip happenings on the island are. ⊠ *48 Reid St., Hamilton* ☎ *441/296–5241* ⊕ *www. rockisland.bm.*

6

SPORTS AND THE OUTDOORS

with Beaches and Golf

Updated by
Amy Peniston

Long before your plane touches down in Bermuda, the island's greatest asset becomes breathtakingly obvious—the crystal clear, aquamarine water that frames the tiny, hook-shaped atoll.

So clear are Bermuda's waters that in 1994 the government nixed a local scuba-diving group's plan to create a unique dive site by sinking an abandoned American warplane in 30 feet of water off the island's East End, fairly close to the end of the airport's runway. The government feared that the plane would be easily visible from above—to arriving passengers—and could cause undue distress. It's the incredible clarity of the water that makes Bermuda one of the world's greatest places for exploratory scuba diving and snorkeling, especially among the age-old shipwrecks off the island. The presence of these sunken ships is actually one of Bermuda's ironies—as translucent as the water is, it wasn't quite clear enough to make the treacherous reefs visible to the hundreds of ship captains who have smashed their vessels on them through the centuries.

Thanks to Bermuda's position near the Gulf Stream, the water stays warm year-round. In summer the ocean is usually above 80°F, and it's even warmer in the shallows between the reefs and shore. In winter the water temperature only occasionally drops below 70°F, but it seems cooler because the air temperature is usually in the mid-60s. There's less call for water sports December through March, not because of a drop in water temperature but because of windy conditions. The wind causes rough water, which in turn creates problems for fishing and diving boats, and underwater visibility is often clouded by sand and debris.

Whether it's renting a glass-bottomed kayak for a gentle paddle over the reefs, taking a motorboat for a spin, or spending an adrenaline-filled afternoon wakeboarding, getting out on the water is an essential part of the Bermuda experience. In high season, mid-April through mid-October, fishing, diving, and yacht charters fill up quickly.

Bermudians take their onshore sports seriously, too. Cricket and soccer are the national sports, but road running, golf, field hockey, rugby, and a host of other activities get their share of love. Bermudian soccer stars, such as former Manchester City striker Shaun Goater, have delighted crowds in British and U.S. leagues through the years, and Bermudian sailors hold their own in world competition, as do runners, equestrians, and swimmers. Tennis is quite a big deal here, too, and with 70 courts packed into these 21.6 square miles, it's hard to believe there's room left for horseback riding, cycling, running, and golf.

BEACHES

Bermuda's south-shore beaches are more scenic than those on the north side, with fine, pinkish sand and limestone dunes topped with summer flowers and Bermuda crabgrass. The water on the south shore does get a little rougher when the winds are from the south and southwest, but mainly the pale-blue waves break at the barrier reefs offshore and roll gently onto the sandy shoreline. Because the barrier reefs break up the waves, surfing has not really taken off in Bermuda, though many locals—especially children—love to bodysurf at Horseshoe Bay. Kite-surfing is also becoming increasingly popular. Most Bermudian beaches are relatively small compared with ocean beaches in the United States, ranging from about 15 yards to half a mile or so in length. In winter, when the weather is more severe, beaches may erode—even disappear— only to be replenished as the wind subsides in spring.

Before beginning your adventure, pick up the pocket-sized map of Bermuda available for free in all Visitor Information Centres and most hotels. Complete with bus-and-ferry information, the guide shows beach locations and how to reach them. You can also download maps, brochures, and transportation timetables from the Bermuda Tourism Authority's website at ⊕ *www.gotobermuda.com/official-visitor-guides*.

Few Bermudian beaches offer shade, but some have palm trees and thatched shelters. The sun can be intense, so bring a hat and plenty of sunscreen. You can rent umbrellas at some beaches, but food and drink are rare, so pack snacks and lots of water.

HAMILTON AND CENTRAL PARISHES

Astwood Cove and Park. On weekends you can often find lots of children and families at this small, yet popular beach. The Astwood Park area is shady and grassy, with a great view of the ocean, making it popular among locals for birthday parties, picnics, and weddings. Though accessible via one of Bermuda's main roads, it's quite secluded; the few benches scattered around the area are a great vantage point to share a romantic evening. If you're bringing kids, watch out for the steep climb from the park down to the beach area. **Amenities:** parking (free). **Best for:** solitude; swimming. ⊠ *Off South Shore Rd.* Ⓜ *Bus 7 from Hamilton.*

FAMILY **Elbow Beach.** Swimming and bodysurfing are great at this beach, which is bordered by the prime strand of sand reserved for guests of the Elbow Beach Hotel on the left, and the ultraexclusive Coral Beach Club beach area on the right. It's a pleasant setting for a late-evening stroll, with the lights from nearby hotels dancing on the water. If you're planning a daytime visit during summer months, be sure to arrive early to claim your spot as this popular beach is often crowded. In addition to sun-tanners and joggers, groups of locals also gather here to play football and volleyball. Protective coral reefs make the waters some of the safest on the island and a good choice for families. A lunch wagon sometimes sells fast food and cold drinks during the day, and Mickey's Beach Bar (part of the Elbow Beach Hotel) is open for lunch and dinner, though it

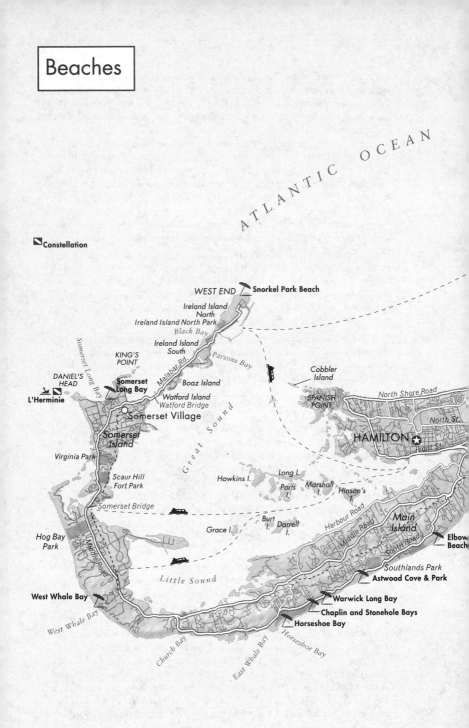

Beaches

Constellation

ATLANTIC OCEAN

WEST END · Snorkel Park Beach

Ireland Island North
Ireland Island North Park
Black Bay
Ireland Island South
Malabar Rd.
Parsons Bay

SOMERSET LONG BAY
KING'S POINT
Boaz Island
Watford Island
Watford Bridge

Cobbler Island
SPANISH POINT
North Shore Road
North St.

DANIEL'S HEAD
L'Herminie
Somerset Long Bay
Somerset Long Bay

Somerset Village

Great Sound

HAMILTON
Front St.

Somerset Island

Virginia Park
Scaur Hill Fort Park
Somerset Bridge

Hawkins I.
Long I.
Ports I.
Marshall I.
Hinson's I.

Burt I.
Darrell I.
Grace I.

Harbour Road
Middle Road
South Road

Main Island

Elbow Beach

Hog Bay Park
Middle Road

Little Sound

Southlands Park
Astwood Cove & Park

West Whale Bay
West Whale Bay

Warwick Long Bay
Chaplin and Stonehole Bays
Horseshoe Bay

Church Bay
East Whale Bay
Horseshoe Bay

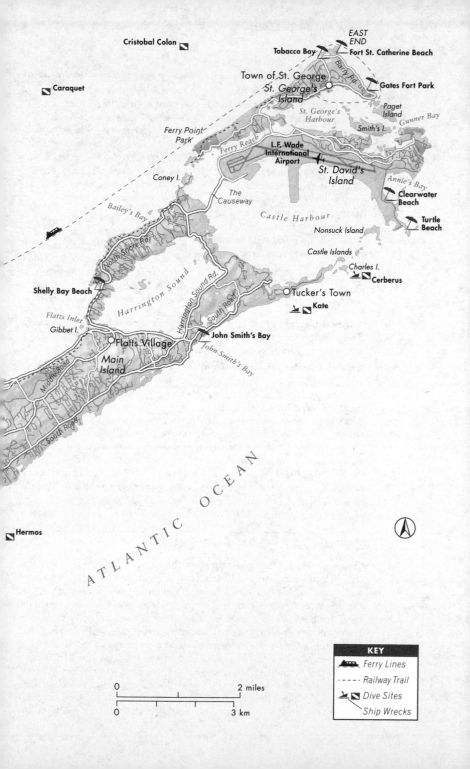

Cristobal Colon

Caraquet

EAST
END

Tobacco Bay

Fort St. Catherine Beach

Town of St. George
St. George's
Island

Gates Fort Park

Barry Rd.

Paget
Island

Gunner Bay

St. George's
Harbour

Smith's I.

Ferry Point
Park

Ferry Reach

L.F. Wade
International
Airport

St. David's
Island

Annie's Bay

Coney I.

The
Causeway

Clearwater
Beach

Bailey's Bay

Castle Harbour

Turtle
Beach

Nonsuck Island

Castle Islands

North Shore Rd.

Charles I.

Cerberus

Harrington Sound

Tucker's Town

Shelly Bay Beach

Harrington Sound Rd.

South Road

Kate

Flatts Inlet

Gibbet I.

Flatts Village

John Smith's Bay

Main
Island

Middle Road

John Smith's Bay

South Road

ATLANTIC OCEAN

Hermos

0   2 miles

0   3 km

KEY
🚢 Ferry Lines
- - - Railway Trail
🤿 Dive Sites
Ship Wrecks

Blushing Beaches

In only a few regions where tropical coral reefs flourish offshore do pink-sand beaches form. What makes Bermuda's sand pink is an amalgam of calcium-rich shells and fragments of invertebrate sea creatures, from minute, single-cell protozoa to spiny sea urchins. Chiefly responsible are *foraminifera* ("foram" for short), a type of protozoan that lives in great profusion in reef environments. The microscopic red *Homotrema rubrum* (red foram) variety is numerous both on the reefs and in the ocean sediments that surround Bermuda,

and their persistent red pigment remains even in the microscopic "skeletons" these animals leave behind when they die. The red gets mixed in with other (predominantly white) reef debris—broken clam and snail shells, fragments of coral—and, when washed ashore, forms the island's signature pink sand.

The most visited pink-sand beaches are Warwick Long Bay Beach and Horseshoe Bay in Southampton. But just about any beach you visit on the south shore will have the famous sand in abundance.

may be difficult to get a table without a reservation. **Amenities:** parking (free); water sports. **Best for:** snorkeling; swimming; walking. ⊠ *Off South Rd.* Ⓜ *Bus 2 or 7 from Hamilton.*

Warwick Long Bay. Different from the covelike bay beaches, Warwick Long Bay has about a ½-mile stretch of sand—the longest of any beach here. Its backdrop is a combination of steep cliffs and low grass- and brush-covered hills. The beach is exposed to some strong southerly winds, but the waves are usually moderate because the inner reef is close to shore. A 20-foot coral outcrop less than 200 feet offshore looks like a sculpted boulder balancing on the water's surface. South Shore Park, which surrounds the bay, is often empty, a fact that only heightens the beach's appealing isolation and serenity. Although there aren't any changing rooms, a summertime concession stand offers snacks for purchase. **Amenities:** parking (free); toilets. **Best for:** solitude; snorkeling; swimming; walking. ⊠ *Off South Shore Rd.* Ⓜ *Bus 7 from Hamilton.*

ST. GEORGE'S AND EASTERN PARISHES

FAMILY **Clearwater Beach.** On the eastern tip of the island in St. David's, Clearwater is a long sandy strip of beach that's popular with serious swimmers and triathletes who use it as a training ground. But don't be intimidated: the young and old also flock here to wade in the shallow water, and there are buoy markers that identify where the beach becomes deeper. Keep your eyes peeled for turtles! Clearwater is one of the few beaches in Bermuda that has a restaurant on the premises called Gombey's, serving kids' picnic favorites such as burgers and fries as well as island classics like Bermudian fish chowder and Jamaican jerk chicken. There's also an in-house bar when the five-o'clock-somewhere mood strikes. Beach bathrooms, lifeguards during the tourist season (April through September), and a playground make this a great choice for families.

Amenities: food and drink; lifeguards; parking (free); toilets. Best for: partiers; sunrise; swimming; walking. ⊠ *Off Cooper's Island Rd., St. David's Island* Ⓜ *Bus 6 from St. George's.*

Fort St. Catherine Beach. Fort St. Catherine is one of the larger north-shore beaches, and the water's deep enough for a serious swim. If and when you get beach-bummed out, head over to the military fort next door, for which this beach is named. A quick tour of the structure will be a welcome break from the strong sun, as there is little shade along the beach. For a romantic evening enjoy a beautiful alfresco meal at The Beach House overlooking Achilles Bay just across the street. **Amenities:** food and drink; parking (free). **Best for:** solitude; snorkeling; sunset; swimming. ⊠ *Coot Pond Rd., St. George's* Ⓜ *Bus 10 or 11 from Hamilton.*

FAMILY **Gates Fort Park.** Named after its neighboring military fort, Gates has a very small beach that is popular with local families. The park is off Barry Road, not far from Alexandra Battery, a favorite diving spot of St. George's children. From the beach you can enjoy an unobstructed view of cruise ships as they navigate the reefs through the Town Cut. **Amenities:** parking (free). **Best for:** solitude; sunrise. ⊠ *Coot Pond Rd., St. George's* Ⓜ *Bus 1, 3, 10, or 11 from Hamilton.*

FAMILY **John Smith's Bay.** Just past Spittal Pond Nature Reserve, this beach consists of a pretty strand of long, flat, open sand. The presence of a lifeguard in summer makes it an ideal place to bring children. The only public beach in Smith's Parish, John Smith's Bay is also popular with locals. Groups of young folk like to gather in the park area surrounding the beach for parties, especially on weekends and holidays, so if you're not in the mood for a festive bunch with music and plenty of beer, this may not be the place for you. Lots of scooter parking is available as is the occasional local food vendor. **Amenities:** lifeguards; parking (free). **Best for:** partiers; snorkeling; swimming. ⊠ *South Shore Rd.* Ⓜ *Bus 1 from Hamilton.*

FAMILY **Shelly Bay Beach.** Known for its sandy bottom and shallow water, Shelly Bay is a good place to take small children. It also has shade trees, a rarity at Bermudian beaches. A large playground behind the beach attracts hordes of youngsters on weekends and during school holidays. There's also a nearby soccer and cricket practice field and a public basketball court. Keep an eye out for the food truck that often stops in the parking lot behind the beach. **Amenities:** parking (free). **Best for:** partiers; swimming. ⊠ *Off North Shore Rd., Hamilton* Ⓜ *Bus 10 or 11 from Hamilton.*

Tobacco Bay. The most popular beach near St. George's—about 15 minutes northwest of the town on foot—this small north-shore strand is huddled in a coral cove surrounded by rock formations. Its beach house serves burgers and salads as well as specialty cocktails. Equipment rentals including umbrellas, chairs, floaties, and snorkel sets, and ample parking are also available. It's a 10-minute hike from the bus stop in the town of St. George's, or you can flag down a taxi. In high season the beach is busy, especially midweek, when the cruise ships are docked; check the website for information on Friday-night events, bonfires, and live music. **Amenities:** food and drink; parking (free); toilets; water sports. **Best for:** snorkeling; swimming. ⊠ *9 Coot's Pond*

6

Rd., St. George's ☎ *441/737–2355 main* ⊕ *www.tobaccobay.bm* Ⓜ *Bus 10 or 11 from Hamilton.*

Turtle Beach. Down a stretch from Clearwater Beach, adjacent to Cooper's Island Nature Reserve, Turtle Beach offers the same tranquility but with a bit less traffic. The water's also a deeper turquoise color here and very calm. If you're lucky, you might even spot a turtle. There's also a lifeguard station with a guard on duty. When your tummy grumbles, it's a short walk to Gombey's Restaurant. **Amenities:** food and drink; lifeguards. **Best for:** solitude; snorkeling; swimming. ⊠ *Cooper's Island Rd., St. David's Island* Ⓜ *Bus 6 from St. George's.*

DOCKYARD AND WESTERN PARISHES

Chaplin and Stonehole Bays. In a secluded area east along the dunes from Horseshoe Bay, these tiny adjacent beaches almost disappear at high tide. Like Horseshoe Bay, the beach fronts South Shore Park; it often experiences a strong wind and surf, so the waters may be too cloudy to snorkel. Wander farther along the dunes and you can find several other tiny, peaceful beaches before you eventually reach Warwick Long Bay. **Amenities:** parking (free). **Best for:** solitude; swimming; walking. ⊠ *Off South Shore Rd.* Ⓜ *Bus 7 from Hamilton.*

FAMILY

Fodor'sChoice

★

Horseshoe Bay. When locals say they're going to "the beach," they're generally referring to Horseshoe Bay, the island's most popular. With clear water, a 0.3-mile crescent of pink sand, a vibrant social scene, and the uncluttered backdrop of South Shore Park, Horseshoe Bay has everything you could ask of a Bermudian beach. An on-site bar and restaurant, changing rooms, beach-rental facilities, and lifeguards add to its appeal. The Annual Bermuda Sand Castle Competition also takes place here. The undertow can be strong, especially on the main beach. A better place for children is **Horseshoe Baby Beach.** Before 2003's Hurricane Fabian, this beach was reached by climbing a trail over the dunes at the western end of Horseshoe Bay. Fabian's storm surge ploughed right through those dunes, creating a wide walkway for eager little beachgoers. Sheltered from the ocean by a ring of rocks, this cove is shallow and almost perfectly calm. In summer, toddlers can find lots of playmates. **Amenities:** food and drink; lifeguards; parking (free); showers; toilets. **Best for:** partiers; swimming; walking. ⊠ *Off South Shore Rd.* Ⓜ *Bus 7 from Hamilton.*

FAMILY

Snorkel Park Beach. This is a popular spot for tourists as well as local families who like to treat their children to a sheltered white-sand beach and pristine views of the water. Enjoy local and American cuisine while sipping a frozen cocktail at Hammerheads Bar and Grill; on-site water-sport and beach equipment rentals are available for the excitement of kids and parents alike. A recently updated playground located outside the park features a 70-foot green moray eel and a replica of the St. David's Lighthouse. If your cruise ship docks in Dockyard, Snorkel Park Beach is just a short walk from the cruise terminal. Before you leave, be sure to stop in the Clocktower Mall and the Craft Market to pick up a souvenir or two. Also nearby are the Bone Fish Bar & Grill, the Frog & Onion Pub, the Bermuda Rum Cake Company, the Dockyard

Ferry Terminal, and an ATM. At night, Snorkel transforms into a lively nightclub area, especially on Monday and Thursday when live DJs spin top 40, soca, reggae, and dancehall hits. **Amenities:** food and drink; parking (free); toilets; water sports. **Best for:** partiers; snorkeling; sunset; swimming. ⊠ *7 Maritime La., Dockyard* ☎ *441/234–6989* ⊕ *www. snorkelparkbeach.com* ⊡ *$5 for adults; check website for special-event prices* Ⓜ *Bus 7 or 8 from Hamilton.*

Somerset Long Bay. Popular with Somerset locals, this beach is on the quiet northwestern end of the island, far from the bustle of Hamilton and major tourist hubs. In keeping with the area's rural atmosphere, the beach is low-key and great for bird-watching. Undeveloped parkland shields the beach from the light traffic on Cambridge Road. The main beach is long by Bermudian standards—nearly ¼ mile from end to end. Although exposed to northerly storm winds, the bay water is normally calm and shallow—ideal for children. The bottom, however, is rocky and uneven, so it's a good idea to put on water shoes before wading. **Amenities:** parking (free). **Best for:** solitude; swimming; walking. ⊠ *Cambridge Rd., Somerset* Ⓜ *Bus 7 or 8 to Dockyard from Hamilton.*

West Whale Bay. This beach can be a secluded oasis if you go at the right time: sunset. To get to the beach, you need to cross a large grassy field and walk down a natural rock formation path. If you're looking to avoid the crowds and experience a breathtaking view, this is your spot. The park also features several picnic tables and public bathroom facilities. **Amenities:** parking (free); toilets. **Best for:** solitude; snorkeling; sunset; swimming. ⊠ *Off Whale Bay and Middle Rds.* Ⓜ *Bus 7 or 8 from Hamilton.*

GOLF

Golf is an important facet of sporting life in Bermuda, where golf courses make up nearly 17% of the island's 21.6 square miles. The scenery on the courses is quite often spectacular, with trees and shrubs decked out in multicolor blossoms against a backdrop of brilliant blue sea and sky. The layouts may be shorter than what you're accustomed to, but they're remarkably challenging, thanks to capricious ocean breezes, daunting natural terrain, and the clever work of world-class golf architects.

Of the six 18-hole courses and one 9-hole layout on Bermuda, four are championship venues: Belmont Hills, the Mid Ocean Club, Port Royal, and Tucker's Point. All are well maintained, but you should not expect the springy bent grass fairways and fast greens typical of U.S. golf courses. The rough is coarse Bermuda grass that will turn your club in your hands. Most clubs have TifEagle or Tifdwarf greens—finer-bladed grasses that are drought-resistant and putt faster and truer than Bermuda grass. Because the island's freshwater supply is limited, watering is usually devoted to the greens and tees, which means the fairways are likely to be firm and give you lots of roll. Expect plenty of sand hazards and wind—*especially* wind.

CLOSE UP

Secrets from a Golf Pro

Golf courses elsewhere are often designed with the wind in mind—long downwind holes and short upwind holes. Not so in Bermuda, where the wind is anything but consistent or predictable. **Quirky air currents** make play on a Bermudian course different every day. The wind puts a premium on being able to hit the ball straight and grossly exaggerates any slice or hook.

The **hard ground** of most Bermudian courses means you must abandon the strategy you use on heavily watered tracks. Your ball will run a lot in the fairway, so don't overestimate the distance to hazards. Around the greens, it's wise to run the ball to the hole rather than chipping. Not only will you find it difficult to get under

the ball on the firm fairways, but your shot will be subject to the vagaries of the wind. If you're in the clinging Bermuda grass rough, your club face is likely to turn if you try to swing through it.

How should you prepare for a Bermuda trip? Practice **run-up shots** from close-cropped lies using a 5- or 6-iron—or a putter from just off the green. Use midirons to practice **punching shots** from the rough, angling back into the fairway rather than trying to advance the ball straight ahead and risk landing in the rough again. Putting surfaces are often undulating and grainier than bent grass, so putts will break less than you expect. They'll also die much more quickly unless you use a firm stroke.

All courses in Bermuda have dress codes: long pants or Bermuda (knee-length) shorts and collared shirts for both men and women. Denim is not allowed. ■TIP➔ **Bermudian men always wear color-coordinated knee-high socks with their shorts on other occasions, but it's okay to go bare-legged on the golf course.**

Courses in Bermuda are rated by the United States Golf Association (USGA), just as they are in the States, so you can tell at a glance how difficult a course is. For example, a par-72 course with a rating of 68 means that a scratch golfer (one who usually shoots par) should be four under par for the round. High handicappers should score better than usual, too.

Reserve tee times before you leave home or ask your hotel concierge to do so as soon as you arrive. This is especially necessary to access the private courses. "Sunset" tee times, available at lower greens fees, generally start at 3 pm, but call ahead to be sure.

HAMILTON AND CENTRAL PARISHES

Belmont Hills Golf Club. Belmont Hills, opened in June 2003, was designed by California architect Algie Pulley Jr. and built on the site of the former Belmont Manor and Golf Club, a haven for celebrities in the early 1900s. "Hills" was added to the course name to reflect the dramatic design features that Pulley used to replace the previous, rather mundane layout. This is now a real shot-making test, heavily contoured and with more water than most other Bermuda courses. The sand in the bunkers is the

From Tee Time to Bed Time

If you stay in a hotel with its own golf course or one that has agreements with some of the golf clubs, it cuts out much of the planning you'll have to make on your own. For instance, the **Fairmont Southampton Resort** has its own 18-hole executive course. Hotels block tee times for guests and provide a shuttle to and from the course.

At the **Tucker's Point Club,** which opened its hotel and spa in the spring of 2009, you can contrast the old and the new in golf course designs without straying very far from the resort. On-site is Roger Rulewich's

fabulous design, laid down atop the old Castle Harbour Golf Club, designed by his mentor, Robert Trent Jones Sr. Literally next door is the classic **Mid Ocean Club,** a Charles Blair Macdonald track redesigned by Jones in 1953. You will have seen Mid Ocean on television during the 2007 and 2008 PGA Grand Slams, and you'll be anxious to try your luck.

When you make your lodging arrangements, check to see what golf packages and perks are available. Many hoteliers are also members at the clubs and are happy to facilitate arrangements.

6

same used at the famed Augusta National, site of the Masters. A waterfall connects two man-made lakes that can come into play on several holes. The final four holes are particularly challenging because of their tight landing areas bordered by out-of-bounds stakes. A bad hit or intervention by the ever-present wind can lead to lost balls and penalties. The pressure continues until the ball is in the hole, because the greens are heavily bunkered and multitiered. Putting surfaces are well-maintained TifEagle grass. Fairways are attractively defined by palm trees, and an automated irrigation system keeps everything lush. The course has the island's only double green, a 14,000-square-foot putting surface on holes 1 and 10.

Highlight Hole: The 7th hole, a 178-yard par 3, is bordered by a waterfall.

Clubhouse: The main clubhouse with a private members' lounge stands on the site of the former Belmont Hotel, overlooking the 9th hole. The building has lovely views of the Great Sound and Hamilton Harbour, plus an airy lounge, bar, and pro shop. ✉ *25 Belmont Hills Dr.* ☎ *441/236–6060* ⊕ *www.newsteadbelmonthills.com* 💳 *$100 daily (including cart), $50 sunset; club rentals $50; lessons $60/½ hr* ⚑ *18 holes, 6017 yards, par 70* ⚐ *Rating: blue tees, 68.8; white tees, 68.4; red tees, 69.4.*

Ocean View Golf Course. If you want to play with locals or just mingle to talk golf, Ocean View is the place to be after the workday ends. Only 10 minutes from Hamilton, it's very popular. Switch tees on your second loop of the 9 holes for an 18-hole round playing 5658 yards to a par of 70. The first hole is a tough par 5 with a long, tight fairway flanked by a coral wall on one side and a drop-off to the shore on the other. The course is aptly named; there are panoramas from many holes as well as from the clubhouse and the restaurant patio. The club has a 260-yard driving range where the wind is often at your back, giving you a pleasant feeling that your drives are longer than they really are.

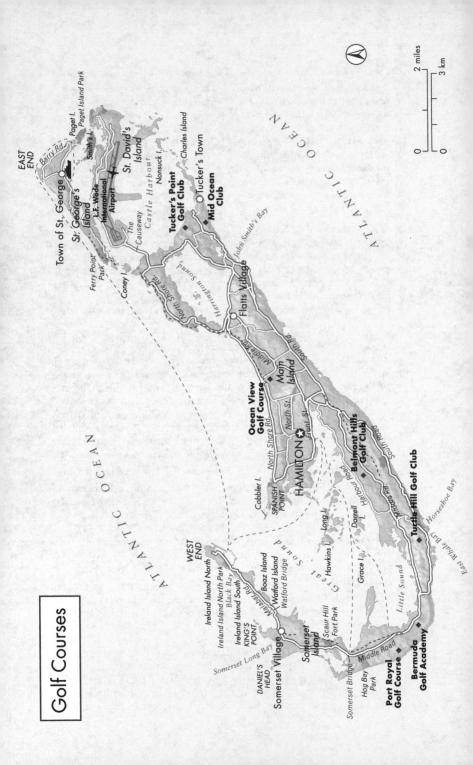

Highlight Hole: The green on the 192-yard, par-3 9th hole is cut into a coral hillside that's landscaped with colorful plants. It's a demanding shot when the wind is gusting from the north or west.

Clubhouse: Inside Ocean View's modest clubhouse is a small bar. Enjoy a cool beverage and the ocean breeze on the outside patio overlooking the north shore. ⊠ 2

> **TAXI TO TEE**
>
> If you bring your own clubs, budget for taxis to get you to the various courses. It's dangerous to carry your golf bag on a scooter, and clubs are not allowed on public buses. Taxis are expensive, but most rides are relatively short.

Barker's Hill ⊕ Off N. Shore Rd. ☎ *441/295–9092* ⊕ *www.ocean-viewgolfclub.com* ✉ *$50 with cart, $50 sunset; club rentals $25* ⌘. *9 holes (9 holes are played "out" followed by the same 9 holes played "in" to total 18), 2940 yards, par 35* ☞ *Lessons available. Rating: 68 playing white then blue tees; 68.7 playing yellow then red tees.*

ST. GEORGE'S AND EASTERN PARISHES

Mid Ocean Club. The elite Mid Ocean Club is a 1921 Charles Blair Macdonald design revamped in 1953 by Robert Trent Jones Sr. *Golf Digest* ranks it among the top 100 courses outside the United States. The club has a genteel air and a great sense of history. Even though it's expensive, a round of play is worthwhile, as you walk with a caddy to savor the traditional golf experience and the scenery. There are many holes near ocean cliffs, but you'll want to linger on the back tee of the last hole, where the view up the coast is spectacular. Overlooking the 18th hole and the south shore, the Mid Ocean's pink clubhouse is classically Bermudian down to the interior cedar trim. The pro shop offers a range of golfing goodies. The dining rooms are for members only, but you can have a drink in the bar. Nonmembers can play midweek; be sure to reserve your tee time early as the calendar books up months in advance. Caddies, club rentals, and shoe rentals are all available. ⊠ 1 *Mid Ocean Dr., Tucker's Town ⊕ Off S. Shore Rd.* ☎ *441/293–1215* ⊕ *www.themidoceanclubbermuda.com* ✉ *$250 for nonmembers ($32 for cart); $65 for caddy; club rentals $52; shoe rentals $12; lessons $120/hr, $70/½hr* ⌘. *18 holes, 6548 yards, par 71* ☞ *Ratings: blue tees, 71.9; white tees, 69.8; red tees, 72.6; yellow tees, 68.6.*

Fodor's Choice
★ **Tucker's Point Golf Club.** If you remember the old Castle Harbour Golf Club, you'll recognize some of the views but not the holes. Roger Rulewich, a former senior designer for the late Robert Trent Jones Sr., mapped out a stunning site layout in 2002, making the most of elevation changes and ocean views. It's longer than nearby Mid Ocean and holds more surprises. On many holes, you tee off toward the crest of a hill, not knowing what lies beyond. Topping the rise reveals the challenge, often involving a very elevated, sculpted green with a scenic vista. The course is fully irrigated and beautifully groomed. The final resort component—the 88-room Tucker's Point Hotel & Spa—opened in spring 2009. If you're not a guest at the hotel, you must have an introduction (your hotelier can do this) for playing and dining privileges.

6

Highlight Holes: There are many outstanding holes, but the par-4 17th is one of the most picturesque in Bermuda, with sweeping views of Tucker's Town and the Castle Islands. A rival is hole 13, where the perspective is the north coast and the Royal Navy Dockyard 20 miles away on the island's western tip.

Clubhouse: The 20,000-square-foot Tucker's Point Golf Clubhouse, a traditional Bermudian British–colonial design with covered verandas and tray ceilings, stands on a hilltop with a commanding view. Within are posh locker rooms, a large pro shop, and superb dining. You can relax with a cocktail or dine alfresco on the second-floor veranda while enjoying a panorama of Castle Harbour and Tucker's Town. ✉ *60 Tucker's Point Dr., off Harrington Sound Rd., Hamilton* ☎ *441/298–6970* ⊕ *www.tuckerspoint. com* ✉ *$150 with cart (weekdays), $180 with cart (weekends); shoe rentals $15; club rentals $50; lessons $150–$200/hr, $75–$100/½ hr* ⌘ *18 holes, 6500 yards, par 70* ☞ *Rating: blue tees, 71.2; white tees, 69.1; red tees, 69.7.*

> ### DON'T REPLACE YOUR DIVOTS
>
> Bermuda grass is so called because it came to the United States from Bermuda, but it actually originated in Africa, where it's called Devil's Grass or Wire Grass. The grass is considered holy in India, where it's used to feed sacred cows. In ancient times Romans boiled it and used the juice to stop bleeding. Bermuda grass is a creeping plant, putting down roots where nodes touch the earth. Once dislodged by your stroke, the mat of grass will not reroot, so don't bother to replace your divots. Instead, fill them with the sand and seed mixture on your cart.

DOCKYARD AND WESTERN PARISHES

FAMILY **Bermuda Golf Academy.** When you just want to practice or have some fun teaching the kids how to play golf in a relaxed environment, head for the Bermuda Golf Academy. The 320-yard driving range is floodlit at night until 10 pm and there are 40 practice bays. If you get a rainy day, fine-tune your game in one of the 25 covered bays. You can also work on sand shots in the practice bunker or sharpen your putting on a practice green.

Especially attractive for families is the 18-hole miniature golf course, which features pagodas, a waterfall, waterways—even a drawbridge to hit over on the 16th hole. The minicourse is lighted at night and takes 45 to 60 minutes to complete. Afterward, have a tasty bite to eat at the food truck parked nearby. ✉ *12 Industrial Park Rd.* ✛ *Off Middle Rd.* ☎ *441/238–8800* ⊕ *www.bermudagolfacademy.com* ✉ *Driving range $6 (40 balls); club rentals $2; miniature golf $12 adults, $8 children; lessons $85/hr.*

Port Royal Golf Course. One of two government-owned courses (Ocean View is the other), Port Royal is a perennial local and visitor favorite. The course reopened in July 2009 after a yearlong renovation that added irrigation, rebuilt tees and returfed them with Bermuda 419 grass, rebuilt and returfed greens with TifEagle grass, and redesigned bunkers. Two holes, 12 and 13, have been rerouted and now play as a par 4 and par 3. The revamped course is 280 yards longer than before. It hosted the PGA Grand Slam October 2009–2014.

One hole affected by the lengthening is the 16th, arguably Bermuda's best-known golf hole, which now plays 235 yards from the back tee. The green of this stunning par 3 occupies a treeless promontory with a backdrop of the blue waters and pink sands of Whale Bay. When the wind is blowing hard onshore, as it frequently does, this can be a tough green to reach. The holes leading up to the 16th are the icing on the cake, with ocean views on 7, 8, 9, and 15. The 1970 Robert Trent Jones Sr. layout has many elevated tees and greens and some clever doglegs. There are plenty of hills, on the back nine in particular.

GOLF TOURNAMENTS

Bermuda Golf Association. The Bermuda Golf Association stages a variety of tournaments beginning in January each year. Overseas entrants are actively encouraged, with the Goodwill Tournament in December the main competition for overseas golfers. For more information contact the Bermuda Golf Association. ⊠ *Victoria Place Bldg., 31 Victoria St., Hamilton* ☏ *441/295–9972* ⊕ *www.bermudagolf.org.*

6

Highlight Hole: Like the much-photographed 16th hole, the 412 yard, par-4 15th skirts the windswept cliffs along Whale Bay. The well-preserved remains of the Whale Bay Battery, a 19th-century fortification, stand next to the fairway.

Clubhouse: The Port Royal clubhouse also underwent renovation and reopened at the end of 2009, with a breezy outdoor patio and stunning panoramic views. ⊠ *5 Port Royal Golf Course Rd.* ⊕ *Off Middle Rd.* ☏ *441/234–0974, 441/234–0974 for automated tee-time reservations* ⊕ *www.portroyalgolf.bm* ⊠ *$180 (with cart); sunset $110 (with cart); shoe rentals $15; club rentals $50; lessons $120/hr, $60/½ hr* ⚑ *18 holes, 6842 yards, par 71* ☞ *Rating: blue tees, 72.4; white tees, 70.2; red tees, 71.9; black tee 74.6.*

Turtle Hill Golf Club. Spreading across the hillside below the high-rise Fairmont Southampton, this executive golf course is known for its steep terrain, giving players who opt to walk (for sunset tee times only) an excellent workout. The Ted Robinson design is a good warm-up for Bermuda's full-length courses, offering a legitimate test of wind and bunker play. The front nine has almost constant views of the ocean and is more difficult than the back nine, with tight holes calling for careful club selection. Club rentals and lessons are also available. Because the hotel and its restaurants are so close, there's no golf clubhouse per se, just a 10th-hole Golf Hut for snacks and drinks. ⊠ *Fairmont Southampton Resort, 101 South Rd.* ☏ *441/239–6952* ⊕ *www.fairmont.com/ southampton-bermuda* ⊠ *$99 before 12 pm (with cart), $69 after 12 pm (with cart), $45 sunset (walking); club rentals $39; lessons $175/ hr, $95/½ hr* ⚑ *18 holes, 2684 yards, par 54.*

OTHER SPORTS AND OUTDOOR ACTIVITIES

BICYCLING

The best and sometimes only way to explore Bermuda's nooks and crannies—its little hidden coves and 18th-century tribe roads—is by bicycle or motor scooter. Arriving at the small shore roads and hill trails, however, means first navigating Bermuda's rather treacherous main roads. They are narrow, with no shoulders, and often congested with traffic (especially near Hamilton during rush hours). Fortunately, there's another, safer option for biking in Bermuda: the Railway Trail, a dedicated cycle path blissfully free of cars.

Despite the traffic, bicycle racing is a popular sport in Bermuda, and club groups regularly whir around the island on evening, weekend, and early-morning training rides. Be prepared for some tough climbs—the roads running north and south across the island are particularly steep and winding—and the wind can sap even the strongest rider's strength, especially along South Shore Road in Warwick and Southampton parishes. Island roads are no place for novice riders. Helmets are strongly recommended on pedal bikes (it's illegal to ride without them on a motor scooter), and parents should think twice before allowing preteens to bike here.

Information on local races or on how to meet up with fellow cyclists for regular group rides is available at ⊕ *www.bermudabicycle.org*. The Winner's Edge bike shop on Front Street in Hamilton is also a good source of information about the local cycling scene; visit its website at ⊕ *www.winnersedge.bm*.

BIKE PATHS

Fodor's Choice **The Railway Trail.** Running intermittently along the length of the old Ber-
★ muda Railway (old "Rattle 'n' Shake"), this trail is scenic and restricted to pedestrian and bicycle traffic. You can enter and exit the trail at several clearly signposted points. One especially lovely route starts at Somerset Bridge and ends 2½ miles later near Mangrove Bay. You can take your bike onto the ferry for a pleasant ride from Hamilton or St. George's to the Somerset Bridge stop. From there, bike to the bridge on the main road, turn right, and ride uphill for about 50 yards until you reach the sign announcing "Railway Trail." Turning onto the trail, you find yourself along a course with spectacular views of the Great Sound. Along the way you pass old Fort Scaur, several schools, and the large pink Somerset Cricket Club. Toward the end of the trail segment, you'll find yourself on Beacon Hill Road opposite the bus depot. Here you can turn around and head back to Somerset Bridge, or, for refreshment, turn left and ride to the main road (you can see Somerset Police Station), and make a sharp right turn to find Mangrove Bay and several small pubs and shops nearby. On the East End of the island, in Hamilton Parish, recent restoration efforts have breathed new life into the already popular Railway Trail. Late 2014 saw the construction of a 740-foot bridge that allows walkers, joggers, and bikers to pass between Crawl Hill and Coney Island. Because parts of the Railway Trail are somewhat isolated and not well lit, you should plan your excursions for daytime hours.

South Shore Road. This main island road covers almost the full length of the island and passes absolutely gorgeous ocean views. South Shore Road—also known as South Road—is well paved and, for the most part, wider than Middle Road, North Shore Road, and Harbour Road, with relatively few hills. However, it's one of Bermuda's windiest and most heavily traveled thoroughfares. Highlights are through Warwick and Southampton, looking down on the popular south shore beaches.

> ## ROAD RASH
>
> The Bermudian slang dictionary *Bermewjan Vurds* defines "road rash" (grazes received from sliding along Bermuda's roads in an accident) as "a skin disease common amongst tourists brave enough to rent mopeds."

Tribe Road 3. Tribe roads are small, often unpaved side roads, some of which date to the earliest settlement of Bermuda in the 17th century. They make for good exploring, though many are quite short and lead to dead ends. Beginning at Oleander Cycles in Southampton, Tribe Road 3 steeply climbs the hillside just below Gibbs Hill Lighthouse, with views of the south shore below. It eventually leads to a point from where you can see both the north and south shores.

BIKE RENTALS

In Bermuda bicycles are called pedal or push bikes to distinguish them from the more common motorized two-wheelers, which are also called bikes. Some of the cycle liveries around the island rent both, so make sure to specify whether you want a pedal or motor bike. If you're sure you want to bicycle while you're in Bermuda, try to reserve rental bikes a few days in advance. Rates are around $40 a day, though the longer you rent, the more economical your daily rate. You may be charged an additional $30 for a repair waiver and for a refundable deposit.

Riding a motor scooter for the first time can be disconcerting wherever you are. Here you have the added confusion that Bermudians drive on the left, and though the posted speed limit is 35 kph (about 22 mph), the unofficial speed limit is actually closer to 50 kph (31 mph; and many locals actually travel faster than that). At most rental shops, lessons on how to ride a motor scooter are perfunctory at best—practice as much as you can before going on to the main road and beware of unusual traffic patterns such as double-laned roundabouts. Though many tourists can and do rent motor scooters, the public transportation system (ferries and buses) is excellent and should not be ruled out.

Oleander Cycles. This agency is known primarily for its selection of motorbikes and scooters for rent and sale. Single and double bikes are available, and a $30 damage waiver is charged. Oleander Cycles' main store is in Paget, but its Southampton location is convenient for The Reefs Resort & Club guests since it's right across the street. There are also small branches in Hamilton, near the St. George's Club, in the Royal Naval Dockyard, and down the road from Grotto Bay Beach Resort. ⊠ *6 Valley Rd.* ⊕ *Off Middle Rd.* ☎ *441/236–5235* ⊕ *www.oleandercycles.bm.*

Smatt's Cycle Livery. Smatt's offers standard moped rentals with helmets. The daily rate is $55 for a single seater, plus the $30 damage-waiver fee. Before a moped is rented, you'll be asked to take a riding test for your safety. There are two additional locations, one in the west end at the Fairmont Southampton Resort, and one at the Rosewood Tucker's Point Hotel & Spa. If you are arriving into Dockyard by cruise ship, the closest shop is the Hamilton branch (accessible via a 20-minute ferry ride). There are also a limited number of bicycles available for rent from the Hamilton and Southampton locations. ⊠ *Fairmont Hamilton Princess, 74 Pitts Bay Rd., Hamilton* ☎ *441/295–1180* ⊕ *www.smattscyclelivery.com.*

BIKE TOURS

Island Tour Centre. This comprehensive recreational company offers an assortment of memorable excursions. The bike tour along the Railway Trail begins in Dockyard with a short boat cruise to the trail, where you will pick up your 21-speed mountain bike. After the leisurely 1½-hour guided ride and commentary, finish with a cool-off swim and a drink at a beach in the Somerset area. The trip is about 3½ hours, including the cruise and biking. It costs $80 per person and includes equipment and drinks. There is a $5 administration fee per reservation. ☎ *441/236–1300* ⊕ *www.islandtourcentre.com.*

BIRD-WATCHING

Forty species of warblers have been spotted in Bermuda, especially in the casuarina trees along the south shore and West End. Other omnipresent species include kiskadee, swifts, cuckoos, flycatchers, swallows, thrushes, kingbirds, and orioles. Bird conservation is a big deal in Bermuda. You can see bluebird boxes on every island golf course, which act as safe nesting sites for this jeopardized species, threatened by development and the invasive sparrow.

The largest variety of birds can be spotted during fall migration, when thousands of birds pass overhead, stop for a rest on their way south, or spend the winter on the island. You might spot the rare American avocet or the curlew sandpiper. In spring look for brightly colored Central and South American birds migrating north. The white-tail tropic bird, a beautiful white bird with black markings and a 12- to 17-inch-long tail (locals call it a "longtail"), is one of the first to arrive. Summer is the quietest season for bird-watching in Bermuda. Late migrants, like the barn swallow and chimney swift, pass by, and if you check the ponds you may see the occasional shorebird.

Bermuda Audubon Society. The society has an excellent book called *A Birdwatching Guide to Bermuda,* by president Andrew Dobson, published by the Arlequin Press. In it are maps, illustrations, and descriptions of birds and their habitats. It also sells a special DVD featuring the history and conservation of Nonsuch Island for $20. Several birding events are organized throughout the year, including the Christmas Bird Count—Bermuda averages over 80 species per count, although 250 species have been recorded. You can find a listing of the Audubon Society's events on its website as well as a bird-watching checklist. Birders may also be interested in David Wingate's successful efforts to repopulate the native cahow bird population via artificial burrows on Nonsuch Island. ☎ *441/238–8628* ⊕ *www.audubon.bm.*

Seymour's Pond Nature Reserve. Seymour's Pond is smaller and less exciting than Warwick and Spittal ponds, but it has the advantage of being a bit farther inland, and therefore both better protected and better suited to serious birders. Twenty-eight species of duck are recorded in Bermuda and you're quite likely to see many of them here. Keep an eye out for moorhens, American coot, and pied-billed grebes, three species known to breed around this location. ⊠ *Middle Rd., near Barnes Corner Park.*

FAMILY **Spittal Pond Nature Reserve.** Stretching placidly within a 60-acre nature reserve, Spittal Pond is an excellent place to view wildlife, especially birds. As long as the water level is not too high, some 30 species of shorebird can be present on the margins of the pond. On a good day in September you might see more than 100 birds. Semipalmated sandpipers are perhaps the most abundant. In winter, herons and egrets roost serenely in the shallow water. Contact the Bermuda National Trust, or visit its website, for more information on planning your own self-guided tour. Don't forget your camera if you take one of the great coastal nature trails. ⊠ *South Rd.* ☎ *441/236–6483* ⊕ *www.bnt.bm.*

Warwick Pond. Warwick Pond, also referred to as Sherwin Nature Reserve, is Bermuda's second-largest freshwater pond and prime bird-viewing territory. Shorebirds and herons gather en masse in the surrounding allspice woodland and cattail marsh during the fall and winter seasons. Note: in the heat of summer, the stagnant water lets off a rather putrid smell. ⊠ *Middle Rd.* ✛ *Near Ettrick Animal Hospital.*

BOATING

Bermuda is gorgeous by land, but you should take to the water to fully appreciate its beauty. You can either rent your own boat or charter one with a skipper. There are literally scores of options to suit all tastes, from champagne cruises at sunset to cruise and kayak ecotours.

CHARTERS AND BOAT RENTALS

More than 20 large power cruisers and sailing vessels, piloted by local skippers, are available for charter. Primarily 30 to 60 feet long, most charter sailboats can carry up to 30 passengers, sometimes overnight. Meals and drinks can be included on request, and a few skippers offer dinner cruises for the romantically inclined. Rates generally range from $500 to $750 for a three-hour cruise, or $800 to $1,500 for a full-day cruise, with additional per-person charges for large groups. Where you go and what you do—exploring, swimming, snorkeling, cruising—is usually up to you and your skipper. Generally, however, cruises travel to and around the islands of the Great Sound. Several charter skippers advertise year-round operations, but the off-season schedule can be haphazard. Skippers devote periods of the off-season to maintenance and repairs or close altogether if bookings lag. Be sure to book well in advance; in the high season do so before you arrive on the island.

Good, Cheap Fun!

Bermuda is notoriously expensive, but if you've blown most of your vacation budget getting here, you can stretch the rest while still having a good time.

Walking Along the South Shore Beaches. There's a 2-mile stretch from Horseshoe Bay in Southampton right down to Warwick Long Bay, which, with a bit of clambering and the odd paddle in the ocean, you can comfortably negotiate. The quiet secluded spots along the rocks are great for bird-watching, and there are a number of tiny coves where you can stop for a picnic.

Cup Match. If you want a real Bermuda experience, come to the island during the annual Cup Match holiday—either the last weekend in July or the first weekend in August. It's essentially the all-star cricket game between the best of the west and the best of the east, but you don't have to like cricket to enjoy the atmosphere. Half the island trots through the ground at some stage during the two-day holiday to listen to the sound of the drums, sample the fried chicken, and wave a flag for Somerset or St. George's. It's also the one time of year when gambling is legal and thousands pack the Crown & Anchor tents to roll the dice for Bermuda's own unique version of the

casino favorite—craps. Entry is $20 for adults, $5 for children.

Rent a Bike. On an island where the speed limit is 35 kph (roughly 20 mph), there's no need to worry about renting a car. Bermuda's strict traffic-control rules mean you're not allowed to anyway. A bike is the best way to discover for yourself the hidden nooks and crannies and secret beaches that the bus routes and the tourist cabs just won't take you to. It costs about $55 a day.

Snorkeling at Tobacco Bay. You don't have to rent a boat or even swim very far offshore to get a close-up look at some of Bermuda's wonderful marine life. Tobacco Bay in St. George's is a favorite spot, where colorful sergeant majors, parrot fish, and clown fish can be seen in the crystal clear water close to the rocks. John Smith's Bay in Smith's Parish, where shoals of tiny fish cast large, dark shadows across the bay, is another great snorkeling destination.

Wildlife Photography. From a patient day's vigil with an ultralong lens, waiting for a shot of a humpback whale, to a frantic pursuit of a pair of longtails dancing in the summer sky, Bermuda is an amateur photographer's dream.

Ana Luna Adventures. The *Ana Luna* is a 45-foot catamaran that provides snorkeling cruises, scuba diving trips, and sunset tours as well as a host of other marine adventures from around $70. The regularly scheduled sailing charters depart daily from Grotto Bay during the summer months and tour Bermuda's northern coastline. Panoramic views of forts, railway artifacts, old docks, and an array of marine life await. There are also romantic sunset voyages and bioluminescent glowworm tours. Planning something extra special? Speak to Captain Nathan to schedule a private adventure aboard the *Ana Luna*. ⊠ *Grotto Bay Beach Resort, 11 Blue Hole Hill, Bailey's Bay, Hamilton* ☎ *441/504–3780* ⊕ *www.analunaadventures.com.*

Bermuda Charters. Captained by Anthony Mello, the elegant and comfortable 45-foot *AJ's Wings* offers guests an array of exciting tours and private charters. Rent the entire boat for three hours (up to six people) for $600 plus $150 for each additional hour and $30 for each additional person. Sunset

> **GOOD TO KNOW**
>
> If you rent a motorboat, be sure to ask for directions to Castle Island Nature Reserve, one of the most secluded and beautiful spots on the island.

cocktail, dinner, and moonlight cruises are also offered with wine and cheese, desserts, and full menus available on request. Bring your binoculars and enjoy the thrill of offshore sailing and whale-watching during the prime spring season (March and April). ☎ *441/534–7669* ⊕ *www. bermudacharters.com.*

FAMILY **Bermuda Waterski and Wakeboard Center.** International competitor Kent Richardson represented Bermuda at nine World Championships and the Pan Am games. He also took a trick skiing bronze medal at the Latin American games, but don't be intimidated—Kent is a patient teacher. His business operates at the same location as Somerset Bridge Watersports at Robinson's Marina from May to September. You can take your pick from waterskiing (regular and barefoot), wakeboarding, cliff jumping, or tubing, or mix it up with a bit of everything. Kent charges by the hour and can take up to six people at a time, ages five and older. ⊠ *Robinson's Marina, Somerset Bridge, Somerset* ☎ *441/335–1012* ⊕ *www.islandwindsbermuda.com.*

Blue Hole Watersports. Blue Hole, based out of the Grotto Bay Resort, has you covered in the East End of the island. Cruise the waters and soak up some rays in a Fun Cat, a low-powered floating deck chair, for $40 per half hour or $60 for an hour. You can rent kayaks; a single costs $20 for the first hour, and a double costs $30 for the first hour, then $15 per additional hour. Blue Hole also offers windsurfing and sunfish sailboat rentals, and paddleboards for around $30 per hour; motorboats start at $120 for two hours plus fuel costs. There's a gorgeous sheltered beach with a small wreck sunk just offshore for snorkelers. A snorkeling set is $8 an hour or $24 for 24 hours. ⊠ *Grotto Bay Beach Resort, 11 Blue Hole Hill, Bailey's Bay, Hamilton* ☎ *441/293–2915, 441/293–2915* ⊕ *www.blueholebermuda.com.*

H2O Sports. Located on the shore of Mangrove Bay in Somerset, H2O offers just about everything there is to do on the water: sailing, boat rentals, kayaking, as well as instruction from experienced mariners; 17-foot-long motorboats are available for rent for $100 for the first hour, plus $30 for each additional hour. Adventurous explorers and independent anglers can take out a 17-foot sailboat at $80 for the first hour, and $10 for each additional; 90-minute sailing lessons are available if you need a refresher. See the island at speed with a guided 75-minute Jet Ski tour for $135 or snorkel at your own pace—gear costs $20 for 24 hours. The staff will happily point out the best snorkeling spots to explore and what marine life to look out for. ⊠ *Cambridge Beaches Resort, 30 Kings Point Rd., Somerset* ☎ *441/234–3082* ⊕ *www.h2osportsbermuda.com.*

6

KS Watersports. This is the one and only place to go for parasailing, Wild-Cat adventure tours, Jet Ski safaris, and sailboat rentals. Its Dockyard location, right next to the ferry stop, is open year-round, and specializes in water sports excursions. An afternoon of parasailing, around an hour and 45 minutes on the water, will get you 8 to 10 minutes of airborne excitement for $110 per person—two people can go up together, on request. For a more low-key day in the sun, check out the KS Watersports locations in King's Square, St. George's, and Pitts Bay Road, Hamilton; they offer Pontoon and Boston Whaler boat rentals and private charters. All three locations run Jet Ski tours, starting from $145, for a 75-minute thrilling adventure. ⊠ *Dockyard Watersports Center, 6 Dockyard Terr., Dockyard* ☎ *441/238–4155 Dockyard, 441/232–4155 Hamilton, 441/297–4155 St. George's* ⊕ *www.kswatersports.com.*

Pompano Beach Club. For a more relaxed aquatic experience, check out Pompano Beach Club. Several low-speed vessels are available including motorized Fun Cat cruisers ($80 per hour), Hobie Cat sailboats ($80 per hour), two-person glass-bottom kayaks ($40 per hour), and paddle-boards ($40 per hour). Discounted rates are offered to Pompano Beach Club hotel guests. The water-sports center is open from May to October. Snorkeling equipment is available to rent at $6 per hour; the club also offers snorkeling trips, harbor cruises, and fishing trips. ⊠ *36 Pompano Beach Rd.* ☎ *441/234–0222* ⊕ *www.pompanobeachclub.com.*

FAMILY **Restless Native Tours.** With a full bar, huge music library, an iPod dock, and onboard souvenir shop, you can be sure that everyone will enjoy cruising on this family-owned and -operated charter catamaran. Restless Native is also unique in its educational approach to chartering—it offers a crash course on Bermuda's fish and a guided snorkeling trip. The 50-by-30-foot pink boat is excellent for dinner charters, evening cocktail cruises, birthday parties, and weddings. Pickup can be arranged at any wharf on the island; charters are available year-round for two to five hours and up to 50 guests. ☎ *441/531–8149* ⊕ *www.restlessnative.bm.*

Rising Son II Catamaran. The *Rising Son II* is a beautiful, 60-foot, 75-passenger catamaran with a full bar, roomy shaded cockpit, and multiple trampolines. Besides offering sailing, swimming, and snorkeling trips, Captain Steve "Squid" Smith and the accommodating crews can arrange for private cocktail parties and even catering. Rates start at $600 for the two hours. You can also book one of the popular cruises, such as the Ultimate Catamaran Sail and Snorkel, which anchors off a quiet sandy bay for snorkeling and kayaking for $75 a head. Keep your eyes peeled for marine life as turtles are often spotted. ⊠ *King's Wharf, Dockyard* ☎ *441/236–1300* ⊕ *www.risingsoncruises.com.*

Somerset Bridge Watersports. Located right next to the Somerset Bridge, this West End outfitter rents 13- and 15-foot Boston Whalers. Rates start at $95 for two hours, $145 for four hours, $200 for six hours, or $260 for eight hours, plus the cost of gas. You can also take a speed tour of the western end of the island on a Jet Ski for $125 for a single and $135 for a double. The tour will take you flying over crystal clear waters, weaving through coral reefs, and under the world's smallest drawbridge. Prices include a paid taxi ride to or from Dockyard; be aware that groups are kept small, so big parties may need to split up. Single and double kayaks are also available starting at $25 and $30 an hour. ✉ *Robinson's Marina, Somerset Bridge, Somerset* ☎ *441/234–0914* ⊕ *www.bdawatersports.com.*

Tam-Marina. Founded in 1967, Tam-Marina has a reputation for lively dinner and cocktail cruises on a fleet of elegant white motor yachts. *Lady Charlotte* and *Lady Tamara* often accommodate large private parties on the Great Sound, whereas *Boss Lady* is smaller and more intimate, tailored for groups of 10 guests or fewer. Join the ranks of celebrities that have cruised aboard these luxurious boats—a plush interior, fully stocked bar, and impeccable service awaits. ✉ *61 Harbour Rd.* ☎ *441/236–0127* ⊕ *www.ladyboats.com.*

Wind Sail Charters. You can rent a 41-, 51-, or 60-foot Morgan yacht, including snorkeling equipment, from Wind Sail. Captain Mike or his daughter, Captain Melissa, will sail to your location and take you for a spin. The rates for six people are $550 and up, depending on the boat, for three hours, making this the most affordable ride on the island. You can also join a group (daytime and sunset) for the bargain price of $50, when available. Lunch catering is available for an extra charge. ☎ *441/734–8547* ⊕ *www.bermudawindsailcharters.com.*

6

CRICKET

Cricket is one of the favorite pastimes on this sports-mad island, a fact that was seen with the national celebrations that followed Bermuda's qualification for the Cricket World Cup in 2007. Bermuda is the smallest country ever to make the finals of the competition, and its cricketeers are treated as heroes in their homeland. The island's cricket season runs from April through September.

Bermuda Cricket Board. The Bermuda Cricket Board was founded in 1938 and is in charge of scheduling, game regulations, and player development. Visit the BCB's website to learn more about its history, review past and upcoming events, and much more. ☎ *441/292–8958* ⊕ *www.cricket.bm.*

Fodor's Choice ★ **Cup Match.** Among Bermuda cricket aficionados, Cup Match in late July or early August is *the* summer sporting event, played over two days. The top players from around the island compete in two teams: the East End team and the West End team. Although the match is taken very seriously, the event itself is a real festival, complete with plenty of Bermudian food and music. Cup Match coincides with two national holidays, Emancipation Day and Somers' Day. Emancipation Day is the celebration of the passing of the Slavery Abolition Act in 1834, which freed Bermuda's slaves, and Somers' Day celebrates Admiral Sir George Somers discovering Bermuda, which led to its settlement in 1609. Cup Match is Bermuda's only venue for legal gambling: the Crown & Anchor tent is pitched at the field each year. Thousands of picnickers and partiers show up during the two-day match. Although the players wear only white, fans wear colors to support their team—light blue on dark blue represents the East End and navy on red represents the West End.

For Love of Cricket

The Oval and Lords are names of English cricket grounds that evoke memories of Britain long ago, a time of cucumber sandwiches and tea poured from china pots—but the cricket scene in Bermuda is definitely Caribbean. The thwack of leather on willow is the same, but overcast skies and frequent breaks as the ground staff move quickly to put the rain covers in place are not for these players. The fans, gathered on grassy knolls and open terraces, are also far removed from those back in England, where the game originated. Polite clapping and hearty hurrahs are not to be heard here. Instead the air is filled with chanting, and the grandstands reverberate to the sound of music. Allegiances are clearly defined, though few miles separate the opposing factions—mothers, fathers, sons, and daughters all cheering on their favorites. As the match comes to a conclusion, the setting sun falls low behind the clubhouse and players and fans mingle to await the dawn of another day of runs, catches, and cries of "Howzat."

General admission tickets are available each day at the stadium entrance and give visitors free rein to spectate, gamble, and explore the grounds and food tents. Drink tickets are also available inside the venue. Although diehard cricket fans tend to stake out bleacher seats closest to the action, most locals don't stay put for the entire match. As the day wears on, the party moves to the elaborate, multitiered scaffolding structure that is erected around the playing field. Though some sections are VIP only, the rest is open to the public and a great place to watch the game below.

The venue alternates each year between the St. George's Cricket Club and the Somerset Cricket Club. ⊠ *St. George's Cricket Club, 56 Wellington Slip Rd., St. George's* ⊕ *www.bermudacupmatch.com* ⊠ *Somerset Cricket Club, 6 Cricket La., Somerset.*

FISHING

Bermuda's proximity to the deep ocean makes it one of the best places in the world for deep-sea fishing. Many of the International Fishing Association's world-record catches were hauled in a few miles off the Bermuda coastline. July and August is marlin season, and anglers from all over the world come to the island in a bid to try to hook monster blue marlin in excess of 1,000 pounds. Deep-sea fishing is not just for the experts, though. Most charter companies are happy to teach amateurs how to hook and reel in a catch—whether it's tuna, wahoo, or even marlin. Some of the charter fishermen let you keep your catch, but they're not obliged to do so. Many of the fishermen rely on sales to restaurants to bolster their businesses, so unless it's a good day they might not give much away. And don't be surprised to find fish you pulled out of the ocean that day on the menu in one of Bermuda's many restaurants that evening. As well as deep-sea fishing, shore fishing is also popular, while some fishermen trawl inside the reefs. If you've got the cash, there's no substitute for the thrill of the open ocean. Scores of operators are on the island, about 20 of which are regularly out on the water. A full list is available at ⊕ *www.gotobermuda.com/sportfishing*. Prices vary depending on the size and quality of the boat.

REEF AND OFFSHORE FISHING

Three major reef bands lie at various distances from the island. The first is anywhere from ½ to 5 miles offshore. The second, the Challenger Bank, is about 12 miles offshore. The third, the Argus Bank, is about 30 miles offshore. As a rule, the farther out you go, the larger the fish—and the more expensive the charter.

Most charter-fishing captains go to the reefs and deep water to the southwest and northwest of the island, where the fishing is best. Catches over the reefs include snapper, amberjack, grouper, and barracuda. Of the most sought-after deepwater fish—marlin, tuna, wahoo, and dol-phinfish—wahoo is the most common, dolphinfish the least. Trawling is the usual method of deepwater fishing, and charter-boat operators offer various tackle setups, with test-line weights ranging from 20 pounds to 130 pounds. The boats, which range from 31 feet to 55 feet long, are fitted with gear and electronics to track fish, including depth sounders, global-positioning systems, loran systems, video fish finders, radar, and computer scanners.

Half-day and full-day charters are offered by most operators, but full-day trips offer the best chance for a big catch because the boat has time to reach waters that are less often fished. Rates are about $900 per boat for half a day (four hours), $1,300 per day (eight hours). Request more information about chartering a fishing boat at Visitor Information Centres in Hamilton, Dockyard, or St. George's.

Atlantic Spray Charters. Half-day and full-day year-round charters are available on Atlantic's 40-foot *Tenacious*. Rates are $850 for the four-hour half day, $1,050 for six hours, and $1,250 for the eight-hour full day, including all the equipment you need, soda and water, and, most important, the knowledge you need to catch the big fish. ⊠ *St. George's* ☎ *441/735–9444.*

Mako Charters. Allen DeSilva, one of Bermuda's most knowledgeable skippers, guarantees a fun day of fishing whether you're a complete beginner or a serious angler. His spacious 56-foot fully air-conditioned boat, *Mako,* based out of Mill's Creek near Hamilton, is one of the best for a safe, comfortable, and exciting cruise. A full, nine-hour charter costs $2,500 for up to four people, with an additional charge per head, up to eight people. Overnight fishing packages, complete with breakfast and lunch, are also available. Allen's website is a great source of information on local fishing competitions and includes lots of photos of past guests and their record-breaking catches. ⊠ *11 Abri La., Spanish Point* ☎ *441/295–0835 office, 441/505–8626 cell* ⊕ *www.fishbermuda.com.*

Overproof. Skipper Peter Rans is a regular in the big-game classic and a master at hooking monster marlin. He navigates a fully equipped 42-foot vessel to the very best spots to help you reel in whatever game fish is in season. His rates vary from $1,000 for half a day to $1,400 for

CLOSE UP

World Cup

Bermuda's angling competitions attract top fishermen from all over the world. The Bermuda Billfish Blast tournament over the Fourth of July weekend coincides with the World Cup—where anglers across the globe compete to land the largest fish on the planet between 8 am and 4:30 pm. Each year more and more boats descend on Bermuda over the holiday weekend. The biggest local tournament is the Bermuda Big Game Classic, with many of the World Cup fishermen sticking around to take part in the three-day festival. The dates vary depending on when the weekend falls, but it's usually around July 15. The lure of monster marlin in excess of 1,000 pounds keeps them coming for the third leg of the Bermuda Triple Crown, the Seahorse Anglers Club tournament, the following week. Marlin season is what a lot of Bermuda's sport fishermen live for. "It's the biggest, baddest fish in the ocean—there's no feeling like landing a marlin," explains Sloane Wakefield of Atlantic Spray Charters. The **Bermuda Game Fishing Association** (☎ 441/292–7131) is a good source of information about tournaments.

eight hours of serious marlin hunting, equipment, bait, and beverages included. ✉ *136 Somerset Rd., Somerset* ☎ *441/238–5663, 441/335–9850 cell* ⊕ *www.overprooffishing.com.*

Playmate Fishing Charters. With Kevin Winter's 30 years of experience fishing Bermuda's waters, you're guaranteed excitement, action, and results aboard the 43-foot, smooth-sailing *Playmate.* Rates go from $1,000 for half a day to $1,350 for the full day, including all bait and tackle plus complimentary soft drinks, with extra costs for tournament fishing. Catering is available upon request. ✉ *4 Mill Point La.* ☎ *441/292–7131, 441/799–8862 boat cell* ⊕ *www.playmatefishing.com.*

SHORE FISHING

The principal catches for shore fishers are pompano, bonefish, and snapper. Excellent sport for saltwater fly-fishing is the wily and strong bonefish, which hovers in coves, harbors, and bays. Among the more popular spots for bonefish are West Whale Bay and Spring Benny's Bay, which have large expanses of clear, shallow water protected by reefs close to shore. Good fishing holes are plentiful along the south shore, too. Fishing in the Great Sound and St. George's Harbour can be rewarding, but enclosed Harrington Sound is less promising. Ask at local tackle shops about the latest hot spots and the best baits. You can also make rental arrangements through your hotel or contact **H2O Sports** *(see Boating, Charters and Boat Rentals).*

RUGBY

Bermuda's rugby season runs from September to April.

World Rugby Classic. The World Rugby Classic, in early to mid-November, brings erstwhile top players, now retired, to the island for a week of play and parties—it's a hugely popular event among Bermuda's expatriate community. A game pass for the week is $100, daily admission is $25. The Classic can provide information about other matches as well. ☎ 441/295–6574 ⊕ *www.worldrugby.bm.*

RUNNING AND WALKING

Top runners flock to the island in January for the Bermuda International Race Weekend, which includes a marathon and 10-km races. Many of the difficulties that cyclists face in Bermuda—hills, traffic, and wind—also confront runners. Be careful of traffic when walking or running along Bermuda's narrow roads—most don't have shoulders.

Runners who favor firm pavement are happiest along the **Railway Trail** *(see Bicycling, above),* a former train route, one of the most peaceful stretches of road in Bermuda.

If you like running on sand, head for the **south shore beaches** *(see Beaches, above).* The trails through the South Shore Park are relatively firm. A large number of serious runners can be seen on Horseshoe Bay and Elbow Beach early in the morning and after 5 pm. Another good beach for running is half-mile-long Warwick Long Bay, the island's longest uninterrupted stretch of sand. The sand is softer here than at Horseshoe and Elbow, so it's difficult to get good footing, particularly at high tide. By using South Shore Park trails to skirt the coral bluffs, you can create a route that connects several beaches. Note that the trails can be winding and uneven in places.

Bermuda Half Marathon Derby. Held on Bermuda Day (May 24), a public holiday, the race brings thousands of locals and visitors, who line the edges of the 13.1-mile course. Even if you aren't a runner, it's great fun to watch. There's also the annual Heritage Day parade, complete with Gombeys, baton twirlers, floats, and musicians, in Hamilton afterward. The procession starts at 1:30 pm from Bernard Park, finishing on Front Street several hours later. ⊕ *www.bermudamarathon.bm.*

Bermuda Triathlons. The Bermuda Triathlon Association holds these sporting events about once a month from April to October. The events are of various lengths and combine a swim, a cycling leg, and a run. The BTA also hosts sprint series throughout summer months. Many of the events take place at Clearwater Beach in St. David's or at Harrington Sound Dock. ⊕ *www.bermudatriathlon.com.*

International Race Weekend. Held in mid-January, there's some serious competition for winning these races; they attract world-class distance runners from countries around the world, but they're open to everyone. The weekend event begins with the Front Street mile race on Friday night, continues with a 10k walk and run on Saturday, and finishes with the marathon on Sunday. Many ambitious participants aim to get three medals in three days! ☎ 441/737–8850 ⊕ *www.bermudaraceweekend.com.*

Mid Atlantic Athletic Club Races. This club hosts many middle- to long-distance running events at various locations across the island throughout the year. The main attraction is the annual Fairmont to Fairmont, a 7.2-mile race that challenges participants to make the trek from the Fairmont

Hamilton Princess to the Fairmont Southampton. The Renaissance 10 Miler and Team Challenge in March and the Fidelity 5k in June are also popular. ☎ 441/239–4803 ⊕ www.maac.bm.

SAILING AND YACHTING

Bermuda has a worldwide reputation as a yacht-racing center. The sight of the racing fleet, with brightly colored spinnakers flying, is striking even if it's difficult to follow the intricacies of the race. The racing season runs from March to November. Most races are held on weekends in the Great Sound, and several classes of boats usually compete. You can watch from Spanish Point and along the Somerset shoreline. Anyone who wants to get a real sense of the action should be on board a boat near the racecourse. The Argo Gold Cup race is held in October, and International Race Week is held at the end of April or beginning of May. In June in alternating years, Bermuda serves as the finish point for oceangoing yachts in three major races starting in the United States. Bermuda also took the international spotlight as the host of the 35th America's Cup in June 2017.

RACES AND EVENTS

Argo Group Gold Cup. This is the event of choice if you're more interested in racing than gawking at expensive yachts. Managed by the Royal Bermuda Yacht Club, the October tournament hosts many of the world's top sailors—some of whom are America's Cup skippers—and includes the elite among Bermudians in a lucrative chase for thousands in prize money. Join in the excitement as the-best-of-the-best compete in Hamilton Harbour. ⊠ *Royal Bermuda Yacht Club, 15 Point Pleasant Rd., Hamilton* ☎ *441/295–2214* ⊕ *www.bermudagoldcup.com.*

Bermuda Ocean Race. This 753-mile race routes competitors down the Chesapeake Bay from Annapolis, Maryland, across the Gulfstream, to the turquoise waters of Bermuda, taking place every other year in June, in even-numbered years. Whether you're a sailing aficionado or just enjoy a fine ocean breeze, be sure to take a stroll to see the hundreds of docked boats at the Royal Hamilton Amateur Dinghy Club after the event. ⊠ *Royal Hamilton Amateur Dinghy Club, 25 Pomander Rd., Hamilton* ☎ *441/236–2250* ⊕ *www.bermudaoceanrace.com.*

Marion (MA)-to-Bermuda Cruising Yacht Race. Only slightly smaller in scale than the Newport-to-Bermuda, this race is held in June of odd-numbered years. Competitors set sail from Marion, Massachusetts, race across the Atlantic, and arrive in Hamilton in just under five days. Contact the Royal Hamilton Amateur Dinghy Club for information on where and when to watch finishers. ⊠ *Royal Hamilton Amateur Dinghy Club, 26 Pomander Rd.* ☎ *441/236–2250* ⊕ *www.marion-bermuda.com.*

Fodor's Choice **Newport (RI)-to-Bermuda Ocean Yacht Race.** Powerhouse yachtsmen flock
★ to this popular and prestigious event in June. The race takes place every two years, in even-numbered years. Even better than watching the finishers is the after-race party—it's open to the public and is always extremely well attended. Contact the Royal Bermuda Yacht Club for more information. ⊠ *Royal Bermuda Yacht Club, 15 Point Pleasant*

Rd., Hamilton ☎ *241/295–2214*
⊕ *www.bermudarace.com.*

FAMILY
Fodor's Choice
★

Non-Mariners Race. Though not as prestigious as other Bermuda sailing yacht races, this annual race, which takes place in July or August on the Sunday of Cup Match weekend (the annual cricket holiday), is one of the highlights of the year. Held at the Sandys Boat Club at Mangrove Bay, the goal of this race is simple: to see whose boat (constructed on the beach minutes before) can make it out of the harbor without sinking. Easy to watch, as the boats never get very far from land, this race sets the stage for an afternoon of music, barbecue, local political satire, and merrymaking. Legend has it that someone even tried to float an old bus one year. ⊠ *Sandys Boat Club, 8 Mangrove Bay Rd., Mangrove Bay, Somerset* ☎ *441/234–2248* ⊕ *www.sandysboatclub.com.*

ON A ROLL

Segway. Rent a Segway, a two-wheeled upright power scooter, and tour around historic Dockyard. Pick yours up at the old-fashioned double-decker bus across from Dockyard Glassworks and Bermuda Rum Cake Company. Tours are 1½ hours long and cost $80, which includes Segway training. Times are 10 am, noon, 2 pm, and 4 pm during summer months. ⊠ *Corner of Camber Rd. and Dockyard Terr., Dockyard* ☎ *441/236–1300* ⊕ *www.segway.bm.*

RENTALS

Outfitters like **Blue Hole Watersports** and **H2O Sports** *(see Boating, Charters and Boat Rentals)* have a range of craft to rent and also offer lessons for beginners.

Royal Hamilton Amateur Dinghy Club. If you're a sailor, it's worth checking out Royal Hamilton Amateur Dinghy Club, which is the main center for sailors in Hamilton and offers lessons for beginners. It's also the only "Royal" Dinghy Club in the world! If you know what you're doing and fancy taking part in some amateur racing, this is the place to be on a Wednesday evening between late April and mid-September. Just turn up at the dock from about 5:30 pm—skippers are always looking for willing crew members. There's also a club barbecue afterward and everyone is welcome. ⊠ *25 Pomander Rd.* ☎ *441/236–2250* ⊕ *www.rhadc.bm.*

SCUBA DIVING

Bermuda has all the ingredients for classic scuba diving—reefs, wrecks, underwater caves, a variety of coral and marine life, and clear, warm water. Although you can dive year-round (you will have to bring your own gear in winter, when dive shops are closed), the best months are May through October, when the water is calmest and warmest. No prior certification is necessary, and novices can expect to dive in water up to 25 feet deep after several hours of instruction. Many hotels, including Grotto Bay Beach Resort and Fairmont Southampton, offer discounted scuba rates or Dive and Stay packages that enable guests to learn the basics in a pool, on the beach, or off a dive boat, and culminate in a reef or wreck dive.

6

The easiest day trips involve exploring the south-shore reefs that lie inshore. Be sure to bring an underwater camera as these reefs may be the most dramatic in Bermuda. The ocean-side drop-off exceeds 60 feet in some places, and the coral is so honeycombed with caves, ledges, and holes that opportunities for discovery are pretty much infinite. Despite concerns about dying coral and dwindling fish populations, most of Bermuda's reefs are still in good health. No one eager to swim with multicolor schools of fish or the occasional barracuda will be disappointed. ■TIP➜ **In the interest of preservation, the removal of coral is illegal and subject to hefty fines.**

Dive shops around Bermuda prominently display a map of the outlying reef system and its wreck sites. Only 38 of the wrecks from the past three centuries are marked. They're the larger wrecks that are still in good condition. The nautical carnage includes some 300 wreck sites—an astonishing number—many of which are well preserved. As a general rule, the more recent the wreck or the more deeply submerged it is, the better its condition. Most of the well-preserved wrecks are to the north and east, and dive depths range between 25 feet and 80 feet. Several wrecks off the western end of the island are in relatively shallow water, 30 feet or less, making them accessible to novice divers and even snorkelers.

Blue Water Divers and Watersports. The major operator for wrecks on the western side of the island, Blue Water Divers offers lessons, tours, and rentals. The lesson-and-dive package for first-time divers, including equipment, costs $150 for one tank or $200 for two tanks. A one-tank dive for experienced divers costs $130, and a two-tank dive is $180. Prices include all necessary equipment. With two tanks—the more commonly offered package—you can explore two or more wrecks in one four-hour outing. This operator is not to be confused with Dive Bermuda, despite the Web address. ⊠ *Robinson's Marina, Somerset Bridge, Somerset* ☎ *441/234–1034* ⊕ *www.divebermuda.com.*

Dive Bermuda. This is an environmentally friendly dive shop as instructors go out of their way to protect Bermuda's reefs and fish. Dive Bermuda has been awarded National Geographic Dive Centre status and is the only center on the island to offer courses sanctioned by the world-renowned environmental organization. It has also received an environmental excellence award from PADI (Professional Association of Diving Instructors). For $195 you can opt for a Discover Scuba Diving course, which includes a lesson, dive, and equipment. For experienced divers, a single-tank dive costs $95 and a double-tank dive costs $150. Group rates and multiple dives cost less. Dive Bermuda has a second location at Grotto Bay Beach Resort in Hamilton Parish. ⊠ *Fairmont Southampton Resort, 101 South Shore Rd.* ☎ *441/238–2332* ⊕ *www.bermudascuba.com.*

CLOSE UP

Wreck Diving

If you've heard the stories of the Bermuda Triangle, then you won't be surprised to hear that there are more than 20 ships wrecked off the island. Actually it's got more to do with the craggy reefs that surround the island than that old myth, but each wreck has a story, and most dive operators here know it. Graham Maddocks, a 20-year veteran of Bermuda's waters and owner of Triangle Diving, gave us a history lesson on five of Bermuda's most interesting wrecks.

Constellation. Jaws author Peter Benchley based his follow-up novel *The Deep,* set in Bermuda, around the *Constellation* wreck. A cargo ship bound for Venezuela during World War II, she was carrying building materials, morphine, and 700 bottles of whiskey when her hull was broken apart on the reef. Some of the building materials remain, but the rest of her cargo is long gone.

The Cristobel Colon. This massive Spanish cruise liner is the biggest of Bermuda's shipwrecks, at 499 feet long. It crashed into the reefs off the north shore in 1936 after its captain mistook an offshore communications tower for the Gibbs Hill Lighthouse. It was crewed by Spanish dissidents from the civil war in Puerto Rico. (They were eventually rounded up and hanged for treason in Spain.) The *Cristobel* sat in Bermuda's waters for several years and many of its furnishings can be found in Bermudian homes today. The British eventually sank its empty shell by using it for target practice during World War II.

The Hermes. Probably the most popular wreck dive in Bermuda, the *Hermes* remains fully intact sitting in 80 feet of water off the south shore. It's one of the few wrecks that you can actually get inside and explore. It arrived in Bermuda with engine trouble and was ultimately abandoned by its crew. The Bermuda Government took possession of the 165-foot steel-hulled ship and sank it as a dive site in the early 1980s.

The Pelinaion. This 385-foot Greek cargo steamer was another victim of World War II. The British had blacked out the lighthouse in a bid to stop the Germans from spying on Bermuda. The captain had a perfect record, had sailed past Bermuda many times, and was months away from retirement when he made this journey from West Africa to Baltimore in 1940, carrying a cargo of iron ore. Without the lighthouse to guide him, he couldn't find the island until he struck the reef off St. David's. You can still see the ship's steam boiler and engine as well as some of the cargo of iron ore.

The Xing Da. A modern-day pirate ship, the *Xing Da* was carrying a "cargo" of Chinese immigrants to be smuggled into the United States in 1996. Crewed by members of the Chinese mafia, the Triad, it had arranged to meet a smaller boat 145 miles off Bermuda for the immigrants to be transferred and taken into the States. Instead, they found themselves surrounded by the U.S. Marines. The boat was given to the government as a dive site in 1997.

6

SNORKELING

The clarity of the water, the stunning array of coral reefs, and the shallow resting places of several wrecks make snorkeling in the waters around Bermuda—both inshore and offshore—particularly worthwhile. You can snorkel year-round, although a wet suit is advisable for anyone planning to spend a long time in the water in winter, when the water temperature can dip into the 60s. The water also tends to be rougher in winter, often restricting snorkeling to the protected areas of Harrington Sound and Castle Harbour. Underwater caves, grottoes, coral formations, and schools of small fish are the highlights of these areas.

Some of the best snorkeling sites are accessible only by boat. As the number of wrecks attests, navigating around Bermuda's reef-strewn waters is no simple task, especially for inexperienced boaters. If you rent a boat yourself, stick to the protected waters of the sounds, harbors, and bays, and be sure to ask for an ocean-navigation chart. These charts point out shallow waters, rocks, and hidden reefs.

For trips to the reefs, let someone else do the navigating—a charter-boat skipper or one of the snorkeling-cruise operators. Some of the best reefs for snorkeling, complete with shallow-water wrecks, are to the west, but where the tour guide or skipper goes often depends on the tide, weather, and water conditions. For snorkelers who demand privacy and freedom of movement, a boat charter (complete with captain) is the only answer, but the cost is considerable—expect to pay upward of $550 for three hours and up to six people. By comparison, half a day of snorkeling on a regularly scheduled cruise generally costs $65 to $85, including equipment and instruction.

SNORKELING SITES

Fodor's Choice
★

Church Bay. When Bermudians are asked to name a favorite snorkeling spot, they invariably rank Church Bay in Southampton (at the western end of the south-shore beaches) at, or near, the top of the list. A small cove cut out of the coral cliffs, the bay is full of nooks and crannies, and the reefs are relatively close to shore. Snorkelers should exercise caution here (as you should everywhere along the south shore), as the water can be rough. Bring your own snorkeling equipment, underwater camera, and fish food with you. ⊠ *South Rd.*

John Smith's Bay. This popular snorkeling spot off the south shore of Smith's Parish has several reefs close to the shore as well as the added safety of a lifeguard overseeing the beach. Beware, this site occasionally experiences rip currents. ⊠ *South Rd.*

FAMILY **Tobacco Bay.** This beautiful bay is tucked in a cove near historic Fort St. Catherine's beach. Tobacco Bay offers wonderful snorkeling, public facilities, and equipment rentals, and there's a snack bar near the shore. This site is the most popular in St. George's and can get crowded. ⊠ *9 Coot's Pond Rd., St. George's* ⊕ *www.tobaccobay.bm.*

Warwick Long Bay. On South Shore in Warwick, this ½-mile of beach is usually secluded and quiet. It's the perfect spot to check out Bermuda's underwater life without bumping into any other snorkelers. You'll have plenty of room to explore, and there's an inner reef very close to the shore. ⊠ *South Rd.*

West Whale Bay. Tiny West Whale Bay, off the western shore near the Port Royal Golf Course in Southampton, is quiet and usually uncrowded. The beach disappears during high tide, though, so check tide times first. ⊠ *Whale Bay Rd.*

SNORKELING CRUISES AND OUTFITTERS

Snorkeling cruises, offered from April to November, are a less expensive albeit less personal way to experience the underwater world. Some boats carry up to 40 passengers to snorkeling sites but focus mostly on their music and bars (complimentary beverages are usually served on the trip back from the reefs). Smaller boats, which limit capacity to 10 to 16 passengers, offer more personal attention and focus more on the beautiful snorkeling areas themselves. Guides on such tours often relate interesting historical and ecological information about the island. To make sure you choose a boat that's right for you, ask for details before booking. Most companies can easily arrange private charters for groups.

Fantasea Bermuda. You're spoiled for choice with this one-stop recreational company. There are snorkeling tours, diving, sightseeing cruises, glass-bottom boat trips, and even banana-boat rides. The whale-watching tours in March and April are immensely popular, when you can get close to the majestic humpbacks as they migrate north. Take your pick of a cruise-and-kayak or boat-and-bike ecotour for a closer look at some of the prettiest spots on the island. The three-hour Catamaran Coral Reef Snorkel aboard a luxury catamaran costs $70, while a 90-minute rum-tasting sunset sail costs $60. Most tours depart from Dockyard, near the cruise ship terminal. Fantasea tours are booked through Island Tour Centre; its website has a detailed list of daily activities, which you can book online. ☎ *441/236–1300* ⊕ *www.islandtourcentre.com.*

Jessie James Cruises. Prepare for 2½ memorable hours with Jessie James Cruises. Depending on weather, you'll stop at two of three exciting locations: a shipwreck, a secluded island beach, and one of Bermuda's beautiful coral reefs. Snorkeling equipment, masks, and vests are provided; plus you can peer into the turquoise waters right through the glass bottom of the boat. The 31-foot *Pisces* holds up to 17 people and departs from Dockyard. ☎ *441/747–2204* ⊕ *www.jessiejames.bm.*

Restless Native Tours. Captain Kirk Ward has regularly scheduled sailing and snorkeling trips to the outer reefs on a 50-by-30-foot catamaran. With breezy hammocks, a shady cabin, plus fresh cookies on board, it's hard to resist this popular outfitter. The tours depart from the center of Heritage Wharf and King's Wharf in the Royal Naval Dockyard—prepare for a crash course in Bermuda's marine life! ☎ *441/531–8149* ⊕ *www.restlessnative.bm.*

FAMILY **Snorkel Park Beach.** This family-friendly venue has all the water sports you could want in one location. It's tucked away through a limestone tunnel in the northwest corner of Dockyard, next to the National Museum of Bermuda, but it's just a stone's throw from the cruise-ship pier. Jet Ski tours are offered for $145 per hour and $270 for two hours.

Kayaks can be put to good use for $25 an hour, or you can rent a paddleboat for the same price. Snorkeling equipment is available starting at $10 an hour. The kids will love the free buckets and sand toys as well as the huge waterslide. Scuba dives and power snorkel excursions can also be arranged and there's the Hammerheads Bar and Grill on-site to keep parents busy. Daily opening hours follow the seasonal cruise ship schedule; the beach is closed from November through end of April. ⊠ 7 *Maritime La., Dockyard* ☎ *441/234–6989* ⊕ *www.snorkelparkbeach. com* ⊠ *$5 for adults, free for children 12 and under; check website for special event prices.*

SNORKELING EQUIPMENT RENTALS

Snorkeling equipment and, sometimes, underwater cameras are available for rent at most major hotels and at several marinas. Cambridge Beaches Resort, Grotto Bay Beach, Resort Rosewood Tucker's Point, Pompano Beach Club *(see also Boating, Charters and Boat Rentals)*, and Fairmont Southampton Resort have dive operators either on-site or less than five minutes away. A deposit or credit-card number is usually required when renting equipment.

Rum Bum Beach Bar. Snorkel gear, umbrellas, and sun loungers are available at this beachside bar and restaurant. A mask and snorkel set will set you back $20 for the day, plus a $20 deposit. ⊠ *94 South Shore Rd.* ☎ *441/238–0088* ⊕ *www.rumbumbeachbar.com.*

SOCCER

Football (soccer) season runs from September through April in Bermuda. One of Bermuda's two national sports, football is massively popular among Bermudians, who often crowd matches in the evening and on weekends. You can watch local action in various age divisions battle it out on fields around the island, or enjoy a cold pint of beer while cheering on your favorite international team at one of Hamilton's popular watering holes: **The Docksider Pub & Restaurant** or **Flanagan's Outback Sports Bar.**

TENNIS

Bermuda has one tennis court for every 600 residents, a ratio that even the most tennis-crazed countries would find difficult to match. Many are private, but the public has access to more than 70 courts in 20 locations. Courts are inexpensive and seldom full. Hourly rates for nonguests are about $15 to $20. You might want to consider bringing along a few fresh cans of balls, because balls in Bermuda cost $6 to $8 per can—two to three times the rate in the United States. Among the surfaces used in Bermuda are Har-Tru, clay, cork, and hard composites, of which the relatively slow Plexipave composite is the most prevalent. Despite Bermuda's British roots, the island has no grass court.

Wind, heat (in summer), and humidity are the most distinct characteristics of Bermudian tennis. From October through March, when daytime temperatures rarely exceed 80°F, play is comfortable throughout the day. But in summer the heat radiating from the court (especially hard courts) can make play uncomfortable between 11 am and 3 pm, so some clubs take a midday break. Most tennis facilities offer lessons, ranging from $30 to $60 for 30 minutes of instruction, and racket rentals for $4 to $10 per hour.

Coral Beach & Tennis Club. Introduction by a member is required to play at this exclusive club, which was once the site of the USTA-sanctioned XL Capital Bermuda Open tournament. Coral Beach has eight clay courts, three of which are floodlighted. Resident pros are on hand to arrange private lessons, which run upward of $100 per hour. The club also hosts several well-attended senior and junior tournaments throughout the year. Tennis whites are required. ⊠ *34 South Shore Rd.* ☎ *441/236–2233* ⊕ *www.coralbeachclub.com.*

Elbow Beach Tennis Facility. This facility is fortunate to have as its director of tennis David Lambert, who is also a former president of the Bermuda Lawn Tennis Association. There are five Plexipave courts on hand, three with lights, and hours of play are 8 am to 7 pm daily. Courts cost $12 per hour for guests of Elbow Beach Resort or $15 per hour for members of the public. Lessons and match play can be arranged for hotel guests or other visitors at $50 per half hour, $85 for the hour. This facility also rents and repairs rackets. ⊠ *Elbow Beach Resort, 60 South Shore Rd.* ☎ *441/236–8737* ⊕ *www.elbowtennisbda.com.*

Fairmont Southampton Tennis Club. Despite their position at the water's edge, the Plexipave hard courts here are reasonably shielded from the wind, although the breeze can be swirling and difficult. Six courts are at hand, costing $19 per non-hotel guest per day; hours of service are daily from 8:30 am to 6 pm. You can also book a complete tennis package, which includes luxury Fairmont accommodations, breakfast, and lessons. Racket rentals are $10 per day and balls are available for $10 per pack. Book time with a pro for $115 per hour for up to two players. ⊠ *Fairmont Southampton, 101 South Shore Rd.* ☎ *441/236–6950.*

The Grotto Bay Tennis Club. A little more than a stone's throw from the L.F. Wade International Airport, Grotto Bay has four Plexipave cork-based courts, two of which are equipped with lights for nighttime play. Hourly bookings are available for $10, from 8 am to 7 pm, or $15 after 7 pm. Resident tennis pros offer lessons (individual and small group) for adults and juniors starting at around $30 per half hour. Tennis attire is required. ⊠ *11 Blue Hole Hill, Bailey's Bay, Hamilton* ☎ *441/293–3420* ⊕ *www.grottobaytennis.com.*

Pomander Gate Tennis Club. There are five hard courts available (four with lighting) at this scenic club located off Hamilton Harbour. Temporary membership is available for $40 per family per week; court rentals are $6 per session (one hour of play time during the day or 45 minutes at night). Be aware that nighttime play incurs an extra $7 charge to run the lights. Hours of play are 8 am to 9 pm. ⊠ *21 Pomander Rd.* ☎ *441/236–5400* ⊕ *www.pgtc.bm.*

W.E.R. Joell Tennis Stadium. This government-run facility is the busiest of Bermuda's tennis courts, the inland location ideal for combating strong winds and hosting year-round tournaments. Of the eight all-weather courts available, five are Plexi-Cushion and three are Har-Tru. Three courts in the main stadium have floodlights. Hours are from 8 am to 9 pm weekdays and from 9 am to 6 pm on weekends. Rates are $12 per hour during the day and $22 per hour at night; small discounts are available for seniors and young adults. Tennis attire is required, and lessons are available from on-site pros on request. ⊠ *2 Marsh Folly Rd.* ☎ *441/292–0105.*

TENNIS TOURNAMENTS

Bermuda Lawn Tennis Association. Established in 1964, the association is the governing body for tennis in Bermuda and hosts all the important tennis events on the island. The BLTA headquarters are located at the popular W.E.R. Joell Tennis Stadium, a short taxi ride from the city of Hamilton. Visit the website for an up-to-date calendar of tournaments and events. ⊠ *W.E.R. Joell Tennis Stadium, 2 Marsh Folly Rd.* ☎ *441/296–0834* ⊕ *www.blta.bm.*

International Beach Tennis Tournament. The pink sand of Horseshoe Bay hosts the island's beach tennis tournaments at the end of August. A cross between tennis and beach volleyball, the three-day tournament features "stars" of the game, plus an amateur division that anyone can enter. If you're not visiting in August, the Bermuda Beach Tennis Association runs regular pickup games at Elbow Beach every Saturday from 12 pm to 3 pm throughout the summer. ⊠ *Horseshoe Bay Beach, South Rd.* ☎ *441/334–8669* ⊕ *www.bermudabeachtennis.com.*

WHALE-WATCHING

During March and April the majestic humpback whales pass Bermuda as they migrate north to summer feeding grounds. Watching these giant animals as they leap out of the ocean is an awe-inspiring spectacle. You can see them from Elbow Beach or West Whale Bay on a clear day, if you're prepared to wait. But if you want to get a close-up view, you can book a tour with an operator like **Fantasea Bermuda** *(see Snorkeling Cruises and Outfitters)* or spring for a private offshore charter.

SHOPS AND SPAS

Updated
by Robyn
Bardgett

If you're accustomed to shopping in Neiman Marcus, Saks Fifth Avenue, and Bergdorf Goodman, the prices in Bermuda's elegant shops won't bother you. The island is a high-end shopping paradise; designer clothing and accessories, from MaxMara to Coach, tend to be sold at prices comparable to those in the United States but at least without the sales tax.

That doesn't mean bargain hunters are out of luck in Bermuda. Crystal, china, watches, and jewelry are often less expensive here and sometimes even on par with American outlet-store prices. Perfume and cosmetics are often sold at discount prices, and there are bargains to be had on woolens and cashmeres in early spring, when stores' winter stocks must go. The island's unforgiving humidity and lack of storage space mean sales are frequent and really meant to sweep stock off the shelves.

Art galleries in Bermuda attract serious shoppers and collectors. The island's thriving population of artists and artisans—many of whom are internationally recognized—produces well-reputed work, from paintings, photographs, and sculpture to miniature furniture, handblown glass, and dolls. During your gallery visits, look for Bruce Stuart's abstract paintings, Graeme Outerbridge's vivid photographs of Bermudian architecture and scenery, and Chesley Trott's slim wood and bronze sculptures.

Bermuda-made specialty comestibles include rum and rum-based liqueurs and delicious local honey, which you can find in most grocery stores. Nearly every restaurant and pantry in Bermuda contains a bottle of Sherry Peppers Sauce from Outerbridge Peppers Ltd., and these essential condiments make tasty gift additions to home pantries. The original line of products has expanded to include Bloody Mary mix, pepper jellies, and barbecue sauce, and all can be found in grocery stores on the island.

BERMUDA SHOPPING PLANNER

BUSINESS HOURS

Shops are generally open Monday to Saturday from 9 to 5 and closed on Sunday, although some shops and supermarkets are open from 1 to 6 on Sunday. From April to October some of the smaller Front Street shops stay open late and on Sunday. The shops in the Clocktower Mall at the Royal Naval Dockyard are usually open from Monday to Saturday 9:30 to 6 (11 to 5 in winter) and Sunday 11 to 5. Some extend their hours around Christmas. Almost all stores close for public holidays.

TOP 5 BERMUDA SHOPPING

Shop for a few pairs of Bermuda shorts, available in an array of bright island-inspired colors from the island's own brand TABS (which stands for The Authentic Bermuda Shorts).

Spice up your souvenirs with a bottle of Outerbridges Original Sherry Peppers Sauce and Devilishly Hot Sherry Peppers Sauce to add zip to soups, stews, drinks, and chowders—available at local grocery stores.

Take home the island's citrus and jasmine scents with the Bermuda Blue fragrance, available at A.S. Cooper & Sons and Gibbons Company.

Traditional black rum cakes from the Bermuda Rum Cake Company in the Dockyard make popular (and delicious) gifts and cost $14.95 duty-free.

Pick up a Bermudian cookbook or a beautiful coffee-table book of local art or photography from the Bermuda Book Store.

SHOPPING DISTRICTS

Hamilton has the greatest concentration of shops in Bermuda, and Front Street is its pièce de résistance. Lined with small, pastel-colored buildings, this most fashionable of Bermuda's streets houses sedate department stores and snazzy boutiques, with several small arcades and shopping alleys leading off it. A smart canopy shades the entrance to the 55 Front Street Group, which houses Crisson's. Modern Butterfield Place has galleries and boutiques.

St. George's Water Street, Duke of York Street, Hunters Wharf, and Somers Wharf are the sites of numerous renovated buildings that house branches of Front Street stores, as well as artisans' studios. Historic King's Square offers little more than a couple of T-shirt and souvenir shops.

In the West End, Somerset Village has a few shops, but they hardly merit a special shopping trip. The Clocktower Mall, however, in a historic building at the Royal Naval Dockyard, has a few more shopping opportunities, including branches of Front Street shops and specialty boutiques. The Dockyard is also home to the Craft Market, the Bermuda Arts Centre, and Bermuda Clayworks.

KEY DESTINATIONS

Department stores such as A.S. Cooper & Sons and Gibbons Company are excellent one-stop shopping destinations, but you may have more fun exploring the boutiques on Front and Reid Streets and streets branching off them. For crafts, head to the Royal Naval Dockyard, where you can find artisans' studios and a permanent craft market. The town of St. George's has a bit of everything, including lots of small, unique boutiques, where you can find the perfect island outfit or a Bermuda-cedar model of a famous ship.

DUTY FREE

The duty-free shop at the airport sells liquor, perfume, cigarettes, rum cakes, and other items. You can also order duty-free spirits at some of the liquor stores in town, and the management will make arrangements to deliver your purchase to your hotel or cruise ship. If you choose to shop in town rather than at the airport, it's best to buy liquor at least 24 hours before your departure, or by 9:30 on the day of an afternoon departure, in order to allow time for delivery. With liquor, it pays to shop around, because prices vary. Grocery stores usually charge more than liquor stores. U.S. citizens age 21 and older who have been out of the country for 48 hours are allowed to bring home 1 liter of duty-free liquor.

WATCH OUT

Bermuda Customs. It's illegal to export shipwreck artifacts or a Bermuda-cedar carving or item of furniture that's more than 50 years old without a special permit from Bermuda Customs. ⊠ *Custom House, 40 Front St., Hamilton* ☎ *441/295–4816* ⊕ *www.customs.gov.bm.*

HAMILTON AND CENTRAL PARISHES

Whether you are shopping for souvenirs, gifts, new clothes, or jewelry, Hamilton and the Central Parishes are the places to head for all your shopping needs. Hamilton has Bermuda's largest concentration of stores. The main shopping streets are Front Street and Reid Street, but don't forget about all the side streets and alleyways, where some of the best stores are.

DEPARTMENT STORES

A.S. Cooper & Sons. Cooper's is best known for its extensive inventory of crystal and china, with pieces and sets by Waterford, Wedgwood, Villeroy & Boch, and Portmeirion, many sold at 15% to 20% less than U.S. prices. The store also carries tasteful Bermudian souvenirs, jewelry, fragrances, and cosmetics on the ground level. Brands on sale include Estée Lauder, Clinique, Clarins, Bobbi Brown, Lancôme, and Elizabeth Arden. The main store also carries its private-label clothing collection for women and a ladies' sportswear department, which carries Calvin Klein, Ralph Lauren, vineyard vines, DKNY Jeans, Jones New York, Nic and Zoe, along with a children's and juniors' department. There are several branches, including one at the Fairmont Southampton resort and in Dockyard. Cooper's also owns Astwood Dickinson jewelry stores. ⊠ *59 Front St., Hamilton* ☎ *441/295–3961* ⊕ *www.ascooper.bm.*

Brown & Co. Although there are several standout sections in this sprawling shop, including a perfume department, home decor, and a fun assortment of upscale Bermuda-inspired gifts and trinkets, it's now also the location of The Body Shop and sells a large range of its natural and ethically produced products. Look for the deliciously scented body butters and the popular gift sets. ⊠ *35 Front St., Hamilton* ☎ *441/279–5442* ⊕ *www.brown.bm.*

Fodor's Choice **Gibbons Co.** One of Bermuda's oldest retailers (still run by the Gibbons
★ family) has transformed itself into a contemporary department store
with a wide range of men's, women's, and children's clothing. Brands
include Calvin Klein, Mango, and DKNY, and there's a substantial
lingerie selection, as well as Gap clothing and products, active and
swim wear, accessories, and fashion jewelry. The perfume and cosmetics department stocks many French, Italian, English, and American
lines at duty-free prices. The housewares department is the exclusive
supplier of Denby tableware, which sells at a much lower price than
in Canada or the United States. The shoe department stocks brands
including Nine West, TOMS, and Anne Klein. Gibbons also owns and
operates a separate store, in the nearby Washington Mall, that sells
bed, bath, and home decor; M.A.C. Cosmetics on Front Street; and the
perfume stores in Dockyard and St. George's. ⊠ *21 Reid St., Hamilton*
☎ *441/295–0022* ⊕ *www.gibbons.bm.*

Marks & Spencer. A franchise of the large British chain, Marks and Sparks
(as it's called by everyone in Bermuda and England) is usually filled with
locals attracted by its moderate prices for men's, women's, and children's clothing. Summer wear, including swimsuits, cotton jerseys, and
polo shirts, is a good buy, as is underwear—but don't forget everything
is in U.K. sizes rather than U.S. The chain's signature line of food and
treats, plus wine from all over the world, is tucked away at the back of
the store. ⊠ *18 Reid St., Hamilton* ☎ *441/295–0031.*

ANTIQUES AND COLLECTIBLES

Bermuda Monetary Authority. This agency issues and redeems Bermuda
currency, and also oversees financial institutions operating in and
through Bermuda. At its offices in Hamilton, it sells collectors' coins,
including replicas of the old Bermuda "hogge" money of the early 17th
century. Cahow, Hawksville turtle, and gold shipwreck coins are among
the many other pieces for sale. ⊠ *BMA House, 43 Victoria St., Hamilton*
☎ *441/295–5278* ⊕ *www.bma.bm.*

ART GALLERIES

Art House Gallery. Watercolors, oils, and limited-edition color litho-
graphs by Bermudian artist Joan Forbes are displayed in this gallery.
During the summer the gallery is open Monday, Wednesday, and Friday
from 10 to 4, Saturday from 10 to 1, or by appointment. ⊠ *80 South
Shore Rd.* ☎ *441/236–6746* ⊕ *www.arthousebermuda.com.*

Bermuda Society of the Arts. The island's oldest arts organization has four
galleries, and many highly creative society members sell their work
at the perennial members' shows and during special group exhibits.
You can find watercolor, oil, and acrylic paintings; pastel and charcoal
drawings; and some photographs, collages, and sculptures. Admission is free. ⊠ *17 Church St., 3rd fl. West Wing, City Hall, Hamilton*
☎ *441/292–3824* ⊕ *www.bsoa.bm.*

7

Birdsey Studio. Renowned artist Alfred Birdsey, who painted Bermuda scenes for more than 60 years, died in 1996, but thanks to his daughter, Jo Birdsey Linberg, the studio remains open and the tradition continues. Watercolors cost from $100 and oils from $350 to $1,000. Prints of Birdsey's paintings are also available on note cards for $15. The studio is usually open weekdays 10:30 to 1, but call before you visit, as appointments are preferred. ⊠ *5 Stowe Hill* ☎ *441/236–6658.*

> ## TIME OF YOUR LIFE
>
> While shopping on Reid Street, glance up and admire a famous city landmark hanging from the Phoenix Centre. The clock was imported from Boston in 1893 by watchmaker Duncan Doe. When you're at the Clocktower Mall in Dockyard, you'll notice the clocks on the two 100-foot towers tell different times. This isn't an error; one was installed to show the actual time and the other the time of the high tide.

Gallery One Seventeen. Former Windjammer Gallery manager Danjou Anderson has created his own purpose-built commercial gallery space showcasing top Bermudian artists. Over 60 artists are represented including many well-known names such as Otto Trott, Sharon Wilson, and Christopher Marson. ⊠ *117 Front St., Hamilton* ☎ *441/295–1783* ⊕ *www.gallery117bda.com.*

Picturesque Bermuda. Roland Skinner is one of the island's most loved photographers. He captures the island's architecture, landscapes, and flora. The Front Street gallery, which recently moved into the main A.S. Cooper shop, showcases his portfolio, with photos selling from $100 to $800. ⊠ *A.S. Cooper & Sons Main Store, 59 Front St., Hamilton* ☎ *441/295–3961* ⊕ *www.ascooper.bm.*

BOOKS

Bermuda Book Store. Owner Hannah Willmott doesn't believe in wasting space, so she crammed as many books as she could into her small bookstore. The shop is known for its cozy atmosphere and is well stocked with best sellers, children's books, and special Bermuda titles (including some out-of-print books), plus diaries and calendars. ⊠ *3 Queen St., Hamilton* ☎ *441/295–3698* ⊕ *www.bdabooks.bm.*

Bookmart. The island's largest bookstore carries plenty of contemporary titles and classics, plus a complete selection of books on Bermuda. Paperbacks and children's books are in abundance, as well as a wide selection of popular beauty, technology, and travel books. The Hallmark store at the front of the shop offers the expected greeting cards, balloons, party supplies, and little gift items. Its café has a balcony overlooking Front Street, perfect for grabbing a sandwich or a drink after a hard day's shopping. ⊠ *Brown & Company, 3 Reid St., Hamilton* ☎ *441/279–5443* ⊕ *www.bookmart.bm.*

CERAMICS AND GLASSWARE

Bluck's. A dignified establishment in business for more than 165 years, Bluck's is the island's only store devoted exclusively to crystal and china. Royal Crown Derby, Royal Copenhagen, and Herend china compete with Lalique, Waterford, Baccarat, and Kosta Boda crystal in glorious displays, and enamel boxes sit primly in their display cases. The courteous staff provides price lists upon request. ⊠ *4 Front St., Hamilton* ☎ *441/295–5367* ⊕ *www.blucksbermuda.com.*

CIGARS

House of Cigars: Chatham House. In business since 1895, this shop looks like an old-time country store. Thick, gray, lusty cigar smoke fills the air, and a life-size statue of a Native American princess greets you as you walk in. You can find top-quality cigars from the Dominican Republic, Jamaica, and Cuba (Romeo y Julieta, Bolivar, Partagas, Punch), Briar pipes, tobacco, and Swiss Army knives. ⊠ *63 Front St., Hamilton* ☎ *441/292–8422.*

CLOTHING

CHILDREN'S CLOTHING

Blukids. The Italian brands' affordable clothing line for children (newborn up to size 14 for boys and girls) is surprisingly high quality for the prices. Styles are modern and practical and always on trend. Some of the standouts in the line include clothing featuring popular characters such as Spiderman, Hello Kitty, and Mickey Mouse. ⊠ *Washington Mall, 12 Reid St., Hamilton* ☎ *441/292–5065.*

FAMILY **Pirates Port.** It's small and crowded but it has bargains on casual clothing for girls and boys from toddlers to teens. There's also a Pirates Port women's wear store immediately opposite. ⊠ *Washington Mall, lower level, 7 Reid St., Hamilton* ☎ *441/292–1080.*

MEN'S CLOTHING

A.S. Cooper Man. This division of the classy department store is first-rate, with a staff who are reserved and courteous, but very helpful when needed. It is full of men's casual and dress clothes, plus accessories such as belts and wallets. The store is the exclusive Bermuda supplier of Polo Ralph Lauren. It also stocks brands such as Lacoste, Vineyard Vines, Perry Ellis, Izod, and Helly Hansen. ⊠ *29 Front St., Hamilton* ☎ *441/295–3961.*

The Edge. You can find contemporary menswear at this welcoming shop, with brands from around the world, such as Haight and Ashbury. There are also plenty of shoes, ties, belts, shades, and accessories to choose from. ⊠ *25 Reid St., Hamilton* ☎ *441/295–4715.*

Sports Source. Popular with locals, Sports Source offers men's and youth's urban wear and hip-hop gear. The labels are trendy, but the prices are reasonable. There's also a good selection of sneakers, football

CLOSE UP

Bermuda Shorts in the Office

You may have heard of Bermuda's peculiar business fashion, and you may even have seen pictures of businessmen in shorts and long socks, but nothing can quite prepare you for the first sighting. First-time visitors have been spotted snickering in shop doorways after discovering the bottom half of a blazer-and-tie-clad executive on his cell phone. After all, where else in the world could he walk into a boardroom wearing bright-pink shorts without anyone batting an eyelid? Only in Bermuda. These unique, all-purpose garments, however flamboyantly dyed, are worn with complete seriousness and pride. Bermudians would go so far as to say it's the rest of the world that is peculiar, and they have a point—particularly in the steaming humidity of the summer months.

What is surprising is how the original khaki cutoffs evolved into formal attire. They were introduced to Bermuda in the early 1900s by the British military, who adopted the belted, baggy, cotton-twill version to survive the sweltering outposts of the empire. By the 1920s Bermudian pragmatism and innovation were at play as locals started chopping off their trousers at the knees to stay cool. Tailors seized on the trend and started manufacturing a smarter pair of shorts, and men were soon discovering the benefits of a breeze around the knees.

But for an island that has a love affair with rules, there was always going to be a right and a wrong way to wear this new uniform. Bermudas had to be worn with knee-high socks, and a jacket and tie were the only acceptable way of dressing them up for business. But it didn't stop there. Obsession with detail prevailed, fueled by gentlemen who were disturbed at the unseemly shortness of other men's shorts. A law was passed to ensure propriety, and the bizarre result was patrolling policemen, armed with tape measures and warning tickets, scouring the capital for men showing too much leg. Officially, shorts could be no more than 6 inches above the knee, although 2 to 4 was preferable.

Other rigid but unwritten rules made it unheard-of to wear them in hotel dining rooms after 6 pm or in churches on Sunday morning, and even to this day they are out of bounds in the Supreme Court, although in 2000 legislation was changed to allow them to be worn, even by ministers, in the House of Assembly. Viewed as conservative and respectable menswear for almost any occasion, they can be seen paired with tuxedo jackets and are even acceptable (provided they are black) at funerals.

But if Bermuda shorts are practical, smart dress for men, where does that leave the island's women during the sticky summer months? Wearing brightly colored cotton dresses and skirts, it would seem. Shorts are not considered ideal business wear for women and are only really acceptable in a casual setting. In a country where pink is a man's color and men's bare legs are all but mandatory for six months of the year, perhaps the men feel the need to stamp their masculine pride on their pants.

—Vivienne Sheath

jerseys, and shorts. The store has another location at 49 Middle Road, Warwick. ⊠ *Washington Mall, Reid St., Hamilton* ☎ *441/292–9442.*

MEN'S AND WOMEN'S CLOTHING

The Booth. Named after owner Darren Booth, this shop sells trendy men's and women's attire, including DC shoes, G-Shock watches, and jackets by Helly Hansen and North Face. It also stocks skateboards, backpacks, and a good selection of luggage. ⊠ *51 Reid St., Hamilton* ☎ *441/296–5353.*

Fodor's Choice ★ **Calypso.** Bermuda's fashionable set comes to this boutique to spend on Italian leather shoes and sophisticated designer wear such as Eileen Fisher. Calypso has the island's largest selection of swimwear, including Vilebrequin. Pick up a straw hat and sunglasses to make the perfect beach ensemble. Eclectic novelty items from Europe make great gifts. Calypso's sister shop in Butterfield Place, Voila!, carries Longchamp handbags and Johnston & Murphy men's shoes. There are branches at the Fairmont Southampton Resort and Clocktower Mall at Dockyard. ⊠ *45 Front St., Hamilton* ☎ *441/295–2112* ⊕ *www.calypso.bm.*

English Sports Shop. This shop specializes in knitwear, but walk through the front door and you can't miss the selection of colorful Bermuda shorts and knee-high socks. Upstairs is a good supply of men's business and formal wear and children's clothes. Menswear and suits are from Hugo Boss, Profuomo, and Michael Kors. Women's clothing and accessories are at the back of the store on the ground level. There are branches at Fairmont Southampton Resort, Somerset Village, and one on Water Street in St. George's. ⊠ *49 Front St., Hamilton* ☎ *441/295–2672.*

FH Boutique. Housed in the newly renovated Hamilton Princess & Beach Club, FH Boutique curates high-end and dressy island wear "For Him" and "For Her." There's a selection of upmarket international labels including perfectly tailored Thomas Pink shirts and clothing and accessories from Elie Tahari, as well as jewelry and clothing from local designers and vendors. In the same retail arcade is sister store Resort Life + Style shop with a focus on casual resort wear and swimwear as well as boat-friendly SWIMS shoes. Between both stores, you will find all you need to put together the perfect island outfit. ⊠ *Hamilton Princess Hotel, Beach Club and Marina, 76 Pitts Bay Rd., Hamilton* ☎ *441/298–4035* ⊕ *luxury.bm/fh.*

French Connection. This chic urban-wear shop carries trendy skirts, pants, tops, and accessories for day and night. Women's clothing is on the ground level and men's is on the lower level. Follow the locals to the 50%–75% end-of-season sales. ⊠ *15 Reid St., Hamilton* ☎ *441/295–2112* ⊕ *www.calypso.bm.*

Jeans Express. If you didn't pack denim for those cool Bermuda evening breezes, then this store—crammed with every style of Levis—is the place to go. All shapes and sizes are catered to and—with no sales tax—prices are comparable to the United States (or cheaper). The store also sells Dockers casual clothing. ⊠ *30 Queen St., Hamilton* ☎ *441/295–0084.*

7

Makin' Waves. Casual clothing and swimsuits by big-name brands Roxy, Billabong, O'Neill, Reef, and Quicksilver are sold at this beachy shop. There are plenty of shorts, T-shirts, and summer dresses to choose from, and surf gear is a specialty. You can also take your pick from Oakley sunglasses, incense, shell jewelry, beach bags, flip-flops, water shoes, and snorkeling and dive gear. There's another store on Camber Road in Dockyard. ⊠ *11 Church St., Hamilton* ✤ *At the junction of Church St. and Wesley St.* ☏ *441/292–4609* ⊕ *www.makinwaves.bm.*

Mambo. Need a slice of Italian chic? Stop by this tiny shop that stocks funky Italian labels such as Diesel and Alcott, as well as a large selection of True Religion jeans. ⊠ *Old Cellar La., Front St., Hamilton* ☏ *441/295–3003.*

Stefanel. This long-running fashion brand brings the very latest in quality Italian-made casual, business, and dress wear, made of primarily natural fibers in neutral colors. ⊠ *12 Reid St., Hamilton* ☏ *441/295–5698.*

Fodor's Choice
★

TABS. Designed by Bermudian Rebecca Singleton, TABS (which stands for The Authentic Bermuda Shorts) offers the quintessential Bermuda short for men, women, and children in modern fits and fabrics. The cotton-twill and cotton-linen shorts are lined with fun prints and available in a variety of vibrant island-inspired colors, such as oleander pink, loquat yellow, and lagoon green. You can even have your shorts customized with a word or letters embroidered on the inside fly of the shorts (it takes two weeks, but you can have them shipped to you). Tailored swim shorts, limited-edition collections, and accessories (traditional Bermuda socks) are also available. The Reid Street store also stocks jewelry designed by local Rebecca Little. ⊠ *Walker Arcade, 12 Reid St., Hamilton* ☏ *441/704–8227* ⊕ *www.tabsbermuda.com* ☉ *Closed Sun.*

27th Century Boutique. Khakis, polo shirts, and dress shirts predominate in this boutique's sizable men's section, and women can find colorful dresses, sparkly tank tops, and great-fitting black pants alongside office-appropriate blouses. Owner Sharon Bartram can help you assemble a perfect outfit—she has an excellent eye for style and detail. ⊠ *92 Reid St., Hamilton* ☏ *441/292–2628.*

WOMEN'S CLOTHING

Atelerie. A boutique that wouldn't feel out of place in a stylish New York City neighborhood, Atelerie carries designer labels such as Diane von Furstenburg, Cynthia Vincent, and Helmut Lang in this beautifully designed space. The selection of jewelry may be the highlight here. Layer up with long chains from GINETTE NY and brightly colored gemstone earrings from Coralia Leets. ⊠ *9 Reid St., Hamilton* ☏ *441/296–0280* ⊕ *www.atelerie.com* ☉ *Closed Sun.*

Benetton. This branch of the Italian brand has a wide variety of casual-chic women's and children's clothing, in brash, bright colors and more subdued tones. ⊠ *24 Reid St., Hamilton* ☏ *441/295–2112* ⊕ *www.calypso.bm.*

Boutique C.C. This English Sports Shop–owned store sells quality career wear for women of every age, but the highlight is the selection of evening wear. Look for reasonably priced cocktail dresses and classic suits along with stylish contemporary separates and trendy accessories. ✉ *1 Front St., Hamilton* ☎ *441/295–3935.*

Eve's Garden Lingerie. Silk and satin panties, boxers, brassieres, and night-gowns, in sizes small to full figure, are tucked away in this discreet shop at the back of the Emporium Building. You can also find massage oils and an adult section. The store also houses the Bra Boutique, which sells a wide range of top-quality lingerie for all shapes and sizes. ✉ *Emporium Bldg., 69 Front St., Hamilton* ☎ *441/296–2671.*

Jazzy Boutique. Purses, faux-gem jewelry, Spandex, jeans, and colorful accessories lure shoppers looking for the latest in urban fashion to this affordable store. There's also a good selection of shoes, and its plus-size shop—Jazzy Plus—is nearby. ✉ *Washington Mall, 7 Reid St., Hamilton* ☎ *441/295–9258.*

MaxMara. Prices for this Italian designer's clothing average about 20% less in Bermuda than in the United States, although the accessories sell at much the same as U.S. prices. Although the boutique is much smaller than its counterpart on Madison Avenue, it still has a good selection of conservative casual wear and evening attire. You'll find the labels MaxMara, SportMax, and Studio. ✉ *57 Front St., Hamilton* ☎ *441/295–2112* ⊕ *www.calypso.bm.*

Modblu. Featuring popular names in women's clothing and jewelry and a mix of casual and dressy pieces, this bright and airy addition to the Bermuda shopping scene offers a positive love-yourself vibe with its flattering and stylish selections. Shoppers will find breezier items from Raga, denim and trendier pieces from Blank NYC, and dresses from Cooper & Ella. Local designers featured here include jewelry label Airy Heights and sunglasses and watch designer Kapten & Son. ✉ *46 Reid St., Hamilton* ☎ *441/405–3250* ⊕ *www.modblubermuda. com* ☾ *Closed Sun.*

Revelation Boutique. Cool, contemporary linen and cotton clothing is the focus of Paulette Wedderburn's shop, which also has an impressive collection of formal wear. ✉ *27 Queen St., Hamilton* ☎ *441/296–4252* ☾ *Closed Sun.*

Sisley. Follow the trendsetters to this store to get your hands on the latest women's fashions including suits, party dresses, and casual basics. A sister store to Benetton, Sisley is known for its edgy, contemporary designs with feminine flair. ✉ *Front St., Hamilton* ✛ *Corner of Par-La-Ville Rd.* ☎ *441/295–2112* ⊕ *www.calypso.bm.*

Vibe. Funky clothes, shoes, and accessories at reasonable prices make Vibe a choice shop for women who want to keep up with the latest styles. ✉ *5 Burnaby St., Hamilton* ☎ *441/296–4883.*

Women's Secret. This Spanish brand offers a good range of fun and feminine underwear, lingerie, nightwear, loungewear, sportswear, and swimwear. ✉ *14 Reid St., Hamilton* ☎ *441/295–2112* ⊕ *www.calypso.bm.*

7

COSMETICS AND BEAUTY

M.A.C. Cosmetics. This chic store of the popular M.A.C. Cosmetics brand has every beauty, makeup, and skin-care product you could ever want. Its trained makeup artists offer walk-in makeovers. ✉ *53 Front St., Hamilton* ☎ *441/295–8843* ⊕ *www.gibbons.bm.*

The Perfume Shop. In addition to being the exclusive Bermuda agent for Guerlain's complete line of cosmetics and skin care products, The Perfume Shop boutique stocks perfume, soap, lotions, and bubble bath. It's also the island's exclusive seller of Chanel and Dior makeup. There's a branch in the Clocktower Mall, Dockyard, and Bermuda Island Shop on Water Street in St George's. ✉ *Gibbons Co. Perfume Department, 21 Reid St., Hamilton* ☎ *441/295–5535* ⊕ *www.gibbons.bm.*

> ### SUPERSTAR GROCER
>
> Dai James, a manager at Lindo's in Warwick, has become something of a cult hero as the star of a series of wacky TV adverts. Don't be surprised to hear locals asking Mr. Jones, "Can you wrap?" In one advert he mistakenly starts to rap when a customer asks him to wrap her tomatoes.

ELECTRONICS

iClick. This large store is crammed full of the latest Apple gadgets and accessories. A full-service center is also available with technicians on hand to help if you get pink sand in your phone. ✉ *20 Reid St., Hamilton* ☎ *441/542–5425* ⊕ *www.ptech.bm/iclick* ⊙ *Closed Sun.*

FOOD AND CANDY

FAMILY **Treats.** You can find bulk candy in just about every flavor here, but the greatest draws to this tiny store are the fun, seasonal gifts and cute baby toys. Look out for the educational and science toys. There's also a selection of wooden toys, board games, and a wide selection of LEGO. ✉ *Washington Mall, lower level, 7 Reid St., Hamilton* ☎ *441/296–1123.*

GROCERY STORES

A1 Paget. This grocery store is near several Paget accommodations and it's an easy enough walk to do with bags of shopping. You could also stop here to grab snacks and drinks before hitting nearby Elbow Beach. ✉ *1 Valley Rd., junction of Middle Rd.* ☎ *441/236–0351* ⊕ *www.marketplace.bm.*

ABC Natural Foods. Housed beside the Seventh Day Adventist Church in the City of Hamilton, ABC is filled with mostly vegan and lacto-ovo food options but you can also find natural beauty and body products and a vegan café inside the shop where you can grab a refreshing smoothie. ✉ *41 King St., Hamilton* ☎ *441/292–4111* ⊙ *Closed Sat.*

Arnold's Family Market. Close to several centrally located guesthouses, this grocery store is always open, even on public holidays. The Arnold's Express store in Hamilton—on Front Street—is open until midnight. ✉ *113 St. John's Rd.* ☎ *441/292–3310.*

Down to Earth Health Food. This natural-food and health shop sells everything from tea and supplements to organic body products and home cleaners. Don't leave without grabbing a fruit smoothie or a vegetable juice from the bar in the corner. There's seating on the porch. ✉ *56 Reid St., Hamilton* ☎ *441/292–5639.*

Esso City Tiger Market. Day or night, this gas station sells a good range of fast food and sandwiches, as well as cigarettes, hot drinks, chips, soda, and aspirin. This is the only true 24-hour place on the island. ✉ *37 Richmond Rd., Hamilton* ☎ *441/295–3776.*

Lindo's Family Foods, Ltd. Lindo's is a medium-size store with a good selection of groceries, plus organic foods, fresh seafood, and fine imported French and Italian cheese and pâtés. It's within walking distance of several Warwick accommodations. There's a Devonshire location as well, and both have a pharmacy. ✉ *128 Middle Rd.* ☎ *441/236–1344* ⊕ *www.lindos.bm.*

MarketPlace. The island's largest grocery store, and the chain's headquarters, MarketPlace offers homemade hot soups, stir-fries, salads, dinners, and desserts for about $8 a pound. It's the place locals go for lunch; many are drawn by the healthy-eating and organic sections. ✉ *Church St., Hamilton* ✦ *Near Parliament St.* ☎ *441/295–6006* ⊕ *www.marketplace.bm.*

Miles Market. Miles is the Balducci's of Bermuda, with a large selection of upscale or hard-to-find specialty food items. The deli encompasses the finest imported and local meats and fish. There's also a mouthwatering range of pastries, cakes, and Godiva chocolates. Many items are on the expensive side, but the quality and selection are without rival. The supermarket delivers anywhere on the island. ✉ *96 Pitts Bay Rd., Hamilton* ✦ *Near Fairmont Hamilton Princess* ☎ *441/295–1234* ⊕ *www.miles.bm.*

Modern Mart. Part of the MarketPlace chain, but smaller than its flagship Hamilton store, this location has all the essentials. It's easily accessible from Paraquet Apartments and other south shore hotels. It's also the nearest food stop to Elbow Beach. ✉ *104 South Rd.* ☎ *441/236–6161* ⊕ *www.marketplace.bm.*

Rock On–The Health Store. Nutritional supplements, sports supplements, diet books, natural teas and remedies, and environmentally friendly toiletries are among the goods offered. But its biggest sellers are probably its protein shakes and bars. The staff is knowledgeable. ✉ *Butterfield Pl., 67 Front St., Hamilton* ☎ *441/295–3468.*

Shelly Bay MarketPlace. This branch of the MarketPlace chain is the only large grocery store on North Shore Road. It stocks everything you could need. There's also a huge parking lot and a handful of other stores nearby. ✉ *110 N. Shore Rd., Hamilton* ☎ *441/293–0966.*

The Supermart. English products, including the Waitrose brand, are the specialties of this grocery store. You can pick up a picnic lunch at the well-stocked salad-and-hot-food bar. ✉ *125 Front St., Hamilton* ✦ *Between Court and King* ☎ *441/292–2064* ⊕ *www.supermart.bm.*

JEWELRY AND ACCESSORIES

Fodor's Choice
★ **Alexandra Mosher Studio Jewellery.** After her line of elegant pink-sand-inspired jewelry took off at craft markets and Harbour Nights, artist Alexandra Mosher opened up a light and airy store to showcase her beautiful designs. The shop is as much a work of art as her jewelry, with a pink-sand-beach-inspired mosaic at the entrance of the store designed by local artist Nikki Murray-Mason. Mosher's designs grace the necks, wrists, and fingers of locals and visitors alike; look no further for the perfect souvenir of time spent in Bermuda. There's a smaller, equally beautifully designed, outpost in the Washington Mall. ⌂ *5 Front St., Hamilton ✛ Corner of Par-La-Ville* ☎ *441/236–9009* ⊕ *www.alexandramosher.com.*

Astwood Dickinson. Established in 1904, this store has built a reputation for its exquisite unmounted stones; upscale jewelry, including designs by Cartier and Hearts on Fire; and a wide range of Swiss watches. Baume & Mercier, Omega, and Tag Heuer watches, among other famous names, are sold at U.S. prices with the benefit of no sales tax. The shop's Bermuda Collection, designed and created in the workshop, ranges from 18-karat gold charms to bejeweled pendants representing the island's flora and fauna. There's also a location in the retail arcade at the Hamilton Princess Hotel & Beach Club. ⌂ *Orbis House, 25 Front St., Hamilton* ☎ *441/292–5805* ⊕ *www.ascooper.bm/ascoopers/astwood-dickinson.*

Atlantic Jewellery Studio. Stocked to the brim with brightly colored baubles, Atlantic Jewellery has many handcrafted statement pieces. Find necklaces, bracelets, earrings, and chunky rings featuring every variation of colorful gemstones. ⌂ *Washington Mall, lower level, 7 Reid St., Hamilton* ☎ *441/542–1554* ⊕ *www.atlanticjewellery.bm.*

Crisson's. The only store in Bermuda carrying Rolex, Crisson's attracts well-heeled customers who come here to buy merchandise at U.S. prices with no sales tax. The shop also carries an extensive selection of David Yurman, and there is an in-store Pandora store selling a large selection of charms and jewelry. Earrings are a specialty, and there's a large selection, as well as a handful of gold bangles and beads. There are smaller branches at 16 Queen Street, Fairmont Southampton Resort, and the Clocktower Mall. ⌂ *55 Front St., Hamilton* ☎ *441/295–2351* ⊕ *www.crisson.com.*

E. R. Aubrey. Gold, sapphires, colored pearls, and tanzanite are the specialties of this Hamilton jeweler. The store also carries a large selection of certified diamonds and promises to match prices as long as they can be verified. There are additional locations on Queen Street and in the Clocktower Mall. ⌂ *101 Front St., Hamilton* ☎ *441/296–3171* ⊕ *www.eraubrey.com.*

Everrich Jewelry. This bargain jewelry store stocks countless styles of basic gold and silver chains, earrings, bangles, and rings. ⌂ *28 Queen St., Hamilton* ☎ *441/295–2110.*

Gem Cellar. Jewelers here make Bermuda-theme charms selling for $65 and up, including the Longtail national bird, the Hog Penny, and the Gombey dancer. They can also produce custom-designed gold and silver jewelry in two to three days. ⊠ *Walker Arcade, 47 Front St., Hamilton* ☎ *441/292–3042.*

Kirk's Designs. Owner Kirk Stapff says he can design and produce any piece of jewelry you desire, "from A to Z." Just bring him an idea, and he'll work with you to create it. ⊠ *Butterfield Pl., 67 Front St., Hamilton* ☎ *441/296–9428.*

1609 Design. Known for its Bermuda-made and Bermuda-inspired designs including delicate necklaces—perfect for layering—with gems in soothing tropical palettes, gemstone bracelets, and a selection of pretty earrings from artist Joanna Stapff, 1609 is also a great resource for handmade cards and canvas bags or coasters printed with Bermuda scenes. ⊠ *Old Cellar La., 47 Front St., Hamilton* ☎ *441/336–1326* ⊙ *Closed Sun.*

Sunglass & Watch Shop. The shop has rebranded to sell what it does best: trendy watches from G-Shock and Dolce & Gabbana, as well as many other brands. It's expanded to create room for one of the island's best selections of sunglasses—Prada, Gucci, Marc Jacobs, and Ray-Ban, to name a few. This shop is also a good place for watch repairs and battery or strap replacements. ⊠ *13 Reid St., Hamilton* ☎ *441/292–7933* ⊕ *www.sunglassandwatchshop.bm.*

Swiss Timing. Head here for watches, clocks, and jewelry from across Europe, including Germany, England, and Italy. The store has a great range of birthstone rings, earrings, necklaces, and bracelets, and you can have items custom designed. ⊠ *95 Front St., Hamilton* ☎ *441/295–1376.*

Walker Christopher. Here you can work with a jeweler to design your own exclusive piece or choose from classic diamond bands, strands of South Sea pearls, and the more contemporary hand-hammered chokers. The workshop also produces a line of Bermuda-inspired gold jewelry and sterling silver Christmas ornaments. ⊠ *9 Front St., Hamilton* ☎ *441/295–1466* ⊕ *www.walkerchristopher.com.*

MUSIC

The Music Box. This independent shop is crammed full of all sorts of musical items from guitars to stereos and other electronics. Inside is a diverse collection of new CDs and DVDs, as well as CD/DVD players and accessories. There's a handful of music books on sale, and the shop is happy to do special orders. ⊠ *58 Reid St., Hamilton* ☎ *441/295–4839.*

Sound Stage. Small but fairly comprehensive, Sound Stage stocks new-release, mainstream CDs and DVDs. All genres of music are covered. ⊠ *Washington Mall, upper level, 20 Church St., Hamilton* ☎ *441/292–0811.*

NOVELTIES AND GIFTS

Flying Colours. This family-owned and -operated shop, established in 1937, has the island's largest selection of T-shirts, with creatively designed logos in hundreds of styles. The shop also carries everything for the beach—hats, towels, sarongs, flip-flops, sunglasses, toys for playing in the sand—plus high-quality souvenirs and gifts, like shell jewelry. ⊠ *5 Queen St., Hamilton* ☎ *441/295–0890* ⊕ *www.flyingcolours.bm.*

> ### IN A FORMER LIFE
>
> It may be hard to believe, but the shops at Old Cellar Lane used to be stables, sheltering horses and carriages for patrons of local businesses in a sort of municipal "parking lot."

Hodge Podge. This cluttered little shop, just around the corner from the Ferry Terminal and Visitor Information Centre, offers pretty much what its name implies: postcards, sunblock, sunglasses, and T-shirts. It also sells imported shells and shell jewelry at low prices. ⊠ *3 Point Pleasant Rd., Hamilton* ☎ *441/295–0647.*

The Irish Linen Shop. Along with the expected (and authentic) Irish linens, this home decor shop's stock is from all over the world and includes fine table and bed linens from Le Jacquard Francais, Sferra, Julia B., and Yves Delorme. There is also a selection of furniture along with an exclusive range of gifts from Michael Aram, Mariposa, and Cire Trudon. ⊠ *31 Front St., Hamilton* ☎ *441/295–4089* ⊘ *Closed Sun.*

Fodor's Choice ★ The Island Shop. Brightly colored island-theme artwork for ceramics, linens, and pillows is designed by owner Barbara Finsness. A number of her original watercolors are available for purchase. She also stocks the store with cedar-handle handbags embroidered with Bermuda buildings, shell napkin rings, plates, monogrammed guest towels, rugs, chunky jewelry, and elegant gifts, as well as candles and bath products. There are also branches at Somers Wharf, St. George's, and at the Fairmont Southampton Resort. ⊠ *3 Queen St., Hamilton* ☎ *441/292–5292* ⊕ *www.islandexports.com.*

Pulp & Circumstance. If it's an original, quality gift you're after, look no further. What used to be two separate stores is now one bumper store crammed full of goodies. There are modern picture frames in all shapes and sizes, photo albums, ceramics, candles, bath products, and gifts for babies. There's also a great selection of greeting cards and other stationery items. ⊠ *4 Washington La., Hamilton* ☎ *441/542–9586.*

Sail On. A unique collection of women's clothing, footwear, accessories, jewelry, and eclectic gifts can be found at this local favorite for more than two decades. ⊠ *Washington Mall, 7 Reid St., Hamilton* ☎ *441/295–0808.*

Urban Cottage. What started out as a warehouse of Bermuda and world treasures collected by store owner Nicole Golden has turned into a Front Street boutique with a wide selection of housewares, jewelry, gifts, and clothing. The shop still has the distressed patina of a warehouse and still continues to showcase Bermuda treasures such as old road signs. ⊠ *11 Front St., Hamilton* ☎ *441/532–1152* ⊕ *www.urbancottagebermuda.com.*

PHOTO EQUIPMENT

P-Tech. Point-and-shoot digital cameras, SLR cameras, digital photo frames, camcorders, and other small electronics such as iPod docking stations and tech accessories are all here. Brands to look for are Nikon, Canon, and Olympus. There's also a small photo department on the corner of Church and Queen Streets with self-service photo booths as well as a full-service photo lab. ⊠ *5 Reid St., Hamilton* ☎ *441/295–5496* ⊕ *www.ptech.bm.*

SHOES AND HANDBAGS

Boyle, W. J. & Son Ltd. Bermuda's leading footwear chain sells a wide range of men's, women's, and children's shoes. The Trends location on Reid Street in Hamilton has the most up-to-the-minute foot fashions, although the Sports Locker location on Queen Street in Hamilton has a good stock of running shoes and a wide range of fashion sneakers such as Converse and Keds. The Church Street store specializes in children's shoes. There are also locations on Water Street in St. George's and in Somerset Village. ⊠ *Boyle's Bldg., 31 Queen St., Hamilton* ☎ *441/295–1887.*

> ### QUIK FIX
>
> **Heel Quik.** Local shoes-in-distress swear by the friendly expert same-day service at Heel Quik. The store also cuts keys and carries shoe-care products and umbrellas. ⊠ *Washington Mall, upper level, 7 Reid St., Hamilton* ☎ *441/295-1559.*

Calypso. Women looking for quirky, snazzy footwear should visit Calypso's main store first. The shoe and bag section is small but with choice, supertrendy, sometimes weird styles and colors. Items may cost a little more than you want to spend but you'll want them anyway. Serious bargains can be had during sales. Calypso has branches at the Fairmont Southampton Resort and Clocktower Mall in Dockyard. ⊠ *45 Front St., Hamilton* ☎ *441/295–2112* ⊕ *www.calypso.bm.*

The Harbourmaster. Kipling luggage and bags, among other brands, are sold at this store, which prides itself on having "everything pertaining to travel." Wallets, handbags, and gifts round out the stock. ⊠ *Washington Mall, lower level , 7 Reid St., Hamilton* ☎ *441/295–5333.*

Island Sole. Opened in 2012 by two podiatrists, Island Sole believes that fashion and comfort can meet in a shoe. The shop is stocked with all manner of shoes from flip-flops by Telic to comfortable high heels. Casual and dress shoes are available for both men and women. ⊠ *60 Victoria St., Hamilton* ☎ *441/292–4523.*

Fodor's Choice ★ **Lusso.** This is the ultimate island boutique for designer footwear for men and women, with shoes from Ferragamo, Jimmy Choo, and Fendi. The shop merged with sister shop Cecile and the ready-to-wear collections include Emilio Pucci, Missoni, and Marchesa. The real standout is the selection of Lily Pulitzer as well as swim collections from Gottex and Manual Canovas. ✉ *51 Front St., Hamilton* ☎ *441/295–6734.*

Perry Collections. This stylish store is worth a look, with an impressive collection of women's dress and casual shoes, including Coach, Kate Spade, and Guess. It also sells handbags, wallets, jewelry, and belts. The standout of the store is the Stuart Weitzman in-store boutique, which sells designs exclusive to Perry Collections. Men shouldn't feel left out, as they are catered to with brands such as Donald Pliner, Guess, and LaCoste. ✉ *2 Reid St., Hamilton* ✛ *Corner of Queen St.* ☎ *441/296–0014.*

The Shoe Centre. The Shoe Centre is a short distance from the shops of Front and Reid Streets, but well worth the walk if you want a bargain. There's a good selection of men's, women's and children's shoes starting from about $20. Don't miss the bargain basement on the lower level. ✉ *42 Dundonald St., Hamilton* ☎ *441/292–5078.*

SPAS

Exhale at Hamilton Princess & Beach Club. If you're in need of a quick pick-me-up, the city location of the Exhale Day Spa offers a full array of body treatments, massages, as well as its butt-busting barre classes. ✉ *Hamilton Princess Hotel & Beach Club, 76 Pitts Bay Rd., Hamilton* ☎ *441/298–6046* ⊕ *www.exhalespa.com* ☞ *$155, 60-min. deep tissue massage; $220, 90-min. Thai massage. Services: acu-healing, changing rooms, facials, fitness classes, gym with cardiovascular machines, nails, outdoor spa pool, waxing, well-being boutique, Zen lounge.*

Rosewood Tucker's Point Spa. If you're looking for an extra indulgence and a little down time, Sense Spa at The Rosewood Tucker's Point Hotel is the island's most luxurious. With 12 treatment rooms and 14,000 square feet, there are a wide range of rejuvenating treatments available in a pristine and relaxing environment. ✉ *Rosewood Tucker's Point, 60 Tucker's Point Dr.* ☎ *441/298–4000* ⊕ *www.rosewoodhotels.com* ☞ *$180, 50-min. deep tissue massage; $245, 80-min. cedar warming massage; $300–$650 packages. Hair salon. Services: aquatic therapy, facials, hair and scalp treatments, nail treatments, waxing.*

The Spa at Elbow Beach. For the most pampering treatments in Bermuda, The Spa at Elbow Beach includes personal and couples spa suites overlooking the Atlantic. The suites include personal showers, vanity area, granite bath, and daybeds on private balconies outside the suite. Treatments blend island and Asian influences and use ESPA products. Although not the largest, this is the most lavish, personal, private, and relaxing spa on the island. ✉ *Elbow Beach Hotel, 60 South Shore Rd.* ☎ *441/239–8900* ☞ *$225, 80-min. oasis massage; $375–$435 packages. Gym with: cardiovascular machines, free weights, weight-training equipment. Services: aromatherapy, baths, body wraps, facials, foot treatments, maternity massages, scrubs.*

SPORTING GOODS

CB Wholesale and Dive. The best prices for dive gear are found, naturally, at Bermuda's most complete dive shop. You can find a large selection of wet suits, fishing gear, and wakeboards as well as children's mask-and-snorkel sets. ⊠ *15 Burnaby St., Hamilton* ☎ *441/292–3839.*

International Sports Shop. This store caters to all sporting needs including exercise equipment, football shirts, and exercise wear. The shop also specializes in sporting equipment and promotional products. ⊠ *2 Church St., Hamilton* ⊹ *Corner of Bermudiana Rd.* ☎ *441/295–4183* ⊕ *www.issl.bm* ☉ *Closed Sun.*

The Pro Shop. Tucked away beneath the ground level, this shop sells men's and women's running and tennis clothes, football jerseys, and sneakers from all the main brands at reasonable prices. ⊠ *Kenwood Bldg., 17 Reid St., Hamilton* ☎ *441/292–7487.*

Sports 'R' Us. This store has Bermuda's largest selection of running shoes, plus gear and equipment for most sports. ⊠ *Shoppers Fair Bldg., 61 Church St., Hamilton* ☎ *441/292–1891.*

SportSeller. Big-name exercise gear, knapsacks, and running shoes are available at this shop, which also sells Speedo swimwear, sunglasses, and water bottles of every shape and size. Come here to get the best fit in running shoes from a very knowledgeable staff. ⊠ *Washington Mall, lower level, 7 Reid St., Hamilton* ☎ *441/295–2692.*

Winners Edge. This store sells everything to do with cycling including exercise wear, water bottles, and helmets, and it's the only store in Bermuda to sell Cannondale and Trek equipment. The owners and staff include some of Bermuda's top cyclists; they'll be able to answer just about any biking question you throw at them. ⊠ *73 Front St., Hamilton* ☎ *441/295–6012* ⊕ *www.winnersedge.bm.*

TOYS

The Annex Toys. Upstairs at the Phoenix Pharmacy, this large toy department has an up-to-date selection of toys and games for all ages. There's a good supply of kites and beach toys, as well as shelves full of board games and puzzles. Phoenix Kidz, located in the same space, stocks baby equipment and essentials. There's also a small selection of children's clothes and accessories. ⊠ *Phoenix Centre, 3 Reid St., Hamilton* ☎ *441/279–5450* ⊕ *www.annextoys.bm.*

Nest. All the gear you need for baby and toddler is stocked in this well-edited shop. Toys include the Plan line of wooden toys as well as a great selection of Chewbeads. The shop also stocks a large selection of Honest brand products and plenty of items to help organize your child's room into a stylish retreat. There is a small selection of kids' clothing and shoes as well as gorgeous maternity wear. ⊠ *44 Reid St., Hamilton* ☎ *441/296–6378* ⊕ *www.nestbermuda.com* ☉ *Closed Sun.*

FAMILY **People's Pharmacy.** Head to the back of this large pharmacy where you will find Little People's for one of the island's biggest selections of toys and games—from cuddly toys and rattles for babies to computer

CLOSE UP

Yo, Ho, Ho and a Bottle of Rum

One of the distinct pleasures of a visit to Bermuda is getting to sample a bit of island rum and rum-based products. Gosling's Black Seal Rum is perhaps the best loved by locals. It's darker and thicker than the usual stuff, with a hint of a caramel flavor—especially when mixed with carbonated ginger beer to make a Dark 'n' Stormy, a famous Bermuda drink (treat it with respect and caution).

Gosling's is one of Bermuda's oldest companies, and its Hamilton liquor shop was established in 1806. Gosling's Black Seal Rum was sold in barrels until just after World War I, and inherited its name from the black sealing wax that sealed the barrel corks. In its 151-proof variety, Black Seal will test the strongest

drinker. Many prefer to buy it in the standard 80 proof.

Bermuda's rum swizzle, another popular drink, also uses the ubiquitous Black Seal Rum, along with a splash of club soda, lime juice, and sugar. Gosling also produces three liqueurs that are big favorites— Bermuda Gold, Bermuda Banana Liqueur, and Bermuda Coconut Rum. These liqueurs can be ordered everywhere, from poolside bars to late-night jazz clubs. They're even found in cakes, as you soon discover in gift shops and on restaurant menus. Classic Bermuda rum cakes are a delicious, nontoxic way to taste the island's famous export. Fear not if rum's not your thing: Guinness and Heineken are among the widely available imported beers.

games and board games for teens. The shop also stocks a large selection of organic and natural baby products. ⊠ *62 Victoria St., Hamilton* ☎ *441/292–7527* ⊕ *www.peoplespharmacy.bm.*

WINES AND SPIRITS

Burrows Lightbourn. This wine and spirits merchant has a great selection in stores all over the island. Visitors who want to take duty-free alcohol back home make significant savings on the retail price. There are two other locations including one on York Street in St. George's and the other located on Harbour Road. ⊠ *127 Front St., Hamilton* ☎ *441/295–1554.*

Front Street Wine & Spirits. Here's your one-stop shop for candy, wines, beer, souvenirs, and assorted snacks. ⊠ *57 Front St., Hamilton* ☎ *441/292–6620.*

Gosling's Ltd. The maker of Bermuda's Black Seal Rum also stocks wines and other liquors at its stores. The helpful and knowledgeable staff provides excellent advice. The store also sells T-shirts, ties, and hats with Gosling's logo, a black seal. There's another branch on Dundonald Street in North Hamilton. ⊠ *Front and Queen Sts., Hamilton* ☎ *441/298–7337* ⊕ *www.goslingsrum.com.*

ST. GEORGE'S AND EASTERN PARISHES

If you want to combine shopping with a leisurely stroll, Water Street and Duke of York Street in St. George's have a variety of stores which you can browse at your ease. St. George's is the perfect day trip, as you can pick up some bargains, stop for lunch, and go sightseeing in the same location. There are also a handful of stores in Flatts Village, which you may want to visit on your way to the Bermuda Aquarium, Museum & Zoo.

ART GALLERIES

Bermuda Memories. Local artists, including Jill Amos Raine, display their work depicting Bermuda's houses, scenery, and wharfs in this specialty shop. You can also pick up pieces made by Dockyard Glass as well as grab one of its famous Bermuda rum cakes. ⊠ *Water St., St. George's* ☎ *441/297–3908.*

BOOKS

The Book Cellar. In a small space underneath the Tucker House, this shop crams in a surprisingly large selection of books about Bermuda and an interesting assortment of novels in addition to contemporary best sellers. ⊠ *5 Water St., St. George's* ☎ *441/297–0448* ⊘ *Closed Sun.*

7

CERAMICS AND GLASSWARE

Vera P. Card. Lladro and Swarovski silver crystal figurines are available at almost identical prices elsewhere, but this store has the largest selection, including pieces specifically made for the shop, such as the Bermuda Moongate by Lladro. The shop's collection of more than 250 Hummel figurin... ...ne of the world's largest. Limited-edition porcelain plates and v... ...picting Bermuda scenes cost $69 to $300. There are also bright... ...ted chiming cuckoo clocks. Fine and costume jewelry are also sol... ...2 *Water St., St. George's* ✛ *Above Carriage House restaurant* ☎... ...*295–1729* ⊘ *Closed Sun.*

CLOTHING

Davison's of Bermuda. Davison's ups the souvenir T-shirt game by offering a great selection of shirts with stylish logos in great fits and designs. It also offers brightly printed dresses and separates for women and light, comfortable clothes for men, and a large selection of children's clothes from infant to about nine years. The store includes plenty of gift ideas and accessories as well as the perfect beach hat and bags. There are branches on Front Street in Hamilton, in the Fairmont Southampton Resort, and the Clocktower Mall in Dockyard. ⊠ *16 Water St.* ☎ *441/296–9552* ⊘ *Closed Sun.*

Flatts Men's Wear. Owner Mick Adderley runs this popular out-of-town shop selling men's clothing, shoes, and accessories, including Dickies work clothes. It also has a small selection of specially made clothes in big-and-tall sizes. ⊠ *13 N. Shore Rd., Flatt's Village* ☎ *441/292–0360* ⊘ *Closed Sun.*

Frangipani. This little store sells colorful women's fashions with a Southeast Asian island–resort look. Cotton, silk, and rayon leisure wear are the backbone of the stock. Don't miss the hand-strung, brightly colored, beaded necklaces, bracelets, and earrings, as well as eye-catching bags. There's also a location in the Washington Mall in Hamilton. ⊠ *13 Water St., St. George's* ☎ *441/297–1357* ⊘ *Closed Sun.*

COSMETICS AND BEAUTY

Fodor's Choice **Lili Bermuda (Bermuda Perfumery).** This historic perfumery, which began in
★   1928, creates and manufactures all its own perfumes, using the scents of Bermuda's flowers and citrus trees as inspiration. New perfumes are constantly being created, but try out Coral and Lili for women and Navy, 32 North, and Somers for men. You can also tour the facilities to learn how modern and traditional techniques of perfumery are combined. There's also a small museum dedicated to the history of perfumery. The Perfumery opened the Lili Bermuda Boutique in Hamilton at 67 Front Street where you can also test out and purchase all of the scents. ⊠ *Stewart Hall, 5 Queen St., St. George's* ☎ *441/293–0627* ⊕ *www.lilibermuda.com* ⊘ *Closed Sun.*

CRAFTS

The Bounty. The spicy smell of cedar is the first thing to greet you in this tiny shop, where owner Kersley Nanette handcrafts teak and cedar model ships. The focus is on tall ships of the 17th and 18th centuries. Prices range from $150 to $5,000. Models of the *Sea Venture* and *Deliverance* are especially popular. Call for an appointment weekdays 9 to 5. ⊠ *2A Old Maid's La., St. George's* ☎ *441/297–2143* ⊘ *Closed Sun.*

FOOD AND CANDY

GROCERY STORES

Harrington Hundreds. Harrington Hundreds is a must for those observing special diets or seeking unusual ingredients. As well as all your usual groceries, it has the island's best selection of wheat-free foods, including gluten-free pastas, breads, and cookies. It's within walking distance of Spittal Pond. ⊠ *99 S. Shore Rd.* ☎ *441/293–1635.*

Somers Supermarket. Despite its small size, Somers has a large selection, with hot food, salads, and sandwiches made fresh daily. It offers delivery service within St. George's, and it's open Monday to Saturday from 7 am to 10 pm, and Sunday from 8 to 6. ⊠ *41 York St., St. George's* ☎ *441/297–1177.*

JEWELRY AND ACCESSORIES

Davidrose. Specializing in one-of-a-kind and specially designed jewelry, husband-and-wife-team David and Avrel Zuill can create anything you dream up. The St. George's design studio is filled with their unique statement pieces and, with a view over St. George's Harbour, is the perfect place to find inspiration for your next fine piece of jewelry. ⊠ *20 Water St., St. George's* ☎ *441/293–7673* ⊕ *www.davidrose.bm.*

NOVELTIES AND GIFTS

Bermuda Linens and Gifts. Specialty items include hand-embroidered table, bed, and bath linens; christening gowns; and infant wear. There's also selection of home decor and gifts. ⊠ *16 Somers Wharf, St. George's* ☎ *441/296–0189* ⊕ *www.bermudalinens.com.*

Paradise Gift Shop. You can find every permutation of gift in this shop—from "Bermuda" T-shirts to plates to funky knickknacks. ⊠ *7 King's Sq., St. George's* ☎ *441/297–0670.*

Regali by Luxury Gifts Bermuda. Located in the lobby of Rosewood Tucker's Point, this boutique is more than just a hotel gift shop. There is a gorgeous selection of flowy summer dresses, bathing suits, cover-ups, and hats on one side with a selection of high-end gifts from Jonathan Adler as well as specialty spa and beauty products on the other. Men can also pick up shirts from local menswear line Coral Coast Clothing, and there is a lovely selection of clothing and gifts for babies and toddlers. The shop also stocks a small selection of travel necessities and snacks. ⊠ *Rosewood Tucker's Point, 60 Tucker's Point Dr.* ☎ *441/298–4035* ⊕ *luxurygiftsbermuda.com.*

Robertson's Drug Store. This is so much more than a pharmacy, as it's crammed full of goodies. It stocks great greetings cards, many toiletries and beauty products, and one of the best selections of unusual toys can be found downstairs. ⊠ *24 York St., St. George's* ☎ *441/297–1828.*

Trustworthy Gift Shop at The Globe Hotel. Proceeds from the sales of Bermuda-inspired coffee-table books, key chains, serving trays, spoons, ceramics, pens, and bags at this gift shop benefit the Bermuda National Trust. Look out for their specially designed bluebird boxes. This is where you can find some of the most upscale gifts to take back home. ⊠ *The Globe Hotel, 32 Duke of York St.* ☎ *441/297–1423* ⊕ *www.bnt. bm* ☉ *Closed Mon., Fri., and Sun.*

WINES AND SPIRITS

Bermuda Duty Free Shop. Before you head home, this airport store invites you to put together your own package of Bermuda liquors at duty-free prices. Gosling's Black Seal Rum and rum cakes are among the native products. ⊠ *L.F. Wade International Airport, 3 Cahow Way, St. George's* ☎ *441/293–2870.*

DOCKYARD AND WESTERN PARISHES

New stores continue to spring up as the West End begins to threaten Hamilton as a shopping hot spot. Dockyard is the place to go for those quirky gifts you won't be able to find anywhere else. Don't miss the Bermuda Craft Market, Bermuda Glassworks, and Bermuda Rum Cake Company, and just around the corner you have the Clocktower Mall

7

with its quaint indoor selection of little stores and boutiques. Just a few miles along the road you will find the village of Somerset, which has a few stores to browse.

ART GALLERIES

Bermuda Arts Centre at Dockyard. Sleek and modern, with well-designed displays of local art, this gallery is in one of the stone buildings of the former Royal Naval Dockyard. The walls are adorned with paintings and photographs, and glass display cases contain exquisitely crafted ceramics, jewelry, and wood sculpture. Exhibits change every month. Several artists' studios inside the gallery are open to the public. Much of the work on show is for sale; there's also a small shop selling prints and a variety of art-related gifts. ⊠ *4 Maritime La., Dockyard* ☎ *441/234–2809* ⊕ *www.artbermuda.com.*

Carole Holding Print & Craft Shops. Prices for artist Carole Holding's watercolors of Bermuda's scenes and flowers range from $12 for small prints to more than $5,000 for framed originals. The artist's prints can also be found on linen, china, and clothing, including T-shirts and aprons, and she has her own line of jams, chutneys, and rum cakes. The shop also sells crafts by local artists, and there's a branch at the Clocktower Mall, Dockyard. ⊠ *Fairmont Southampton Resort, 101 South Shore Rd.* ☎ *441/238–7310* ⊕ *www.caroleholding.com.*

CLOTHING

Crown & Anchor. Housed in a former ship captain's home, the nautically designed shop with it's whitewashed exposed beams and model sailboats is the perfect showcase for the nautically inspired clothing. Find polos and khaki shorts for men and striped T-shirt dresses and colorful beach dresses that can be easily dressed up or down for women. ⊠ *Royal Naval Dockyard, 4 Dockyard Terr., Dockyard* ☎ *441/296–9558.*

CRAFTS

Bermuda Craft Market. The island's largest permanent craft outlet is in the Dockyard's old Cooperage building, which dates from 1831. Dozens of artists show their work here, and this is the place to go to find that unusual gift, from Bermuda-cedar hair clips to Bermuda chutney and jam. Hand-painted glassware, sterling-silver jewelry, and sand sculptures are also among the pretty offerings. ⊠ *The Cooperage, 4 Maritime La., Dockyard* ☎ *441/234–3208* ⊕ *www.bermudacraftmarket.com.*

Jon Faulkner Gallery. Customized house-number and name plaques and tableware are among the brightly painted pottery pieces created in this little shop. Faulkner's salt-fire pottery and porcelain fare are some of the standout pieces. There's also a walk-in Paint Your Own Pottery Studio where you can create your own masterpieces. ⊠ *7 Camber Rd., Dockyard* ☎ *441/234–5116* ⊕ *www.jonfaulknergallery.com.*

FOOD AND CANDY

GROCERY STORES

Heron Bay MarketPlace. Part of the island-wide MarketPlace chain, this one has a large selection of fresh vegetables, as well as meats and seafood. It's a convenient dive to Marley Beach but not on foot. ⊠ *227 Middle Rd.* ☎ *441/238–1993* ⊕ *www.marketplace.bm.*

Somerset MarketPlace. The largest grocery store on the island's western end, it's convenient to Cambridge Beaches, but take a moped or taxi. ⊠ *48 Somerset Rd., Somerset* ☎ *441/234–0626* ⊕ *www.marketplace.bm.*

NOVELTIES AND GIFTS

Fodor's Choice ★ **Dockyard Glassworks and Bermuda Rum Cake Company.** Pull up an armchair and watch as artists turn molten glass into vases, plates, miniature tree frogs, and other collectibles. Afterward help yourself to the rum-cake samples. Flavors include traditional black rum, chocolate, coconut, rum swizzle (with tropical fruit juices), coffee, banana, and ginger. You can buy the cakes duty-free or pick up a specially presented cake in a tin. Black rum fruitcake and loquat cakes are also sold. If you buy glassware, the company will pack the purchase and deliver it to your hotel or cruise ship for a small fee. ⊠ *Bldg. No. 9, 1 Maritime La., Dockyard* ☎ *441/234–4216* ⊕ *www.dockyardcompany.com.*

Island Outfitters. This shop has everything you need for your beach vacation, from hats to flip-flops to cover-ups. Bermuda-inspired dresses, shorts, and hats from local children's clothing designer Aqua Designs are carried here. ⊠ *6 Dockyard Terr.* ☎ *441/238–4842.*

Littlest Drawbridge Gift Shop. Bermuda-cedar treasures, such as bowls, candle holders, and letter openers, are the highlight of this closet-size shop. Resort wear, handcrafted pottery, pens, and incense cones are also on sale. ⊠ *Clocktower Mall, Dockyard* ☎ *441/234–6214.*

SPAS

Cambridge Beaches Ocean Spa. Sunlight dapples the indoor swimming pools at the Cambridge Beaches Ocean Spa, inside a traditional Bermudian cottage with pink-stucco walls and a ridged roof. The glass dome that covers the pool is opened in warm weather, allowing salt-tinged ocean breezes to drift into the villa. The treatments offered here are hard to find outside Europe. ⊠ *Cambridge Beaches, 30 Kings Point Rd.* ☎ *441/234–3636* ⊕ *www.cambridgebeaches.com* ⊂ *$120, 50-min. Swedish massage; $293–$632 packages. Hair salon, lap pool, relaxation pool, sauna, steam room. Gym with: cardiovascular machines, free weights, yoga. Services: body therapy, body wraps, facials, men's treatments, nail treatments, waxing.*

Three Graces Day Spa at Pompano Beach Club. With two of its three treatment rooms overlooking the calming waters of the South Shore, Three Graces Day Spa at Pompano Beach Club offers a full range of individual and couples' treatments, including baths, scrubs, and massages. There's another location, with a full salon, at the Newstead Belmont Hills in

Paget. ✉ *Pompano Beach Club, 36 Pompano Beach Rd.* ☎ *441/234–0333* ⊕ *www.threegracesdayspa.com* ☞ *$139, 50-min. deep tissue massage; $189, 80-min. hot-stone massage; $135–$399 packages. Hair salon. Services: baths, body treatments, body wraps, couple's treatments, facials, nail treatments, scrubs, waxing, and tinting.*

Willow Stream Spa. The Fairmont Southampton's Willow Stream Spa is the island's largest facility. Besides a complete health club, including personal trainers, there are a garden-enclosed indoor pool, a sundeck overlooking the ocean, two Jacuzzis, three lounges, steam rooms, inhalation rooms, and 15 treatment rooms. Specially designed lengthy treatments combine baths, wraps, and massage conducted with the utmost skill. ✉ *Fairmont Southampton, 101 South Shore Rd.* ☎ *441/239–6924* ☞ *$179, 60-min. aromatherapy massage; $279, 90-min. stress relief. Hair salon, indoor pool, sauna, steam room. Gym with: cardiovascular machines, free weights, weight-training equipment. Services: aromatherapy, bath, body wraps, facials, nail treatments, reflexology, scrubs. Classes and programs: fitness analysis, personal training, yoga.*

CRUISING TO BERMUDA

Updated by
Amy Peniston

Wouldn't you like to arrive in Bermuda relaxed, unpacked, and already in vacation mode? Although Bermuda is only a two-hour flight from most East Coast cities, a cruise is more than simply transportation. There's nothing quite as traditional, or gracious, as a Bermuda arrival by sea.

In today's bigger-and-newer-is-better marketplace, major cruise lines are divesting their fleets of smaller and older ships. Unfortunately, those were the only cruise ships able to squeeze through the entrances into Hamilton and St. George's harbors. As a result, few ships call in these ports, and most vessels dock only at King's Wharf. In any case, you'll have access to the entire island by taxi, moped, public bus, high-speed ferry, or shore excursion.

Departure points for Bermuda cruises run the length of the Eastern Seaboard, including Baltimore, Boston, New York, Norfolk, and Philadelphia. Departures are sometimes scheduled from other mid-Atlantic ports, such as Charleston, as well as those in Florida, so check with the cruise line or your travel agent. The Bermuda cruise season runs from mid-April through mid-November. However, a few ships make occasional port calls during off-season months.

Increasingly popular are round-trip itineraries originating in northeastern embarkation ports that include a single day or overnight port call in Bermuda before continuing south to the Bahamas or Caribbean. In addition to these Bermuda/Bahamas and Bermuda/Caribbean itineraries, "special" voyages or one-way ship-repositioning cruises are often available at the beginning or end of the usual Bermuda season, when cruise lines move their ships to the Caribbean for winter months.

CHOOSING A CRUISE

Your choice of cruise line to Bermuda is narrowed by the government's firm control over the annual number of cruise ships and visitors to the island. That figure has increased in recent years, allowing more passengers to experience all Bermuda has to offer while still receiving the best service and hospitality. Although most ships to Bermuda are big, floating-resort type vessels, each has its own personality, which is determined by its amenities, theme, and, of course, passengers.

Your cruise experience will be shaped by several factors. To decide whether a particular ship's style will suit you, you need to consider your lifestyle and vacation expectations and then do a bit of research: Is there a full program of organized activities each day? What happens in the evening? What kind of entertainment is offered after dark? How often will you need to dress up for dinner? Are there facilities for kids and teens?

Space and passenger-to-crew ratios are equally important. The latter indicates the number of passengers served by each crew member—the lower the ratio, the better the level of service. The space ratio (the gross tonnage of a ship divided by its passenger capacity) allows you to compare ships' roominess. The higher the ratio, the more spacious the vessel feels: at 40:1 or higher a ship will feel quite roomy. Less than 25:1 will cramp anyone's style.

ACCOMMODATIONS
CABIN SIZE

The term "stateroom," used on some ships, is usually interchangeable with "cabin." Price is directly proportional to size and location of your chosen accommodations, and most cabins are more compact than you would expect. The higher you go in the ship, the more expensive the quarters tend to be.

Suites are the roomiest and best-equipped accommodations, but they may differ in size, facilities, and price even on the same ship. Steward service may be more attentive to passengers staying in suites; top suites on some ships are even assigned private butlers. Most suites have a sitting area with sofa and chairs, but sleeping areas aren't necessarily separated from it with more than a curtain. However, some top suites have entirely private bedrooms, walk-in closets, and a guest bathroom. Occasionally the main bathroom has a separate shower and a whirlpool bath.

LOCATION

Today's cruise ships have stabilizers that make seasickness mostly a problem of the past. However, if you're susceptible to motion sickness, try to book a cabin amidships (close to the middle of the ship) as the bow (front) and stern (back) pitch up and down far more when the waves are uncooperative. Ships also experience a side-to-side motion known as roll. The closer your deck is to the true center of the ship—which is halfway between the bottom of the hull and the highest deck and midway between the bow and the stern—the less you will feel the ship's movement. Some cruise lines charge more for cabins amidships; most charge more for higher decks.

Outside cabins have portholes or windows (which cannot be opened). Upper-deck views from outside cabins may be partially obstructed by lifeboats or overlook a public promenade. Because outside cabins are more desirable, most newer ships are configured with only or mostly outside cabins; outside cabins on upper decks are increasingly being built with private verandas. Cabins that overlook a public promenade have mirrored windows, so that passersby can't see in by day; after dark, you'll need to draw your curtains.

TOP 5 BERMUDA CRUISING

Climb up Gibbs Hill Lighthouse for an expansive view of the inlets and harbors.

Absorb Bermuda's nautical and military history at the Bermuda Maritime Museum.

Ride on the ferries to rub shoulders with Bermudians.

Attend the summertime street festival called Harbour Nights, held every Wednesday in Hamilton.

Marvel as ships gingerly inch through the cuts at Hamilton harbor with *very* little room to spare.

8

Inside cabins on older vessels are often smaller, and some are oddly shaped. On newer ships, inside cabin floor plans are virtually identical to those of outside cabins. As long as you don't feel claustrophobic without a window—and most cruise lines hang curtains or place mirrors on the wall to create the illusion—inside cabins are generally an excellent value.

Cruise brochures in print and online show a ship's layout deck by deck, and include the approximate location and shape of every cabin and suite. Use the deck plan to make sure the cabin you choose is not directly above or below public rooms or near the ship's engine, both of which can be noisy; and make sure that you're close to stairs or an elevator if you want to avoid walking down a long passageway every time you return to your cabin. If you can access detailed layouts of typical cabins, you can determine what kind of beds each cabin has, whether it has a window or a porthole, and what furnishings are provided.

SHARING

Most cabins are designed to accommodate two people. When more than two share a cabin, the third and fourth passengers are usually offered a substantial discount, thereby lowering the per-person price for the entire group. An additional discount is sometimes offered when children share a cabin with their parents.

COSTS

The average daily price of a Bermuda cruise varies dramatically depending on several circumstances. The cost of a cruise on a luxury line such as Regent Seven Seas Cruises or Crystal Cruises may be three to five or more times the cost of a cruise on a mainstream line such as Royal Caribbean or Norwegian Cruise Line. Although Bermuda has a relatively short cruising season, you can often save money by cruising in April, before the island experiences ideal beach weather, or late in the season, but that is the time when hurricanes are most likely.

Solo travelers should be aware that single cabins have virtually disappeared from cruise ships. Taking a double cabin can cost twice the advertised per-person rates (which are based on double occupancy); passengers traveling on their own must pay a single supplement, which usually ranges from 125% to 200% of the double-occupancy per-person rate. Some cruise lines will find same-sex roommates for singles; each then pays the per-person, double-occupancy rate.

EXTRAS

Aside from the cost of your cruise there are additional expenses to consider, such as airfare to the embarkation port city. These days virtually all cruise lines offer air add-ons, which are sometimes less expensive than the lowest available airline fare. Shore excursions can also be a substantial expense; the best shore excursions are not cheap. But if you skimp too much on your excursion budget you can deprive yourself of an important part of the Bermuda cruising experience. Finally, there will be many extras added onto your shipboard account during the cruise, including drinks (both alcoholic and nonalcoholic), activity fees (you pay to play bingo), dining in specialty restaurants, spa services, and even cappuccino and espresso on most ships.

TIPPING

Tipping is another add-on. At the end of the cruise, it's customary to tip your room steward, dining-room waiter, and the person who buses your table. You should expect to pay an average of $11 to $14 per day in tips. Most major cruise lines do not use the traditional method of tipping the service staff in cash at the end of the cruise, opting instead to add the recommended amount per day to your onboard account, which you may adjust upward or downward according to the level of service you receive. Bar bills generally include an automatic 15%–18% gratuity, so the one person you don't need to tip is your bartender. Some high-end cruise lines have no-tipping-required policies, though most passengers tip anyway. Each cruise line offers guidelines.

THE BERMUDA CRUISE FLEET

To avoid overcrowding, the Bermudian government limits the number of regular cruise-ship visits to the island. Cruise lines with weekly or monthly sailings are Norwegian Cruise Line, Carnival Cruise Lines, Celebrity Cruises, and Royal Caribbean International. In addition, cruise lines such as Azamara Club Cruises, Disney Cruise Lines, Seabourn Cruises, Silversea Cruises, MSC Cruises, Regent Seven Seas Cruises, Princess Cruises, Oceania Cruises, and Viking Ocean Cruises may have a Bermuda port call on their schedules.

MAINSTREAM CRUISE LINES

Generally speaking, the mainstream lines have two basic ship sizes— large cruise ship and megaship—in their fleets. These vessels have plentiful outdoor deck space, and many have a wraparound outdoor promenade deck that allows you to stroll or jog the ship's perimeter. In the newest cruise ships traditional meets trendy. You can find atrium lobbies and expansive sun and sports decks, picture windows instead of portholes, and cabins that open onto private verandas. For all these resort-style innovations, the newest ships still feature onboard classics—afternoon tea, complimentary room service, and lavish pampering. The smallest cruise ships carry 1,000 passengers at most, whereas the largest accommodate more than 3,000 passengers and are filled with diversions.

If you're into big, bold, brassy, and nonstop activity, these huge ships offer it all. The centerpiece of most megaships is a three-, five-, or even eleven-story central atrium. However, these giant vessels are most readily distinguished by their profile: the boxy hull and superstructure rise as many as 14 stories out of the water and are capped by a huge sun or sports deck with a jogging track and one or more swimming pools. From their casinos and discos to their fitness centers, everything is bigger and more extravagant than on other ships. You may want to rethink a cruise aboard one of these ships if you like a bit more intimacy, since you'll be joined by up to 3,000 fellow passengers. Keep in mind that megaships are limited to docking at the Royal Navy Dockyard—they are simply too big to slip into the harbors at Hamilton and St. George's.

8

AZAMARA CLUB CRUISES

Designed for exotic, destination-driven itineraries, Azamara offers a more intimate onboard experience, while allowing access to the more unusual ports of call experienced travelers want to visit. The ships are designated resort casual, so there is no necessity to weigh down your luggage with formal attire—even though your butler is on hand to unpack for you if you have booked a suite. Evening entertainment leans toward sophisticated cabaret and jazz. Azamara ships are some of the most smoke-free at sea. Only a single small section in a forward area of the pool deck is designated for smokers. No other areas on the ships allow smoking, including cabins and balconies. Enrichment programs, from culinary demonstrations to seminars by guest speakers and experts on a wide variety of topics, are some of the best on offer.

⊕ *www.azamaraclubcruises.com*

AZAMARA JOURNEY

Between themed parties, concerts, and magic shows, nights are lively aboard *Azamara Journey*. The ship feels comfortable and familiar, with a modest five decks for activities and one staff member to every two guests. Although the price is steep, the longer-than-usual itinerary means you'll get your money's worth.

CARNIVAL CRUISE LINE

The world's largest cruise line originated the Fun Ship concept in 1972 with the relaunch of an aging ocean liner that got stuck on a sandbar during its maiden voyage. Sporting red, white, and blue flared funnels, which are easily recognized from afar, new ships are continuously added to the fleet and rarely deviate from a successful pattern.

Cabins are spacious and comfortable, often larger than on other ships in this price category, and feature the Carnival Comfort Bed sleep system consisting of plush mattresses, luxury duvets, high-quality linens, and cushy pillows. Ship decor on many ships is undergoing a softening and modernizing while new features including new pub, rum- and tequila based pool bars, a Guy Fieri hamburger restaurant, and comedy clubs have been added to most ships. Carnival ships have both flexible dining options and casual alternative restaurants, and the quality of the food is good for a mainstream cruise line.

⊕ *www.carnival.com*

CARNIVAL SUNSHINE

Constructed in 1996 and completely overhauled in 2013, the mid-sized *Carnival Sunshine* is geared toward family fun. As with all Carnival ships, the kid offerings are outstanding, including camps, clubs, gaming, movies, and more. Try your hand at mini-golf and grab a snack at Food Network star Guy Fieri's Burger Joint, then escape to the adults-only Serenity retreat, complete with a pool, bar, and waterfall.

CARNIVAL PRIDE

A dramatic 11-story atrium with dazzling lights and Renaissance-style murals sets the tone for an eye-catching and jaw-dropping experience aboard the *Carnival Pride*. While the complimentary dining options are limited, the ship offers a handful of a la carte and reservations-only alternatives. Happily, activities are plentiful; kids love the poolside theater and sky-high waterpark, while adults will enjoy nightly game shows and the EA-branded Sports Bar.

CARNIVAL HORIZON

The brand new *Carnival Horizon*, which debuted in early 2018, takes fun to a whole new level with bowling, mini-golf, and two theaters, one IMAX and one 3D. Kids will be thrilled to find not only a Dr. Seuss-themed waterpark but a pedal-powered SkyRide high above the Lido deck. Food and drink options are endless, whether you're in the mood for a sit-down dinner, or a handcrafted Cuban cocktail at the Havana Bar & Pool.

CARNIVAL CONQUEST

Poolside fun in the sun is the name of the game aboard the *Carnival Conquest*. Retreat and refuel at one of the dozens of bars and lounges, then head to the 15,000-square-foot health and fitness center to work out, refresh, and do it all over again. Impressive decor features famous paintings and sculptures and the Pissaro Art Gallery is a sight to behold.

CARNIVAL ECSTACY

A dramatic 11-story atrium with dazzling lights and Renaissance-style murals sets the tone for an eye-catching and jaw-dropping experience aboard the *Carnival Ecstacy*. While the complimentary dining options are limited, the ship offers a handful of a la carte and reservations-only alternatives. Happily, activities are plentiful; kids love the poolside theater and sky-high waterpark, while adults will enjoy nightly game shows and the EA-branded Sports Bar.

CARNIVAL ELATION

With three pools, a 9-hole mini-golf course, and a 24-hour pizzeria, it's no surprise that *Carnival Elation* is a hit with families. The ship hosts a variety of clubs and events geared at occupying your kids while you explore the casino or attend a late-night comedy show. Two new eateries, including celebrity chef Guy Fieri's Burger Joint, round out a modest selection of restaurants serving delicious—and complimentary—meals.

CELEBRITY CRUISES

Founded in 1989, Celebrity has gained a reputation for fine food and professional service. The cruise line has built premium, sophisticated ships and developed signature amenities, including a specialty coffee shop, martini bar, large standard staterooms with generous storage, spas, and butler service for passengers booking the top suites. Concierge-class makes certain premium ocean-view and balcony staterooms almost the equivalent of suites in terms of amenities and service. Entertainment choices range from Broadway-style productions, captivating lounge shows, and lively discos to Monte Carlo–style casinos and specialty lounges. Multimillion-dollar art collections grace the entire fleet, and each ship in the fleet has distinguished culinary programs headed by executive chefs and food and beverage managers, who have developed their skills in some of the world's finest restaurants and hotels. Alternative restaurants offer fine dining, but most have an average $40 per-person supplement, much higher than on most other cruise lines.

⊕ *www.celebritycruises.com*

CELEBRITY SUMMIT

Outstanding culinary options and an alfresco Rooftop Terrace make the 2,158-passenger *Celebrity Summit* a popular choice among laid-back foodies who enjoy creative cuisine. The older vessel received a well-needed update in 2016, though it still feels a bit dated in comparison to other modern day mega-ships. Kid programs and activities are modest as are most cabins; upgrade to a suite for personalized butler service and exclusive lounge and restaurant access.

DISNEY CRUISE LINE

Disney Cruise Line launched its ships in 1998 and 1999, and expanded the fleet with a third ship in 2011; a fourth entered service in 2012. Dozens of the best ship designers, industry veterans, and Disney creative minds planned intensely for multiple years to produce these vessels, which make a positive impression on adults and children alike. Exteriors are reminiscent of the great ocean liners of the early 20th century, resplendent with two funnels and black hulls, but interiors are technologically up-to-the-minute and full of novel developments in dining, cabin, and entertainment facilities. Accommodations are especially family-friendly, and most have a split-bathroom configuration with a sink and bathtub in one section and a sink and toilet in the other.

Entertainment leans heavily on popular Disney themes and characters. Parents are actively involved in the audience with their children at shows, movies, "live" character meetings, deck parties, and dancing in the family nightclub. Teens have a supervised, no-adults-allowed club space. For adults, there are no-kids-allowed bars and lounges with live music, dancing, theme parties, and late-night comedy as well as daytime wine-tasting sessions, game shows, culinary-arts and home-entertaining demonstrations, and behind-the-scenes lectures.

Don't expect top chefs and gourmet food; the fare is all-American for the most part. In a novel twist on dining, passengers "rotate" between theme dining rooms, accompanied each night by their waitstaff. Palo, the adults-only Italian restaurant on each ship, requires reservations and has a cover charge. Unlike on many cruise lines, fountain drinks at beverage stations and in dining rooms are complimentary.

⊕ *disneycruise.disney.go.com*

DISNEY MAGIC

Entertainment for all ages is the name of the game aboard the *Disney Magic* by Disney Cruise Line. Kids enjoy a variety of clubs, activities, and a poolside theater; although there's no casino, parents will find plenty of amusement with the live music and family friendly Broadway shows. The 964-foot ship sports 11 decks, three pools, and lighthearted fairy tale-themed decor for a truly magical vacation.

HOLLAND AMERICA LINE

Founded in 1873, Holland America Line (HAL) is one of the oldest names in cruising. Its cruises are classic, conservative affairs renowned for their grace and gentility. As its ships attract a more youthful clientele, Holland America has taken steps to shed its "old folks" image and now offers trendier cuisine, a culinary arts center, and an expanded children's program. Still, these are not party cruises, and Holland America has managed to preserve the refined and relaxing qualities that have always been its hallmark, even on sailings that cater more to younger passengers and families.

Luxury bedding, magnifying makeup mirrors, robes, fresh-fruit baskets, flat-screen TVs, and DVD players are found in all cabins. In addition, suites have duvets, fully stocked minibars, personalized stationery, and access to the exclusive Neptune Lounge. Explorations Café, powered by the New York Times, combines a coffee bar, computer center with Wi-Fi, and cozy library–reading room complete with tabletop versions of the Times crossword puzzles.

Food quality is generally good. In the reservations-required Pinnacle Grill, fresh seafood and premium cuts of beef are used to prepare creative specialty dishes. Canaletto Restaurant serves Italian favorites for dinner with a $10–$15 cover charge. Delicious onboard traditions are afternoon tea, a Dutch Chocolate Extravaganza, and Holland America Line's signature bread pudding.

⊕ *www.hollandamerica.com*

VEENDAM

The petite yet elegant *Veendam* may be on the older side, but it has one major advantage over its oversized kin: it docks in Hamilton, Bermuda's capital. Guests enjoy a wide variety of unique onboard activities from cooking classes with America's Test Kitchen to digital workshops. Renovations in 2009 brought the 1,350-passenger ship up to speed, with new cabins, modernized decor, and improved nightly entertainment.

NORWEGIAN CRUISE LINE

Norwegian Cruise Line (NCL) was established in 1966, when one of Norway's oldest and most respected shipping companies, Oslo-based Klosters Rederi A/S, acquired the *Sunward* and repositioned the ship from Europe to the then-obscure Port of Miami. With the formation of a company called Norwegian Caribbean Lines, the cruise industry as we know it today was born. NCL launched an entirely new concept with its regularly scheduled cruises to the Caribbean on a single-class ship. No longer simply a means of transportation, the ship became a destination unto itself, offering guests an affordable alternative to land-based resorts.

Always a cruise-industry innovator, Norwegian Cruise Line's Freestyle cruising introduced a wider variety of dining options in a casual, free-flowing atmosphere. Noted for top-quality, high-energy entertainment and emphasis on fitness facilities and programs, NCL combines action, activities, and a resort-casual atmosphere.

Main dining rooms serve what is traditionally deemed Continental fare, although in terms of quality it's about what you would expect at a really good hotel banquet. Where NCL stands above the ordinary is in their specialty restaurants, especially the French–Mediterranean Le Bistro (on all ships), the Pan-Asian restaurants, and steak houses (on the newer ships). In addition, you may find an Italian trattoria. Most, but not all, specialty restaurants carry a cover charge and require reservations.

⊕ *www.ncl.com*

NORWEGIAN DAWN

With over a dozen different dining options, three pools, and nightly packed-house entertainment, there's never a shortage of things to do onboard the *Norwegian Dawn*. The lively 2,340-passenger ship fosters a real party atmosphere for kids and adults of all ages. With the variety of cabin types, cruising can fit any budget; just be careful of upcharges, as there are plenty of add-ons available—from food to gaming—that can be hard to resist.

NORWEGIAN BREAKAWAY

As far as mega-ships go, *Norwegian Breakaway* is among the biggest and most extravagant. The floating metropolis dazzles its 3,969 guests with endless options for eating, drinking, and, most importantly, fun. The ship boasts over 25 dining experiences, five multi-story waterslides, mini-golf, and a sports complex unlike any other on the open sea.

NORWEGIAN ESCAPE

Added to the fleet in 2015, the 1,069-foot, 20-deck *Norwegian Escape* entertains a whopping 5,400 passengers. Adults will love the variety of nightly entertainment, lounges, and bars, including Jimmy Buffet's Margaritaville at Sea. Expect plenty of kids though, since the ship is very family friendly, with multiple pools, an outdoor sports complex, and an aqua park.

OCEANIA CRUISES

This distinctive cruise line, founded by cruise-industry veterans with the know-how to satisfy inquisitive passengers with interesting ports of call and upscale touches for fares much lower than you would expect, is owned by Prestige Cruise Holdings. Oceania uses midsize "R-class" ships from the long-defunct Renaissance Cruises fleet, and launched a new ship class in 2011. Varied, destination-rich itineraries are an important characteristic of Oceania Cruises, and most Caribbean sailings are in the 10- to 12-night range. Before arrival in ports of call, lectures are presented on the historical background, culture, and traditions of the islands.

Intimate and cozy public spaces reflect the importance of socializing on Oceania ships. Evening entertainment leans toward light cabaret, solo artists, music for dancing, and conversation with fellow passengers; however, you'll find lively karaoke sessions as well. On sea days jazz or easy-listening melodies are played poolside.

Master chef Jacques Pépin designed the menus for Oceania, and the results are sure to please the most discriminating palate. Oceania simply serves some of the best food at sea, particularly impressive for a cruise line that charges far less than luxury rates. The main open seating restaurant offers trendy French-Continental cuisine with an always-on-the-menu steak, seafood, or poultry choice and vegetarian option. Intimate specialty restaurants require reservations, but there is no additional charge. Unlimited soft drinks, bottled water, specialty coffees and teas, and juices are complimentary.

⊕ *www.oceaniacruises.com*

SIRENA

Updated in 2016, *Sirena* offers a refined and luxurious cruising experience with a price tag to match. The small 684-passenger ship attracts an older demographic, boasting six restaurants, putting greens, and adult entertainment, including comedians and classical concerts. In addition to world-class dining, guests enjoy personalized service and an intimate, country club casual atmosphere.

REGENT SEVEN SEAS CRUISES

Regent Seven Seas Cruises sails an elegant fleet of vessels that offer a nearly all-inclusive cruise experience (including shore excursions) in sumptuous, contemporary surroundings. The line's spacious ocean-view staterooms have the industry's highest percentage of private balconies, and almost all drinks (except some premium brands) are now included.

Subtle improvements throughout the fleet have resulted in features such as Wi-Fi capability and cell phone access. New luxury bedding, Regent-branded bath amenities, flatscreen TVs, DVD players, and new clocks (a real rarity on cruise ships) have been added to all cabins. Top suites also feature iPods and Bose speakers. The ships offer exquisite service, generous staterooms with abundant amenities, a variety of dining options, and superior enrichment programs. Cruises are destination-focused, and most sailings host guest lecturers—historians, anthropologists, naturalists, and diplomats.

Menus may appear to include the usual cruise-ship staples, but the results are some of the most outstanding meals at sea. Specialty dining varies within the fleet; when available, the sophisticated Signatures features the cuisine of Le Cordon Bleu of Paris; Prime 7 offers menus that rival the finest shoreside steak and seafood restaurants. In addition, Mediterranean-inspired bistro dinners are served in the daytime casual Lido buffet restaurants. Wines chosen to complement dinner menus are freely poured each evening.

⊕ *www.oceaniacruises.com*

SEVEN SEAS NAVIGATOR

Sleek and contemporary, thanks to a 2016 refurbishment, *Seven Seas Navigator* is the definition of personalized cruising. The 490-passenger vessel offers 245 spacious ocean-view suites and attracts well-traveled and well-to-do guests. Exciting multi-port itineraries make up for the rather limited dining options and small public areas.

ROYAL CARIBBEAN

Big, bigger, biggest! More than a decade ago, Royal Caribbean launched the first of the modern mega-cruise ships for passengers who enjoy traditional cruising with a touch of daring and whimsy tossed in. These large-to-giant vessels are indoor–outdoor wonders, with every conceivable activity in a resortlike atmosphere, including atrium lobbies, shopping arcades, large spas, expansive sundecks, and rock-climbing walls. Several ships have such elaborate facilities as 18-hole miniature-golf courses and ice-skating rinks. Oasis-class ships, RCI's largest ships, even have surf parks and a zip-line at sea. Plush new bedding has been installed fleet-wide.

8

The centerpiece of Royal Caribbean mega-ships is the multideck atrium, a hallmark that has been duplicated by many other cruise lines. The brilliance of this design is that all the major public rooms radiate from this central point, so you can learn your way around these huge ships within minutes of boarding. Ships in the Vision class are especially bright and airy, with sea views almost anywhere you happen to be. The main problem with RCI's otherwise well-conceived vessels is that there are often too many people on board, making embarkation, tendering, and disembarkation exasperating. However, Royal Caribbean is still one of the best-run and most popular cruise lines.

Royal Caribbean has made great strides in its food offerings. Although Royal Caribbean doesn't place emphasis on celebrity chefs, the line has introduced a more intimate dinner experience in the form of Italian specialty restaurants and steak houses on most ships and has been adding more specialty dining choices fleet-wide.

🌐 *www.oceaniacruises.com*

ANTHEM OF THE SEAS

Entertainment abounds aboard the impressive and technologically savvy *Anthem of the Seas*. The 4,180-passenger ship offers flexible dining options, unique aerial performance shows, and plenty for thrill-seekers, including a skydiving simulator, roller rink, waterpark, and bumper cars. Of the 2,090 cabins, 375 have virtual "balconies," with floor-to-ceiling screens streaming live video of the world outside.

GRANDEUR OF THE SEAS

Affordable cabins and a long list of kid programs make the *Grandeur of the Seas* a popular choice for families. Refurbished in 2012, the 2,446-passenger ship features new specialty dining options, updated cabins, a rock-climbing wall, and a glitzy six-story atrium. Flex your competitive muscles in a variety of onboard activities, from good-natured sporting tournaments to trivia nights and casino contests.

SERENADE OF THE SEAS

The sleek *Serenade of the Seas* emphasizes panoramic views with its impressive glass decor. The mid-sized ship houses 2,501 guests, appealing to all ages with a variety of gaming, sports, fitness, and shopping experiences. The after-hours scene is particularly lively thanks to the expansive casino, entertaining dance parties, and ever-popular rotating Vortex Nightclub on deck 13.

SILVERSEA CRUISES

Intimate ships, paired with exclusive amenities and unparalleled hospitality, are the hallmarks of Silversea luxury cruises. Personalization is a Silversea maxim. Ships offer more activities than other comparably sized luxury vessels, with guest lecturers on nearly every cruise. A multi-tiered show lounge is the setting for classical concerts, big-screen movies, and folkloric entertainers from ashore. All accommodations are spacious outside suites—most with private verandas. Silversea ships have large swimming pools in expansive Lidos. Silversea's third generation of ships introduced even more luxurious features when the 36,000-ton *Silver Spirit* launched late in 2009.

Although these ships schedule more activities than other comparably sized luxury vessels, you can either take part or opt instead for a good book and any number of quiet spots to read or snooze in the shade. Silversea is so all-inclusive that you'll find your room key/charge card is seldom used for anything but opening your suite door.

Dishes from the galleys of Silversea's master chefs are complemented by those of La Collection du Monde, created by Silversea's culinary partner, Relais & Châteaux. Perhaps more compelling is the line's flair for originality. Nightly alternative-theme dinners in La Terrazza (by day, the buffet restaurant) feature regional specialties from the Mediterranean; an intimate dining experience aboard each vessel is Le Champagne—the Wine Restaurant, which is the only Relais & Châteaux restaurant at sea.

🌐 *www.oceaniacruises.com*

SILVER WHISPER

Sophisticated elegance and personalized service await aboard the all-inclusive *Silver Whisper*. Accommodating fewer than 400 guests, the ship emphasizes pampering and relaxation, with extra-long spa treatments and six-course dinners. The all-suite accommodations are pricey, but you get what you pay for: tasteful decor, marble bathrooms, and even your own personal butler.

VIKING OCEAN CRUISES

More widely known for their river cruises in Europe and Asia, Viking debuted Viking Ocean Cruises with their first ship in 2015. Focused on destination-centric cruising with onboard enrichment offerings, the line includes one complimentary shore experience in each port of call. The 928-passenger, all-veranda ships have a Nordic-inspired spa, gym and yoga area, and two pools—including an infinity pool at the back of the ship and a main pool with retractable dome. Onboard amenities include a piano bar, show lounge, cinema, well-stocked library, and boutiques. Internet with Wi-Fi and laundry service are complimentary, as are all soft drinks, specialty coffees and teas, and round-the-clock room service. Wraparound promenade decks are ideal for walking or jogging.

Each ship has a variety of restaurants offering menu choices from regional specialties to heart-healthy options and American classics, as well as more alfresco dining than any other ship at sea. The Restaurant offers a daily-changing menu that highlights fresh local ingredients. The Chef's Table features a curated tasting menu with wine pairings, and the Italian Grill selections include Tuscan favorites. Each meal is accompanied by complimentary tea or coffee, and lunch and dinner service includes complimentary soft drinks, house wine, and beer. There is no reservation fee for any restaurant.

🌐 *www.oceaniacruises.com*

VIKING SEA

Newly christened in 2016, *Viking Sea* is destination-centric, offering longer, multi-stop itineraries and one complimentary excursion per port. Guests must be 16 years of age to sail, though most passengers are 55 or older. In addition to the impeccably outfitted 465 all-balcony rooms and suites, the vessel boasts top-of-the-line amenities, including a Nordic-inspired spa, an open-air gym, and a stunning infinity pool at the rear of the ship.

BEFORE YOU GO

To expedite your preboarding paperwork, most cruise lines have convenient forms on their websites. As long as you have your reservation number, you can provide the required immigration information, reserve shore excursions, and even indicate special requests from the comfort of your home. Less

"wired" cruise lines might mail preboarding paperwork to you or your travel agent for completion after you make your final payment and request that you return the forms by mail or fax. No matter how you submit them, be sure to make copies of any forms you fill out and to bring them with you to the pier to shorten the check-in process.

TRAVEL DOCUMENTS

After you make the final payment to your travel agent, the cruise line will issue your cruise tickets and vouchers for airport-to-ship transfers, or you may be able to print them yourself from the line's website. Depending on the airline, and whether you have purchased an air-sea package, you may receive your flight reservations or e-ticket vouchers at the same time; you may also receive vouchers for shore excursions, although cruise lines generally issue these aboard ship. Should your travel documents not arrive when promised, contact your travel agent or call the cruise line.

Children under the age of 18 who are not traveling with both parents almost always require a letter of permission from the absent parent(s). Airlines, cruise lines, and immigration agents can deny minor children initial boarding or entry to foreign countries without proper proof of identification and citizenship *and* a permission letter from absent or noncustodial parents. Your travel agent or cruise line can help with the wording of such a letter.

A WORD ABOUT PASSPORTS

It is every passenger's responsibility to have proper identification. If you arrive at the embarkation port without it, you will not be allowed to board, and the cruise line will issue no fare refund. Most travel agents know the requirements and can guide you to the proper agency to obtain what you need if you don't have it.

WHAT TO PACK

Cruise wear falls into three categories: casual, informal, and formal. Cruise documents should include information indicating how many evenings fall into each category. You will know when to wear what by reading your ship's daily newsletter—each evening's dress code will be prominently announced.

Time spent ashore touring and shopping calls for shorts topped with T-shirts or polo shirts and comfy walking shoes. In Summer, forget denim, which is too hot, and concentrate on lighter fabrics that will breathe in the heat. Winter months tend to be windy and rainy, so pack a jacket. If you plan to hit the beach, we recommend bringing at least two swimsuits so that you can wear one while the other is drying back in your cabin. Cruises typically allow you to take towels off the boat, but you'll want a coverup as well as sandals or flip-flops. At night, casual means khaki-type slacks and polo or sport shirts for men and sundresses, skirts, or casual pants outfits for women. Golfers should be aware that many golf courses also have dress codes.

Informal dress—sometimes called "resort casual" or "country club casual"—is a little trickier. It applies only to evening wear and can mean different things depending on the cruise line. Informal for women is a dressier dress or pants outfit; for men it almost always includes a sport coat, and a tie is optional. Check your documents carefully.

Formal night means dressing up, but these days even that is a relative notion. You'll see women in everything from simple cocktail dresses to elaborate, glittering gowns. A tuxedo (either all black or with white dinner jacket) or dark suit is required for gentlemen. For children, Sunday best is entirely appropriate.

Men can usually rent their formal attire from the cruise line, and if they do so, it will be waiting when they board. Be sure to make these arrangements in advance; your travel agent can get the details from the cruise line. But if you're renting a tux, buy your own studs: a surefire way to spot a rented tuxedo is by the inexpensive studs that come with it.

An absolute essential for women is a shawl or light sweater. Aggressive air-conditioning can make public rooms uncomfortable, particularly if you're sunburned from a day at the beach.

Put things you can't do without—such as prescription medication, spare eyeglasses, toiletries, a swimsuit, and change of clothes for the first day—in your carry-on. Most cruise ships provide soap, shampoo, and conditioner.

ON BOARD

As you settle in, check out your cabin to make sure that everything is in order. Try the plumbing and set the air-conditioning to the temperature you prefer. Your cabin may feel warm while docked but will cool off when the ship is underway. You should find a copy of the ship's daily schedule in the cabin. Take a few moments to look it over—you'll want to know what time the muster drill takes place (a placard on the back of your cabin door will indicate directions to your emergency station), as well as meal hours and the schedule for various activities and entertainments.

Rented tuxedos are either hanging in the closet or will be delivered sometime during the afternoon; bon-voyage gifts sent by your friends or travel agent usually appear as well. Be patient if you're expecting deliveries, particularly on megaships. Cabin stewards participate in the ship's turnaround and are extremely busy, although yours will no doubt introduce himself at the first available opportunity. It will also be a while before your checked luggage arrives, so your initial order of business is usually the buffet if you haven't already had lunch. Bring along the daily schedule to examine in detail while you eat.

CRIME ON BOARD

Crime aboard cruise ships has occasionally become headline news, thanks in large part to a few well-publicized cases. Most people never have any type of problem, but you should exercise the same precautions aboard ship that you would at home. Keep your valuables out of sight—on big ships virtually every cabin has a small safe in the cabin. Don't carry too much cash ashore, use your credit card whenever possible, and keep your money in a secure place, such as a front pocket that's harder to pick. Single women traveling with friends should stick together, especially when returning to their cabins late at night. When assaults occur, it often comes to light that alcohol, particularly overindulgence in alcohol, is a factor. Be careful about whom you befriend, as you would anywhere, whether it's a fellow passenger or a member of the crew. Don't be paranoid, but do be prudent.

Your cruise is a wonderful opportunity to leave everyday responsibilities behind, but don't neglect to pack your common sense. After a few drinks it might seem like a good idea to sit on a railing or lean over to get a better view of the ship's wake. Passengers have been known to fall. "Man overboard" is more likely to be the result of carelessness than criminal intent.

Do your plans for the cruise include booking shore excursions and indulging in spa treatments? The most popular tours sometimes sell out, and spas can be very busy during sea days, so your next stops should be the shore-excursion desk to book tours and the spa to make appointments if you haven't already done so online. You may even want to take care of those tasks on the way to the buffet.

Dining-room seating arrangements are another matter for consideration. Some people like to check the main dining room to determine where their table is located. If it's not to your liking, or if you requested a large table and find yourself assigned to a small one, you'll want to see the headwaiter. He'll be stationed in a lounge with his charts handy to make changes. The daily schedule will indicate where and when to meet with him. If you plan to dine in the ship's specialty restaurant, make those reservations as soon as possible to avoid disappointment.

PAYING FOR THINGS ON BOARD

Let's step back a moment and take a look at what happened when you checked in at the pier. Because a cashless society prevails on cruise ships, an imprint was made of your credit card or you had to place a cash deposit for use against your onboard charges. Then you were issued a charge card that usually doubles as your stateroom key. Most onboard expenditures are charged to your shipboard account with your signature as verification, with the possible exception of casino gaming—even so, you can often get cash advances against your account from the casino cashier.

An itemized bill is provided at the end of the voyage listing your purchases. In order to avoid surprises, it's a good idea to set aside your charge slips and request an interim printout of your bill from the purser to ensure accuracy. On some ships you can even access your account on your stateroom TV. Should you change your mind about charging onboard purchases, you can always inform the purser and pay in cash or traveler's checks instead. If your cash deposit was more than you spent, you'll receive a refund.

TIPPING

One of the most delicate—yet frequently debated—topics of conversation among cruise passengers involves the matter of tipping. Who do you tip? How much? What's "customary" and "recommended?" Should parents tip the full amount for children or is just half adequate? Why do you have to tip at all?

When transfers to and from your ship are a part of your air and sea program, gratuities are generally included for luggage handling. In that case, do not worry about the interim tipping. However, if you take a taxi to the pier and hand over your bags to a stevedore, be sure to tip him. Treat him with respect and pass along at least $5.

During your cruise, room-service waiters generally receive a cash tip of $1 to $3 per delivery. A 15% gratuity will automatically be added to each bar bill during the cruise. If you use salon and spa services, a similar percentage might be added to the bills there as well. If you dine in a specialty restaurant, it may be suggested that you extend a onetime gratuity for the service staff.

There will be a "disembarkation talk" on the last day of the cruise that explains tipping procedures. If you're expected to tip in cash, which is increasingly rare these days, small white tip envelopes will appear in your stateroom that day. If you tip in cash, you usually give the tip envelope directly to each person on the last night of the cruise. Tips generally add up to about $12 to $16 per person (including children) per day.

Most lines now either automatically add gratuities to passengers' onboard charge accounts or offer the option. If that suits you, then do nothing further. However, you're certainly free to adjust the amounts up or down to more appropriate levels or ask that the charge be removed altogether if you prefer distributing cash gratuities.

DINING

All food, all the time? Not quite, but it's possible to literally eat away the day and most of the night on a cruise. A popular cruise directors' joke is, "You came on as passengers, and you will be leaving as cargo." Although it's meant in fun, it does contain an element of truth. Food—tasty and plentiful—is available 24 hours a day on most cruise ships, and the dining experience at sea has reached almost mythical proportions. Perhaps it has something to do with legendary midnight buffets, the absence of menu prices, or maybe it's the vast selection and availability.

RESTAURANTS

Every ship has at least one main restaurant and a Lido, or casual, buffet alternative. Increasingly important are specialty restaurants. Meals in the primary and buffet restaurants are included in the cruise fare, as is round-the-clock room service on most lines, with Royal Caribbean being the exception—while room service is available 24 hours, there is an automatic per-order charge after midnight. Midday tea and snacks, and late-night buffets are also complimentary on ships that offer them. Most mainstream cruise lines levy a surcharge for dining in alternative restaurants that may, or may not, also include a gratuity, although there generally is no additional charge on luxury cruise lines.

> **GOOD TO KNOW**
>
> It isn't stinginess on the part of the cruise line that forbids bringing snacks ashore. Fruits, vegetables, seeds, plants, and meat are not allowed to be removed from the ship by regulation of the Bermuda government.

You may also find a pizzeria or a specialty coffee bar on your ship—popular favorites cropping up on ships old and new. Pizza is complimentary, but expect an additional charge for specialty coffees at the coffee bar and, quite likely, in the dining room as well. You'll also be charged for alcoholic beverages and soft drinks during meals; iced tea, regular coffee, tap water, and fruit juice are the most common complimentary beverages.

SEATINGS

If your cruise ship has traditional seatings for dinner, the one decision that may set the tone for your entire cruise is your dinner seating. Which is best? Early dinner seating is generally scheduled between 6 and 6:30 pm, and late seating can begin from 8:15 to 8:45 pm. So the "best" seating depends on you, your lifestyle, and your personal preference.

Families with young children and older passengers often choose an early seating. Early seating diners are encouraged not to linger too long over dessert and coffee because the dining room has to be readied for late seating. Late seating is viewed by some passengers as more romantic and less rushed.

Cruise lines understand that strict schedules no longer satisfy the desires of all cruise passengers. Most cruise lines now include alternatives to the set schedules in the dining room, including an open seating option, and casual dinner menus in their buffet facilities, where more flexibility is allowed in dress and meal times. À la carte restaurants are showing up on more ships and offer yet another choice, though usually for an additional charge.

Open seating is primarily associated with more upscale lines; it allows passengers the flexibility to dine any time during restaurant hours and be seated with whomever they please.

CHANGING TABLES

Most cruise lines advise that, although dining preferences may be requested by your travel agent, no requests are guaranteed. Table assignments are generally not confirmed until embarkation; however, every effort is made to satisfy all guests. If there's a problem, see the headwaiter for assistance. Changes after the first evening are generally discouraged; however, there will be a designated place to meet with dining-room staff and iron out seating problems during embarkation day. Check the daily program or ask at the reception desk for the time and location.

SPECIAL DIETS

Cruise lines make every possible attempt to ensure dining satisfaction. If you have special dietary considerations—such as low-salt, kosher, or food allergies—be sure to indicate them well ahead of time and check to be certain your needs are known by your waiter once you're on board. In addition to the usual menu items, spa, low-calorie, low-carbohydrate, or low-fat selections, as well as children's menus, are usually available. Requests for dishes not featured on the menu can often be granted if you ask in advance.

THE CAPTAIN'S TABLE

Legend has it that a nouveau-riche passenger's response to an invitation to dine with the captain during a round-the-world cruise was, "I didn't shell out all those bucks to eat with the help!" Although there are some cruise passengers who decline invitations to dine at the captain's table, there are far more who relish such an experience. You will know you have been included in that exclusive coterie when an embossed invitation arrives in your stateroom on the day of a formal dinner. RSVP as soon as possible—if you are unable to attend, someone else will be invited in your place.

Who is invited? If you're a frequent cruiser, occupy an owner's suite, or if you hail from the captain's hometown and speak his native language, you may be considered. Honeymoon couples are sometimes selected at random, as are couples celebrating a golden wedding anniversary. Unattached female passengers often round out an uneven number of guests. Requests made by travel agents on behalf of their clients sometimes do the trick.

ENTERTAINMENT

It's hard to imagine, but in the early years of cruise travel shipboard entertainment consisted of little more than poetry readings and recitals that exhibited the talents of fellow passengers. Those bygone days of sedate amusements in an intimate setting have been replaced by lavish showrooms where sequined and feathered showgirls strut their stuff on stage amid previously unimagined special effects.

Seven-night Bermuda cruises usually include two original production shows. One of these might be a Las Vegas–style extravaganza and the other a best-of-Broadway show featuring old and new favorites from the Great White Way. Other shows highlight the talents of individual singers, dancers, magicians, comedians, and even acrobats. Don't be surprised if you're plucked from the audience to take the brunt of a comedian's jokes or act as the magician's temporary assistant. Sit in the front row if appearing onstage appeals to you.

Whether it's relegated to a late-afternoon interlude between bingo and dinner or a featured evening highlight, the passenger talent show is often a "don't miss" production. From pure camp to stylishly slick, what passes for talent is sometimes surprising but seldom boring. Stand-up comedy is generally discouraged; however, passengers who want their

DRINKING ON BOARD

The ship's bars are often the social centers, but alcoholic drinks are not usually included in your cruise fare, and bar bills can add up quickly. Drinks at the captain's welcome-aboard cocktail party and at cocktail parties held specifically for repeat cruisers are usually free. But if you pick up that boldly colored welcome-aboard cocktail as your ship pulls away from the dock, you may well be asked to sign for it, and the cost will then be added to your shipboard account. You should expect to pay about the same for a drink on board a cruise ship as you would pay in a bar at home: $6 to $8 for a domestic beer, $8 to $10 for a cocktail, $8 to $14 for a glass of wine, $2 to $3 for a soft drink. On virtually all ships an automatic 15% gratuity will be added to your tab. Also note that specialty coffees like cappuccino—even in the dining room after dinner—will add a $3 to $4 charge to your onboard account. To save money on your bar bill, you can follow a few simple strategies. In lounges, request the less expensive bar brands or the reduced-price drink of the day. On some ships, discounted "beverage cards" for unlimited fountain soft drinks and/or a set number of mixed drinks are available.

In international waters there are, technically, no laws against teenage drinking, but almost all ships require passengers to be over 21 to purchase alcoholic beverages.

performance skills to be considered should answer the call for auditions and plan to rehearse the show at least once.

LOUNGES AND NIGHTCLUBS

If you find the show-lounge stage a bit intimidating and want to perform in a more intimate venue, look for karaoke. Singing along in a piano bar is another shipboard favorite for would-be crooners.

Other lounges might feature easy-listening music, jazz, or combos for pre- and postdinner social dancing. Later in the evening, lounges pick up the pace with music from the 1950s and '60s; clubs aimed at a younger crowd usually have more contemporary dance music during the late-night hours.

CASINOS

A sure sign that your ship is in international waters is the opening of the casino.

The rationale for locating casinos where most passengers must pass either through or alongside them is obvious—the unspoken allure of winning. In addition to slot machines in a variety of denominations, cruise-ship casinos might feature roulette, craps, and a variety of poker games—Caribbean stud poker, Let It Ride, Texas Hold 'Em, and black-jack, to name a few. Cruise lines strive to provide fair and professional gambling entertainment and supply gaming guides that set out the rules of play and betting limits for each game.

Casino hours vary based on the itinerary or location of the ship; as of October 2013, onboard casinos can remain open while docked in Bermuda so long as ships are in port for at least one night. Every casino has a cashier for convenience, and you may be able to charge a cash advance to your onboard account.

OTHER ENTERTAINMENT

Most vessels have a room for screening movies. On older ships and some newer ones, this is often a genuine movie theater; on other ships it may be a multipurpose room or even a giant screen on the Lido deck. Over the course of a weeklong voyage a dozen films may be screened, each repeated several times. Traditional theaters are also used for lectures, religious services, and private meetings.

With a few exceptions, cruise ships equip their cabins with closed-circuit TVs showing movies (continuously on some newer ships), shipboard lectures, and regular programs (thanks to satellite reception). Ships with in-cabin VCRs or DVDs usually provide a selection of movies at no charge (a deposit is sometimes required).

Most medium-size and large ships have video arcades, and nearly all ships now have computer centers and feature Wi-Fi—either bow-to-stern or in hot spots.

SPAS

With all the usual pampering and service in luxurious surroundings, simply being on a cruise can be a stress-reducing experience. Add to that the menu of spa and salon services at your fingertips and you have a recipe for total sensory pleasure. The spas have become among the most popular of shipboard services, so book your bliss time as soon as possible. Some cruise lines allow you to book services in advance.

Some of the more exotic spa offerings sound good enough to eat. A Milk and Honey Hydrotherapy Bath; Coconut Rub & Milk Ritual Wrap or Float; and a Javanese Steam Wrap incorporating cinnamon, ginger, coffee, sea salt, and honey are just a few of the tempting items found on spa menus. Not quite as exotic sounding, other treatments and services are nonetheless therapeutic for the body and soul. Steiner Leisure is the largest spa and salon operator at sea (the company even operates the Mandara and the Greenhouse spas), with facilities on more than 100 cruise ships worldwide.

In addition to facials, manicures, pedicures, massages, and sensual body treatments, other hallmarks of Steiner Leisure are salon services and products for hair and skin. Founded in 1901 by Henry Steiner of London, a single salon prospered when Steiner's son joined the business in 1926 and was granted a royal warrant as hairdresser to Queen Mary in 1937. In 1956 Steiner won its first cruise-ship contract, to operate salons on Cunard Line ships. By the mid-1990s, Steiner Leisure began taking an active role in creating shipboard spas offering a wide variety of wellness therapies and beauty programs for both women and men.

SPORTS AND FITNESS

Onboard sports facilities might include a court for basketball, volleyball, tennis—or all three—a jogging track, or even an in-line skating track. Some Royal Caribbean ships offer such innovative and unexpected features as rock-climbing walls and ice-skating rinks. For the less adventurous, there's always table tennis and shuffleboard.

Naturally, you can find at least one swimming pool, and possibly several. Cruise-ship pools are generally on the small side—more appropriate for cooling off than doing laps—and the majority contain filtered saltwater. But some are elaborate affairs, with waterslides.

Golf is a perennial seagoing favorite of players who want to take their games to the next level and add Bermuda's most beautiful and challenging courses to their scorecards. Shipboard programs can include clinics, use of full-motion golf cages, and even individual instruction from resident pros using state-of-the-art computer analysis. Once ashore, escorted excursions include everything needed for a satisfying round of play, including equipment and tips from the pro, and prescheduled tee times at exclusive courses. ■TIP→ **Unless you find avid golfers with firsthand insight into Bermuda courses who are anxious to make up a group from the ship themselves, you may find it more expedient to book golf outings through the cruise line rather than take your chances at locating a course with a convenient tee time, arranging costly transportation, and being paired with strangers. You may not save time or money by letting the cruise line arrange a golf outing; however, when they do it, they handle the details and make sure you return to the ship on time.**

FITNESS CENTERS

Cruise vacations can be hazardous to your waistline if you're not careful. Eating "out" for all meals and sampling different cuisines tends to pile on unaccustomed calories. But shipboard fitness centers have become ever more elaborate, offering state-of-the-art exercise machines, treadmills, and stair steppers, not to mention weights and weight machines. As a bonus, many fitness centers with floor-to-ceiling windows have the world's most inspiring sea views.

If you prefer a more social atmosphere as you burn off sinful chocolate desserts, there are specialized fitness classes for all levels of ability. High-impact, energetic aerobics are not for everyone, but any class that raises the heart rate can be toned down and tailored to individual capabilities. Stretching classes help you warm up for a light jog or brisk walk on deck, and sit-for-fitness classes are offered for mature passengers or those with delicate joints. Fees are sometimes charged for specialty classes, such as Pilates, spinning, and yoga. Most ships have personal trainers on board to get you off on the right foot, also for a fee.

SHIPBOARD SERVICES
LAUNDRY AND DRY CLEANING

Most cruise ships offer valet laundry and pressing (and some also have dry-cleaning) service. Expenses can add up fast, especially for laundry, as charges are per item and the rates are similar to those charged in hotels. If doing laundry is important to you and you do not want to send it out to be done, some cruise ships have a low-cost or free self-service laundry room (they usually feature an iron and ironing board in addition to washer and dryer). If you book one of the top-dollar suites, laundry service may be included for no additional cost. Upscale ships, such as those in the Regent Seven Seas Cruises and Crystal Cruises fleets, have complimentary self-service launderettes. On other lines, such as

Princess Cruises, Carnival Cruise Lines, and Holland America Line's *Veendam,* you can do your own laundry for about $3 or less per load. Ships in the Royal Caribbean fleet and Norwegian Cruise Line vessels sailing to Bermuda do not have self-service laundry facilities.

LIBRARY

Cruise-ship libraries run the gamut from a few shelves of relatively uninspiring titles to huge rooms crammed with volumes of travel guides, classics, and the latest best sellers. As a rule, the smaller the ship, the more likely you are to find a well-stocked library. The space allotted to the library falls in proportion to the emphasis on glitzy stage shows—on small ships the passengers are more likely to lean toward quiet diversions. On ships with sophisticated entertainment centers in staterooms, you may find videotape or DVD movies as well as books in the library.

PHOTO SHOP

A Bermuda cruise is a series of photo opportunities, and ships' photographers are on hand to capture boarding, sail-away, port arrivals, and other highlights, such as the captain's reception. Photographers seem to pop up everywhere and take far more pictures than you could ever want; however, they're a unique remembrance, and there's no obligation to purchase them. Prices for the prints, which are put on display, range from $15 to $29, depending on size.

Film, batteries, single-use cameras, digital storage cards, and related merchandise may also be available in the ship's photo shop. Some ships' photography staffers are capable of processing your film or your digital prints right on board.

SHORE-EXCURSION DESK

Manned by a knowledgeable staff, the shore-excursion desk can offer not only the sale of ship-sponsored tours, but may also be the place to learn more about ports of call and garner information you'll need to tour independently. Although staff members and the focus of their positions vary widely, the least you can expect is basic information and port maps. Happily, some shore-excursion staff members possess a wealth of information and share it without reservation. On some ships the port lecturer may emphasize shopping and "recommended" merchants, with little to impart regarding sightseeing or the history and culture of ports.

SHORE EXCURSIONS

Shore excursions are optional tours organized by the cruise line and sold aboard the ship. Most tours last two to four hours and all are meant to optimize your time on the island—the cruise line does the research about what to see and do, and you just go along for the ride. You'll sometimes pay more for these ship-packaged tours than if you booked them independently, either before you leave home or after arriving in port. However, with only two or three days at your disposal, the convenience, and assurance that a spot on the tour you're looking forward to is available, may be worth the price. Popular tours often sell out and may not be obtainable at any price once you are ashore. Fees are generally $40–$60 per person for walking tours, $45–$85 per person for island tours, $50–$90 for snorkeling trips, and $150–$185 for diving trips. Prices for children are usually less. For exact durations and pricing, consult your cruise line. Also keep in mind that tour fees and time estimates can vary.

Naturally, you're always free to explore on your own. With its excellent taxi service, Bermuda is a good, although pricey, island for hiring a car and driver. Four-seater taxis charge $7.90 for the first mile and $2.75 for each subsequent mile. A personalized taxi tour of the island costs $50 per hour for up to four passengers and $70 an hour for up to seven, excluding tip. If you can round up a group of people, this is often cheaper than an island tour offered by your ship. Tip drivers 5%. Rental cars are prohibited (with the exception of two-person electric cars from Current Vehicles ⊕ *www.currentvehicles.com*), and while you can rent scooters, this can be dangerous for the uninitiated and is not recommended. Public transportation, including buses and ferries, is convenient to all cruise terminals and the sale of all-day passes might even be offered by the shore-excursion desk on your ship. For a full list of transportation options, visit Bermuda Tourism's website at ⊕ *www.gotobermuda.com/what-to-do/transportation*.

GOING ASHORE

Three Bermuda harbors serve cruise ships: Hamilton (the capital), St. George's, and King's Wharf at the Royal Naval Dockyard. In Hamilton, cruise ships tie up right on the city's main street, Front Street. A visitor information center is next to the ferry terminal, also on Front Street and nearby; maps and brochures are displayed in the cruise terminal itself. St. George's accommodates a handful of smaller cruise ships every year at Penno's Wharf, located just minutes from the heart of the city. A visitor information center is at King's Square, near the Town Hall and within walking distance of the pier. King's Wharf, in the Royal Naval Dockyard at the westernmost end of the island, is the busiest of the three cruise-ship berthing areas, and it is where the largest vessels dock. Although Dockyard appears isolated on a map, it is well connected to the rest of the island by taxi, bus, and ferry. Three visitor information centers can be found along the piers and adjacent to the ferry dock.

Before anyone is allowed to proceed down the gangway, however, the ship must be cleared for landing. Immigration and customs officials board the vessel to examine paperwork and sort through red tape. It may be more than an hour before you're allowed ashore. Your ship ID acts as your boarding pass, which you'll need to get back on board. You may also be advised to take a photo ID ashore, such as your passport or driver's license.

A WHOLE NEW WORLD

Experience a whole different type of Bermuda nightlife—reserve a night snorkel tour from your ship's shore excursion desk. The island's coral reef comes alive when the sun goes down as nocturnal creatures of the deep emerge from the safety of their caves and crevices. Participants are provided with a dive light as well as snorkel gear, but the real treat is when the lights are turned off to reveal the extraordinary effects of bioluminescence—microscopic creatures that create light as you swim through them.

One advantage of a Bermuda itinerary is that cruise ships remain docked at night, which affords the opportunity to dine ashore and sample the nightlife. There's a downside to onboard life, though. Although most shipboard services—dining, lounges, and the fitness center and spa—continue to hum along as usual, duty-free shops and casinos are required by Bermuda government regulations to remain closed when in port. In addition, professional entertainment in the show lounge is curtailed, although a movie might be screened there instead. Some ships offer a "Bermuda Night" tropical-theme deck party.

ON THE SEASHORE

For a "free" souvenir, sea glass (broken bits of glass and china that have been tumbled by the sea to make them nice and smooth) is deposited in fairly large quantities by the surf at Alexandra Battery Beach Park. The beach park is easy to find on any local map and only about a mile walk from St. George's.

RETURNING TO THE SHIP

Cruise lines are strict about sailing times, which are posted at the gangway and elsewhere and announced in the daily schedule of activities. Be sure to be back on board at least a half hour before the announced sailing time or you may be stranded. If you're on a shore excursion that was sold by the cruise line, however, the captain will wait for your group before casting off. That's one reason why many passengers prefer ship-packaged tours.

If you're not on one of the ship's tours and the ship sails without you, immediately contact the cruise line's port representative, whose phone number is usually listed on the daily schedule of activities. You may be able to hitch a ride on a pilot boat, although that is unlikely. Passengers who miss the boat must pay their own way to the next port, and for a Bermuda cruise that means the U.S. disembarkation port (to where you will not be allowed to fly unless you have brought a valid passport).

8

DISEMBARKATION

All cruises come to an end eventually, and it hardly seems fair that you have to leave when it feels like your vacation has just begun, but leave you must. The disembarkation process actually begins the day before you arrive at your ship's home port. During that day your cabin steward delivers special luggage tags to your stateroom, along with customs forms and instructions.

The night before you disembark, you'll need to set aside clothing to wear the next morning when you leave the ship. Many people dress in whatever casual outfits they wear for the final dinner on board, or change into travel clothes after dinner. Also, do not forget to put your passport or other proof of citizenship, airline tickets, and medications in your hand luggage.

After you finish packing, attach your new luggage tags (they are color- or number-coded according to post-cruise transportation plans and flight schedules). Follow the instructions provided and place the locked luggage outside your stateroom door for pickup during the hours indicated.

A statement itemizing your onboard charges is delivered before you arise on disembarkation morning. Plan to get up early enough to check it over for accuracy, finish packing your belongings, and vacate your stateroom by the appointed hour. Any discrepancies in your onboard account should be taken care of before leaving the ship, usually at the purser's desk.

Room service is not available on most ships on the last morning; however, breakfast is served in the main dining room and the buffet restaurant. After breakfast, there's not much to do but wait comfortably in a lounge or on deck for your tag color or number to be called. Disembarkation procedures can sometimes be drawn out by passengers who are unprepared. This is no time to abandon your patience or sense of humor.

Remember that all passengers must meet with customs and immigration officials before disembarkation, either on the ship or in the terminal. Procedures vary and are outlined in your instructions. In some ports, passengers must meet with officials at a specified hour (usually very early) in an onboard lounge; in other ports, customs forms are collected in the terminal, and passports or other identification papers are examined there as well.

Once in the terminal, locate your luggage and proceed to your motor coach or taxi, or retrieve your vehicle from the parking lot.

CUSTOMS AND DUTIES
U.S. CUSTOMS
Before a ship lands, each individual or family must fill out a customs declaration, regardless of whether anything was purchased abroad. If you have less than $800 worth of goods, you will not need to itemize purchases. Be prepared to pay whatever duties are owed directly to the customs inspector, with cash or check.

U.S. Customs might preclear your ship when you sail in and out of certain ports. It's done on board before you disembark. In most ports you must collect your luggage from the dock and then stand in line to pass through the inspection point. This can take up to an hour.

U.S. CITIZENS Duties are the same for returning cruise passengers as for all other travelers, with a few exceptions. On certain Caribbean itineraries that include a visit to Bermuda, you're entitled to bring back $800 worth of goods duty-free. ⇨ *For general customs and duty information, see Customs and Duties in Travel Smart Bermuda.*

NON-U.S. CITIZENS If you hold a foreign passport and will be returning to your home country within hours of docking, you may be exempt from all U.S. Customs duties. Everything you bring into the United States must leave with you when you return home. When you reach your own country, you will have to pay appropriate duties there.

TRAVEL SMART
BERMUDA

GETTING HERE AND AROUND

It's easy to get to Bermuda by air from the United States, and the price is cheaper than it once was, as more discount airlines have added flights from major East Coast hubs. For those who would rather cruise than fly, there are options as well, with the Bermuda cruise season starting in late spring and going through early fall.

▮ AIR TRAVEL

Flying time to Bermuda from most East Coast cities is about 2 hours; from Toronto, 3 hours; and 7 hours from London Gatwick.

Most flights arrive around noon, making for particularly long waits to get through immigration; however, British Airways flights and a couple of American Airlines flights from New York arrive in the evening.

At many airports outside Bermuda, travelers with only carry-on luggage can bypass the airline's front desk and check in at the gate. But in Bermuda everyone checks in at the airline's front desk. U.S. customs has a desk here, too, so you won't have to clear customs at home when you land. Passengers returning to Britain or Canada will need to clear customs and immigration on arrival.

Airlines and Airports Airline and Airport Links.com. ⊕ *www.airlineandairportlinks.com.*

Airline Security Issues Transportation Security Administration. ⊕ *www.tsa.gov.*

AIRPORTS

Bermuda's gateway is L.F. Wade International Airport (BDA), formerly Bermuda International Airport, on the East End of the island. It's approximately 9 miles from Hamilton (30-minute cab ride), 13 miles from Southampton (40-minute cab ride), and 17 miles from Somerset (50 minutes by cab). The town of St. George's is about a 15-minute cab ride from the airport.

Airport Information L. F. Wade International Airport (BDA). ☎ *441/293–2470* ⊕ *www.bermudaairport.com.*

▮TIP→ Ask the local tourist board about hotel and local transportation packages that include tickets to major museum exhibits or other special events.

GROUND TRANSPORTATION

Taxis, available outside the arrivals gate, are the usual and most convenient way to leave the airport. The approximate fare (not including tip) to Hamilton is $35; to St. George's, $15; to south-shore hotels, $45; and to Sandys (Somerset), $50. A surcharge of $1 is added for each piece of luggage stored in the trunk or on the roof. Fares are 25%–50% higher between midnight and 6 am and all day on Sunday and public holidays. Fifteen percent is an acceptable tip.

CEO Transport Ltd. has a range of vehicles available to transport guests to hotels and guesthouses. Prices range from $15 for shared shuttle service up to $200 for a VIP Meet and Greet Service in a luxury sedan.

Contacts CEO Transport Ltd. ☎ *441/234–4366, 855/859–6454 U.S. toll-free* ✉ *pickmeup@limobermuda.com* ⊕ *www.limobermuda.com.* **BTA Dispatching Ltd.** ☎ *441/296–2121* ⊕ *www.btadispatching.com.* **First Step Taxi Service.** ☎ *441/735–7151.* **Island Taxi Services.** ☎ *441/295–4141* ⊕ *www.bermudaislandtaxi.com.*

FLIGHTS

Nonstop service to Bermuda is available year-round on major airlines from Atlanta, Boston, Newark (NJ), New York

City, Baltimore, Philadelphia, Toronto, Miami, and London, and seasonally from Charlotte and Washington, D.C.

Fares from New York City may be found for less than $300 on some of the budget airlines, but the average price is closer to $500 and can be as high as $800 in peak season, whereas fares from Toronto are typically about $400. Fares from Gatwick vary from $900 in low season to $1,300 in high season on British Airways. Flight regularity and price are subject to rapid change, and airlines recommend that travelers check their websites for up-to-the-minute information.

Airline Contacts Air Canada. ☎ *888/247–2262* ⊕ *www.aircanada.com.* **American Airlines.** ☎ *800/433–7300* ⊕ *www.aa.com.* **Delta Airlines.** ☎ *800/221–1212 for U.S. reservations, 800/241–4141 for international reservations* ⊕ *www.delta.com.* **jetBlue.** ☎ *800/538–2583* ⊕ *www.jetblue.com.* **United.** ☎ *800/864–8331 for U.S. and Canada reservations* ⊕ *www.united.com.* **WestJet.** ☎ *888/937–8538* ⊕ *www.westjet.com.*

▌ BOAT TRAVEL

The Bermuda Ministry of Transport maintains excellent, frequent, and on-time ferry service from Hamilton to Paget and Warwick (the pink line), Somerset and the Dockyard in the West End (the blue line), Rockaway in Southampton (the green line), and on weekdays in summer only, the Dockyard and St. George's (the orange line).

A one-way adult fare to Paget or Warwick is $3.50; to Somerset, the Dockyard, or St. George's, $5. The last departures are from Hamilton at 8 pm. Sunday ferry service is limited and ends around 6 pm. You can bring a bicycle on board free of charge, but you'll pay $4.50 extra to take a motor scooter to Somerset or the Dockyard. Discounted one-, two-, three-, four-, and seven-day passes are available for use on both ferries and buses. They cost $19, $31.50, $44, $48.50, and $62, respectively. Monthly passes are also

available. The helpful ferry operators can answer questions about routes and schedules and can even help get your bike on board. Schedules are published online, posted at each landing, and also available at the Ferry Terminal, Central Bus Terminal, Visitors Information Centres, and most hotels.

Information Ministry of Transport, Department of Marine and Ports Services. ☎ *441/295–4506 Hamilton Ferry Terminal* ⊕ *www.marineandports.bm.*

▌ BUS TRAVEL

Bermuda's pink and blue buses travel the island from east to west. To find a bus stop outside Hamilton, look for either a stone shelter or a pink or blue pole. For buses heading to Hamilton, the pole is pink; for those traveling away from Hamilton, the pole is blue. Remember to wait on the proper side of the road. Driving in Bermuda is on the left. Bus drivers will not make change, so purchase tickets or discounted tokens or carry plenty of coins.

In addition to public buses, private minibuses serve St. George's. The minibus fare depends on the destination, but you won't pay more than $5 or $6. Minibuses, which you can flag down, drop you wherever you want to go in this parish. They operate daily from about 7:30 am to 11 pm. Smoking is not permitted on buses.

Bermuda is divided into 14 bus zones, each about 2 miles long. Within the first three zones, the rate is $3.50 (coins only). For longer distances, the fare is $5. If you plan to travel by public transportation often, buy a booklet of tickets (15 14-zone tickets for $37.50, or 15 three-zone tickets for $25). You can also buy a few tokens, which, unlike tickets, are sold individually. In addition to tickets and tokens, there are one-, two-, three-, four-, and seven-day adult passes ($19, $31.50, $44, $48.50, and $62, respectively). Monthly passes are also available. All bus passes are good for ferry service and are available at the central bus terminal.

Tickets and passes are also sold at many hotels and guesthouses.

Hamilton buses arrive and depart from the Central Bus Terminal. An office here is open weekdays from 7:15 am to 7 pm, Saturday from 7:30 am to 6 pm, and Sunday and holidays from 8:30 am to 5:30 pm; it's the only place to buy money-saving tokens.

Buses run about every 15 minutes, except on Sunday, when they usually come every half hour or hour, depending on the route. Bus schedules are available at the bus terminal in Hamilton and at many hotels. The timetable also offers an itinerary for a do-it-yourself, one-day sightseeing tour by bus and ferry. Upon request, the driver will be happy to tell you when you've reached your stop. Be sure to greet the bus driver when boarding—it's considered rude in Bermuda to ask a bus driver a question, such as the fare or details on your destination, without first greeting him or her.

Bus Information Public Transport Bermuda. ☎ *441/292–3851* ⊕ *www.gov.bm/bus-routes-and-maps.*

■ CAR TRAVEL

You cannot rent a car in Bermuda. The island has strict laws governing over-crowded roads, so even Bermudians are only allowed one car per household. A popular, albeit possibly somewhat dangerous, alternative is to rent mopeds or scooters *(below)*, which are better for negotiating the island's narrow roads. If driving a scooter is not your idea of a good time, you may still be in luck: a new and exciting mode of transport has hit the roads of Bermuda. With cockpit-style seats, a centrally located steering wheel, and foot pedals, the two-person Renault Twizys from Current Vehicles are not only safer than mopeds, they're affordable and fun to drive. These mini electric cars are less than 4 feet wide, which makes them the perfect size for Bermuda's narrow roads, and have a range of up to 80 km

(50 miles) on a single charge. Explore the island in style, comfort, and emission-free good conscience. The company is in the process of building an island-wide charging network, but until then, you'll need to book your stay at an affiliated hotel in order to get your hands on one of these trendy little vehicles.

Current Vehicles. ✉ *Hamilton Princess, 76 Pitt's Bay Rd.* ✍ *info@currentvehicles.com* ⊕ *www.currentvehicles.com.*

■ CRUISE SHIP TRAVEL

⇨ *For information about cruising to Bermuda, see Chapter 8.*

■ MOPED AND SCOOTER TRAVEL

Because car rentals are not allowed in Bermuda, you might decide to get around by moped or scooter. Bermudians routinely use the words *moped* and *scooter* interchangeably, even though they're different. You must pedal to start a moped, and it carries only one person. A scooter, on the other hand, which starts when you put the key in the ignition, is more powerful and holds one or two passengers.

■ TIP➔ Think twice before renting a moped, as accidents occur frequently and are occasionally fatal. The best ways to avoid mishaps are to drive defensively, obey the speed limit, remember to stay on the left-hand side of the road—especially at traffic circles—and avoid riding in the rain and at night.

Helmets are required by law. Mopeds and scooters can be rented from cycle liveries by the hour, the day, or the week. Liveries will show first-time riders how to operate the vehicles. Rates vary, so it's worth calling several liveries to see what they charge. Single-seat scooter rentals cost $55–$75 per day or from about $200–$250 per week. Some liveries tack a mandatory insurance-and-repair charge on top of the bill, whereas others include the cost of insurance, breakdown service, pickup and delivery, and a tank of gas in the quoted price. A $20 deposit may also be charged for the lock, key, and helmet. You must be at least 16 and have a valid driver's license to rent. Major hotels have their own cycle liveries, and all hotels and most guesthouses will make rental arrangements.

GASOLINE

Gas for cycles runs from $3 to $4 per liter, but you can cover a great deal of ground on the full tank that comes with the wheels. Gas stations will accept major credit cards. It's customary to tip attendants—a couple of dollars is adequate.

PARKING

On-street parking bays for scooters are plentiful and easy to spot. What's even better is they're free!

ROAD CONDITIONS

Roads are narrow, winding, and full of blind curves. Whether driving cars or scooters, Bermudians tend to be quite cautious around less-experienced visiting riders, but crowded city streets make accidents all the more common. Local rush hours are weekdays from 7:30 am to 9 am and from 4 pm to 6 pm. Roads are often bumpy, and they may be slippery under a morning mist or rainfall. Street lamps are few and far between outside the cities, so be especially careful driving at night.

ROADSIDE EMERGENCIES

The number for Bermuda's emergency services is ☎ 911. Scooters are often stolen, so to be safe you should always carry the number of your hire company with you. Also, don't ride with valuables in your bike basket, as you are putting yourself at risk of theft. Passing motorists can grab your belongings and ride off without your even knowing it.

RULES OF THE ROAD

The speed limit is 35 kph (22 mph), except in the UNESCO World Heritage site of St. George's, where it is a mere 25 kph (about 15 mph). The limits, however, are not very well enforced, and the actual driving speed in Bermuda hovers around 50 kph (30 mph). Police seldom target tourists for parking offenses or other driving infractions. Drunk driving is a serious problem in Bermuda, despite stiff penalties. The blood-alcohol limit is 0.08. The courts will impose a $1,000 fine for a driving-while-intoxicated infraction, and also take the driver off the road for at least one year. A new law has recently been imposed against using a mobile phone while driving a scooter.

Rental Companies Elbow Beach Cycles Ltd. ☎ *441/296–2300* ⊕ *www.elbowbeachcycles.com.* **Oleander Cycles.** ✉ *6 Valley Rd., off Middle Rd.* ☎ *441/236–5235* ⊕ *www.oleandercycles.bm.* **Smatt's Cycle Livery Ltd.** ✉ *74 Pitt's Bay Rd.* ☎ *441/295–1180* ⊕ *www.smattscyclelivery.com.*

▌TAXI TRAVEL

Taxis are the fastest and easiest way to get around the island; unfortunately, they are also the most costly and can take a long time to arrive. Four-seater taxis charge $7.90 for the first mile and $2.75 for each subsequent mile. Between midnight and 6 am, and on Sunday and holidays, a 25%–50% surcharge is added to the fare. There's a $1 charge for each piece of luggage stored in the trunk or on the roof. Taxi drivers accept only American or Bermudian cash, but not bills larger than $50, and they expect a 15% tip. You can phone for taxi pickup, but you may wait while the cab navigates Bermuda's heavy traffic. Another option is Hitch, a local booking app to arrange transportation on demand. The app is available for both Android and Apple devices. Don't hesitate to hail a taxi on the street.

For a personalized taxi tour of the island, the minimum duration is three hours, at $50 per hour for one to four people and $70 an hour for five or six, excluding tip.

Taxi Companies BTA Dispatching Ltd. ☎ *441/296–2121.* **First Step Taxi Service.** ☎ *441/735–7151.* **Island Taxi Services.** ☎ *441/295–4141* ⊕ *www.bermudaislandtaxi.com.*

ESSENTIALS

◼ ACCOMMODATIONS

Accommodation standards in Bermuda—whether you prefer a guesthouse or a five-star hotel—are generally high, and strongly regulated by the Bermuda Tourism Authority. Prices tend to reflect this quality, however, and you should be warned that there are no true budget options. (Camping is not allowed, and there are no hostels on the island.) Staying in a hotel can mean anything from a luxury resort setting to a more posh family-run property. Another option is to stay in more homelike accommodations—either by renting a room in a guesthouse (a commercial establishment roughly similar to a room in a bed-and-breakfast, though some can be very upmarket) or a cottage.

Be sure you understand the hotel's cancellation policy. Some places allow you to cancel without any kind of penalty—even if you prepaid to secure a discounted rate—if you cancel at least 24 hours in advance. Others require you to cancel a week in advance or penalize you the cost of one night. Small inns and bed-and-breakfasts are most likely to require you to cancel far in advance. Most hotels allow children under a certain age to stay in their parents' room at no extra charge, but others charge for them as extra adults; find out the cutoff age for discounts.

APARTMENT AND HOUSE RENTALS

Rental houses, apartments, and villas are all over Bermuda and may be owned by individuals, consortiums, and developers, so booking might be anything from calling the owner in person to booking through a rental agency or Airbnb.

Contacts Airbnb. ⊕ www.airbnb.com. **Villas International.** ☎ 415/499–9490, 800/221–2260 ⊕ www.villasintl.com. **White Roof B&B.** ✍ info@whiteroofbnb.com ⊕ whiteroofbnb.com.

HOME EXCHANGES

With a direct home exchange, you stay in someone else's home while they stay in yours. Some outfits also deal with vacation homes, so you're not actually staying in someone's full-time residence, just their vacant weekend place.

Exchange Clubs HomeExchange.com. ☎ 800/877–8723 ⊕ www.homeexchange.com.

◼ COMMUNICATIONS

INTERNET

While Internet access and Wi-Fi is widely available in Bermuda, free access is limited. The Bermuda Tourism Authority (BTA) offers free Wi-Fi for one hour at the Visitor Information Centres at the Dockyard and at Kings Square in St. George. The BTA also offers free Wi-Fi for one hour at the Hamilton Ferry Terminal, the Hamilton Bus Terminal, and St. George's Ferry Dock, Penno's Wharf.

Several pubs and restaurants in Dockyard and Hamilton offer free Wi-Fi (provided one orders food or drink). Some hotels offer free Wi-Fi to guests; however, most properties charge for access. The Fairmont Southampton Resort, Fairmont Hamilton Princess, and Rosewood Tucker's Point have fully equipped business centers where guests can use hotel computers for Internet access (connection charges still apply).

TeleBermuda International offers hot spots around the island for $4.99 an hour.

PHONES

The good news is you can now make a direct-dial telephone call from virtually any point on earth. The bad news? You can't always do so cheaply. Calling from a hotel is almost always the most expensive option; hotels usually add huge surcharges to all calls, particularly international ones. As expensive as mobile phone calls can be, they are still usually a much cheaper option than calling from your hotel.

Destination-specific international calling cards from One Communications in Hamilton offer the cheapest way of calling. You can use them on any phone, including public pay phones and mobile phones. You can also get standard international cards from pharmacies, some supermarkets, and many gas stations, which will also get you a better rate than calling directly from the hotel.

The country code for Bermuda is 441. When dialing a Bermuda number from the United States or Canada, simply dial 1 + 441 + local number. You do not need to dial the international access code (011).

CALLING WITHIN BERMUDA

Telephone service in Bermuda is organized and efficient, though service may be interrupted during storms.

When in Bermuda, call ☎ *411* for local phone numbers. To reach directory assistance from outside the country, call ☎ *441/555–1212*.

To make a local call, simply dial the seven-digit number.

You can still find a few pay phones on the streets of Hamilton, St. George's, and Somerset as well as at the airport, cruise ship terminals, ferry landings, some bus stops, and public beaches. Deposit *50¢* (U.S. or Bermudian) before you dial. Most hotels charge from *30¢* to $1 for local calls.

CALLING OUTSIDE BERMUDA

The country code for the United States is 1.

Most hotels impose a surcharge for long-distance calls, even those made collect or with a phone card or credit card. Many toll-free 800 or 888 numbers in the United States aren't honored in Bermuda. Consider buying a prepaid local phone card rather than using your own calling card. In many small guesthouses and apartments, the phone in your room is a private line from which you can make only collect, credit-card, or local calls. Some small hotels have a telephone room or kiosk where you can make long-distance calls.

To call the United States, Canada, and most Caribbean countries, simply dial 1 (or 0 if you need an operator's assistance), then the area code and the number. For all other countries, dial 011 (or 0 for an operator), the country code, the area code, and the number. Using an operator for an overseas call is more expensive than dialing direct. For calls to the United States, rates are highest from 8 am to 6 pm and discounted from 6 pm to 8 am and on weekends.

Access Codes AT&T USADirect. ☎ *800/225–5288.* **MCI Call USA.** ☎ *800/888–8000, 800/888–8888.*

CALLING CARDS

Buy a prepaid phone card for long-distance calls. They can be used with any touch-tone phone in Bermuda, although they can only be used for calls outside Bermuda. Rates are often significantly lower than dialing direct, but the downside is that some hotels will charge you for making the call to your card's 800 number. Phone cards are available at pharmacies, shops, gas stations, and restaurants. The phone companies TeleBermuda and One Communications sell prepaid calling cards in denominations of $5 to $50. The cards can be used around the world as well as in Bermuda.

LOCAL DO'S AND TABOOS

CUSTOMS OF THE COUNTRY

Bermudians tend to be quite formal in attire as well as in personal interactions. Casual dress, including bathing suits, is acceptable at hotels and resorts, but locals seldom venture into Hamilton in anything less than long shorts and sports shirts for men, and slacks-and-blouse combinations or dresses for women. Some restaurants and clubs, particularly those connected to hotels, request that men wear jackets, and more formal establishments require ties during dinner, but there are plenty of places in Hamilton and beyond where you can dress casually and dine well. If you have dinner reservations, you should arrive promptly, but be aware that in other situations the phenomenon known as "Bermuda time" prevails. If you make plans to meet a local, don't be surprised if they're 20 minutes late.

In downtown Hamilton the classic Bermuda shorts are often worn by banking and insurance executives, but the outfit always includes knee-high socks, dress shoes, and jacket and tie. When it comes to dress, err on the formal side. It's an offense in Bermuda to appear in public without a shirt, even for joggers. This rule may seem arcane, but most Bermudians appreciate this decorum. Decorum is also expected at the beach.

GREETINGS

Courtesy is the rule when locals interact with each other. In business and social gatherings use the more formal Mr. and Ms. instead of first names, at least until a friendship has been established, which sometimes takes just a few minutes. Always greet bus drivers with a friendly "Good morning" or "Good afternoon" when you board public buses. This is an island custom, and it's nice to see each passenger offer a smile and sincere greeting when boarding and exiting the bus. In fact, saying "Good morning" to people on the street is also a custom. Obviously, if you're walking down a crowded street, you needn't say it to everyone you pass, but in less crowded situations, especially when eye contact is made, some recognition should be given. You'll be surprised at the friendly response you receive.

In general, respect and appreciation are shown quite liberally to public servants in Bermuda. Although one underlying reason may be the fact that the residents of this small island seem to know everyone, and personal greetings on the streets are commonplace, it also seems that a genuinely upbeat and friendly attitude is part of the national character.

OUT ON THE TOWN

The key to interaction with any Bermudian is to be polite and formal, and that goes for your waiter or any other person serving you. Rudeness will get you nowhere. Public displays of affection are quite okay, but you might want to keep it in moderation; generally people are fairly reserved.

SIGHTSEEING

Bathing suits are best kept for the beach only, and overly skimpy attire is traditionally frowned upon, though attitudes are more tolerant of tourists. Although the problem is far less prevalent than in most places of the world, there are a few street beggars, and it's best not to give them anything—for one, due to Hamilton's small size you're likely to see the same beggar again and again, and if you give them something once they'll repeatedly approach you. A firm but polite refusal is best. You shouldn't eat or drink on the buses, and—as with anywhere else you visit—you'll gain approval by giving up your seat for elderly or pregnant women.

Phone-Card Companies One Communications. ☎ 441/700–7000. TeleBermuda International. ☎ 441/296–9000.

MOBILE PHONES

Most travelers can use their own cell phones in Bermuda, though you should check with your provider to be sure. Cellphone rentals are available from stores in Hamilton, some of which will even deliver the phone to you. A typical charge is $2 a day for the rental; local calls will cost 60¢ a minute. Incoming international calls will also cost 60¢ a minute, but outgoing international calls will cost $1.10 a minute.

■ **TIP→** If you travel internationally frequently, save one of your old mobile phones or buy a cheap one on the Internet; ask your cell phone company to unlock it for you, and take it with you as a travel phone, buying a new SIM card with pay-as-you-go service in each destination.

Contacts Cellular Abroad. ☎ 800/287–5072 ⊕ www.cellularabroad.com. **Mobal.** ☎ 888/888–9162 ⊕ www.mobal.com.

▮ CUSTOMS AND DUTIES

On entering Bermuda, you can bring in duty-free up to 50 cigars, 200 cigarettes, and 1 pound of tobacco; 1 liter of wine and 1 liter of spirits; and other goods with a total maximum value of $50. To import plants, fruits, vegetables, or pets, you must get an import permit in advance from the Department of Environmental Protection. Merchandise and sales materials for use at conventions must be cleared with the hotel concerned before you arrive. Be prepared for a bit of a wait, as the Customs Office has a reputation for being very thorough. If there are a lot of passengers, this process can add an hour or so if you're unlucky. It goes without saying, but you should definitely not bring in any drugs such as marijuana, as drug checks are very thorough and the penalties are harsh.

Information in Bermuda Bermuda Customs. ☎ 441/295–4816 ⊕ www.customs.gov.bm. **Department of Environmental Protection.** ☎ 441/236–4201 ⊕ www.animals.gov.bm.

U.S. Information U.S. Customs and Border Protection. ⊕ www.cbp.gov.

▮ EATING OUT

Bermuda has a surprising number of restaurants serving just about any type of foreign cuisine imaginable: Indian, Thai, Japanese, Chinese, British, French—you name it. Truly Bermudian cuisine is, however, harder to come by. Codfish and potatoes, the national dish, tends to appear on some pub-food menus and also in a number of diner-style restaurants. Vegetarians are generally well catered to, and most places have no problem with young children, but check ahead at some of the higher-class establishments just to make sure.

For information on food-related health issues, see Health, below.

MEALS AND MEALTIMES

Unless otherwise noted, the restaurants listed *in this guide* are open daily for lunch and dinner.

A word of warning to those who are used to eating out late: it can be difficult to find a place that serves food after 10 pm. Your last option is a burger van called Jorjays, which is usually open late into the night on Front Street.

RESERVATIONS AND DRESS

Regardless of where you are, it's a good idea to make a reservation if you can. We only mention them specifically when reservations are essential (there's no other way you'll ever get a table) or when they are not accepted. For popular restaurants, book as far ahead as you can (often 30 days), and reconfirm as soon as you arrive. (Large parties should always call ahead to check the reservations policy.) We mention dress only when men are required to wear a jacket or a jacket and tie.

WINE, BEER, AND SPIRITS

Bermuda's two national drinks, the Dark 'n' Stormy (dark rum and ginger beer) and the rum swizzle (a mixed fruit cocktail with dark and light rum), both rely on the locally produced Gosling's Rum. These drinks are everywhere—so watch out! The only locally produced beers are available at Frog & Onion Pub in Dockyard, and a few restaurants carry locally produced On De Rock brews. Otherwise, available beers are fairly standard North American and European brands, and wines are plentiful. Liquor can't be bought from a liquor store after 9 pm any day of the week.

■ ELECTRICITY

The local electrical current is the same as in the United States and Canada: 110 volt, 60 cycle AC. All appliances that can be used in North America can be used in Bermuda without adapters. Winter storms bring occasional power outages.

■ EMERGENCIES

Police, ambulance, and fire services are all at ☏ 911. Pharmacies usually open around 8 am, some stay open until 9 pm. People's Pharmacy in Hamilton is open from 10 am to 6 pm on Sunday.

Doctors and Dentists Government Health Clinic. ☏ 441/278–6441 ⊕ www.health.gov.bm.

Foreign Consulates American Consulate. ⊠ Crown Hill, 16 Middle Rd. ☏ 441/295–1342 ⊕ bm.usconsulate.gov.

General Emergency Contacts Police, fire, ambulance. ☏ 911. **Sea Rescue.** ☏ 441/297–1010 ⊕ www.rccbermuda.bm.

Hospitals and Clinics King Edward VII Memorial Hospital. ⊠ 7 Point Finger Rd. ⚓ Outside Hamilton near the Botanical Gardens ☏ 441/236–2345 ⊕ www.bermuda-hospitals.bm.

■ HEALTH

The most common types of illnesses are caused by contaminated food and water. If you have problems, mild cases of traveler's diarrhea may respond to Imodium (known generically as loperamide) or Pepto-Bismol. Be sure to drink plenty of fluids; if you can't keep fluids down, seek medical help immediately.

Infectious diseases can be airborne or passed via mosquitoes and ticks and through direct or indirect physical contact with animals or people. Some, including Norwalk-like viruses that affect your digestive tract, can be passed along through contaminated food. Speak with your physician and/or check the CDC or World Health Organization websites for health alerts, particularly if you're pregnant, traveling with children, or have a chronic illness.

SPECIFIC ISSUES IN BERMUDA

Sunburn and sunstroke are legitimate concerns if you're traveling to Bermuda in summer. On hot, sunny days, wear a hat, a beach cover-up, and lots of sunblock. These are essential for a day on a boat or at the beach. Be sure to take the same kind of precautions on overcast summer days—some of the worst cases of sunburn happen on cloudy afternoons when sunblock seems unnecessary. Drink plenty of water and, above all, limit the amount of time you spend in the sun until you become acclimated.

The Portuguese man-of-war occasionally visits Bermuda's waters, so be alert when swimming, especially in summer or whenever the water is particularly warm. This creature is recognizable by a purple, balloonlike float sack of perhaps 8 inches in diameter, below which dangle 20- to 60-inch tentacles armed with powerful stinging cells. Contact with the stinging cells causes immediate and severe pain. Seek medical attention immediately: a serious sting can send a person into shock. In the meantime—or if getting to a doctor will take a while—treat the affected area liberally with vinegar. Ammonia is also an effective antidote to the sting. Although usually encountered in the water, Portuguese men-of-war may also wash up onshore. If you spot one on the sand, steer clear, as the sting is just as dangerous out of the water.

More recently, divers have encountered the highly poisonous lionfish, which is not a native of the waters. Swimmers will be extremely unlikely to come into contact with one, while divers should just exercise caution around the creatures, which are not aggressive unless provoked.

∎ HOURS OF OPERATION

Most branches of HSBC Bermuda are open weekdays from 9 to 4:30. All branches of Butterfield Bank are open weekdays from 9 to 4. Bermuda Commercial Bank (✉ *34 Bermudiana Road, Hamilton*) operates weekdays from 9 to 5. Clarien Bank (✉ *25 Reid Street, Hamilton*) is open weekdays from 8:30 to 4 and Saturday from 9:30 to 1:30.

Many gas stations are open daily from 7 am to 9 pm, and a few stay open until midnight. The island's only 24-hour gas station is Esso City Auto Market in Hamilton, near the Bank of Butterfield, off Par-La-Ville Road.

Hours vary greatly, but museums are generally open Monday through Saturday from 9 or 9:30 to 4:30 or 5. Some close on Saturday. Check with individual museums for exact hours.

Pharmacies are open Monday through Saturday from 8 am to 6 or 8 pm, and sometimes Sunday from around 11 to 6 pm.

Most stores are open Monday through Saturday from around 9 until 5 or 6. Some Hamilton stores keep evening hours when cruise ships are in port. Dockyard shops are generally open Monday through Saturday from 10 to 5, Sunday from 11 to 5. Shops that are open on Sunday—mainly grocery stores and pharmacies—have abbreviated hours.

HOLIDAYS

On Sunday and national public holidays, some shops, businesses, and restaurants in Bermuda close. Buses and ferries run on limited schedules. Most entertainment venues, sights, and sports outfitters remain open. When holidays fall on a Saturday, government and commercial offices close the following Monday, but restaurants and shops remain open.

Bermuda celebrates a two-day public holiday for Emancipation Day/Somers Day and Cup Match in late July or early August, when the whole island comes to a standstill for the annual cricket match between the East and West Ends of Bermuda. National public holidays are New Year's Day, Good Friday, Bermuda Day (late May), National Heroes Day (mid-June), Labour Day (early September), Remembrance Day (early November), Christmas, and Boxing Day (December 26).

∎ MAIL

Mail services in Bermuda can be erratic, so the following should be taken with a pinch of salt. Nevertheless, generally allow 7 to 10 days for mail from Bermuda to reach the United States, Canada, or the United Kingdom, and about two weeks to arrive in Australia or New Zealand.

Airmail postcards and letters for the first 50 grams to the United States and Canada cost $1.15. Postcards to the United Kingdom cost $1.20, letters $1.35 for the first 10 grams. Postcards to Australia and New Zealand cost $1.40, letters $1.55 for the first 10 grams.

If you want to receive mail but have no address in Bermuda, you can have mail sent care of General Delivery, General Post Office, Hamilton HM GD, Bermuda. **Main Branches International Data Express.** ☎ 441/297-7802 ⊕ www.bpo.bm. **Parcel Post.** ☎ 441/297-7875 ⊕ www.bpo.bm.

SHIPPING PACKAGES

Through Parcel Post at Bermuda's post office, you can send packages via either International Data Express (which takes three to five business days to the United States and Canada and three to seven days to the United Kingdom, Australia, and New Zealand) or Air Parcel Post (which takes 7 to 10 business days to the United States, Canada, and the United Kingdom, or two weeks to Australia and New Zealand).

For the first 500 grams, International Data Express rates are $35 to the United States and Canada, $38.50 to the United Kingdom, and $55 to Australia or New Zealand. Air Parcel Post rates run $20 for the first 500 grams to the United States, $20 to Canada, $25 to the United Kingdom, and $28 to Australia or New Zealand.

Most of Bermuda's largest stores offer shipping of purchases. Some may ask you either to buy insurance or to sign a waiver absolving them of any responsibility for potential loss or damage.

Overnight courier service is available to or from the continental United States through several companies. Service between Bermuda and Canada takes one or two business days, depending on the part of Canada; between Bermuda and the United Kingdom, generally two business days; and between Bermuda and Australia or New Zealand, usually three.

In Bermuda, rates include pickup from anywhere on the island. Prices for a document up to the first pound range from $44 to $48 to the United States, from $44 to $48 to Canada, and from $45 to $60 to the United Kingdom, Australia, or New Zealand. For the fastest delivery, your pickup request must be made before about 4 pm. Note that pickups (and drop-off locations) are limited on Saturday, and there's no service on Sunday. Packages sent to Bermuda may take a day longer than documents.

Express Services DHL Worldwide Express. ☎ 441/294-4848. **FedEx.** ☎ 441/295-3854. **International Bonded Couriers (IBC).** ☎ 441/295-2467 ⊕ www.zipx.bm. **Mailboxes Unlimited Ltd.** ☎ 441/292-6563 ⊕ www. mailboxesunlimited.com.

■ MONEY

ITEM	AVERAGE COST
Cup of Coffee	$3
Glass of Wine	$11
Glass of Beer	$8
Sandwich	$10
One-Mile Taxi Ride in Capital City	$10
Museum Admission	Free–$20

The Bermudian dollar is on par with the U.S. dollar, and the two currencies are used interchangeably. (Other non-Bermudian currency must be converted.) You can use American money anywhere, but change is often given in Bermudian currency. Try to avoid accumulating large amounts of local money, which is difficult to exchange for U.S. dollars in Bermuda and expensive to exchange in the United States. ATMs are plentiful, as are the number of venues that will accept credit cards, even for small items.

Since Bermuda imports everything from cars to cardigans, prices are high. At an upscale restaurant, for example, you're bound to pay as much for a meal as you would in a top New York, London, or Paris restaurant: on average, $60 to $80 per person, $120 with drinks and wine. There are cheaper options, of course; the island is full of coffee shops, where you can eat hamburgers and french fries with locals for about $15. The same meal at a restaurant costs about $25.

Prices here are given for adults. Substantially reduced fees are almost always available for children, students, and senior citizens.

ATMS AND BANKS

Your own bank will probably charge a fee for using ATMs abroad; the foreign bank you use may also charge a fee. Nevertheless, you'll usually get a better rate of exchange at an ATM than you will at a currency-exchange office or even when changing money in a bank. And extracting funds as you need them is a safer option than carrying around a large amount of cash.

■ TIP➡ **PINs with more than four digits are not recognized at ATMs in many countries. If yours has five or more, remember to change it before you leave.**

ATMs are found all over Bermuda, in shops, arcades, supermarkets, the airport, and two of the island's banks. Both HSBC Bermuda and the Bank of Butterfield are affiliated with the Cirrus and Plus networks. Note that both banks' ATMs only accept personal identification numbers (PIN) with four digits. Typical withdrawal amounts are multiples of 20 up to 100. Cash point robberies are a rarity in Bermuda, but if you're concerned, Reid Street and Front Street—which have the most banks—are Hamilton's busiest, and hence safest, places to withdraw cash.

CREDIT CARDS

It's a good idea to inform your credit-card company before you travel, especially if you're going abroad and don't travel internationally very often. Otherwise, the credit-card company might put a hold on your card owing to unusual activity—not a good thing halfway through your trip. Record all your credit-card numbers—as well as the phone numbers to call if your cards are lost or stolen—in a safe place, so you're prepared should something go wrong. Both MasterCard and Visa have general numbers you can call (collect if you're abroad) if your card is lost, but you're better off calling the number of your issuing bank, since Master-Card and Visa usually just transfer you to

your bank; your bank's number is usually printed on your card.

Dynamic currency conversion programs are becoming increasingly widespread. Merchants who participate in them are supposed to ask whether you want to be charged in dollars or the local currency, but they don't always do so. And even if they do offer you a choice, they may well avoid mentioning the additional surcharges. The good news is that you *do* have a choice. And if this practice really gets your goat, you can avoid it entirely thanks to American Express; with its cards, DCC simply isn't an option.

Most Bermudian shops and restaurants accept credit and debit cards. The most widely accepted cards are MasterCard, Visa, and American Express.

Reporting Lost Cards American Express. ☎ *800/528–4800 in U.S., 336/393–1111 collect from abroad* ⊕ *www.americanexpress. com.* **Diners Club.** ☎ *800/234–6377 in U.S., 514/877–1577 collect from abroad* ⊕ *www. dinersclub.com.* **Discover.** ☎ *800/347–2683 in U.S., 801/902–3100 collect from abroad* ⊕ *www.discovercard.com.* **MasterCard.** ☎ *800/307–7309 in U.S., 636/722–7111 collect from abroad* ⊕ *www.mastercard.com.* **Visa.** ☎ *800/847–2911 in U.S., 303/967–1096 collect from abroad* ⊕ *usa.visa.com.*

CURRENCY AND EXCHANGE

The local currency is the Bermudian dollar, which is on par with the American dollar. Both are accepted throughout the island. Bermudian dollar notes all feature the Queen's head and are smaller than their U.S. counterparts. It's worth being careful, as the $10 and the $2 notes are similar in color (light blue) and could be easily mistaken for one another.

If you need to exchange Canadian dollars, British pounds, or other currencies, for the most favorable rates change money through banks. Although ATM transaction fees may be higher abroad than at home, ATM rates are excellent because they're based on wholesale rates offered only by major banks.

▮ PACKING

As a rule of thumb, Bermudians dress more formally than most Americans. In the evening, some of the more upscale restaurants and hotel dining rooms require men to wear a jacket and tie and women to dress comparably, so bring a few dressy outfits. But increasingly venues are more accepting of the trend toward "smart-casual." In this case, women should be fine with slacks or a skirt and a dressy blouse or sweater. Bermudian men often wear Bermuda shorts (and proper knee socks) with a jacket and tie for formal events and business meetings.

During the cooler months, bring lightweight woolens or cottons that you can wear in layers to accommodate vagaries of the weather. A lightweight jacket is always a good idea. Regardless of the season, pack a swimsuit, a beachwear cover-up, sunscreen, and sunglasses, as well as a raincoat (umbrellas are typically provided by hotels). Comfortable walking shoes are a must. If you plan to play tennis, be aware that many courts require proper whites and that tennis balls in Bermuda are extremely expensive. Bring your own tennis balls if possible.

Bermuda-bound airlines commonly accept golf-club bags in lieu of a piece of luggage, but there are fairly stringent guidelines governing the maximum amount of equipment that can be transported without an excess baggage fee. The general rule of thumb is one covered bag containing a maximum of 14 clubs, 12 balls, and one pair of shoes.

▮ PASSPORTS

U.S. citizens arriving by air and sea to Bermuda need a valid passport, though cruise-ship passengers on closed-loop cruises (those departing and arriving in the same U.S. port) need only have proof of citizenship and identity (a government-issued photo ID and a birth certificate with a raised seal). U.S. citizens do not need a visa to enter Bermuda for a period less than 90 days.

U.S. Passport Information U.S. Department of State. ☎ 877/487–2778 ⊕ *travel.state.gov/ passport.*

▮ SAFETY

Crime, especially against tourists, is extremely low in Bermuda. Purse snatching is the most common crime tourists should watch out for. Although rare, more serious incidents do happen occasionally, so you should guard against being overly complacent. Don't leave unattended valuables on the beach while going for a swim. Exercise commonsense precautions with wallets, purses, cameras, and other valuables. If you're driving a moped, always travel with your purse or bag concealed inside the seat. Always lock your moped or pedal bike, and store valuables in your room or hotel safe. Although an ocean breeze through a screen door is wonderful, close and lock your hotel room's glass patio door while you're sleeping or out of your room. The "back-of-town" area, in particular Court Street, has a bad reputation historically, though the government has made a number of efforts to clean up the area. Nevertheless, if you do want to go to a venue there, it's worth taking a taxi, just to be on the safe side.

▮TIP→ **Distribute your cash, credit cards, IDs, and other valuables between a deep front pocket, an inside jacket or vest pocket, and a hidden money pouch. Don't reach for the money pouch once you're in public.**

▮ TAXES

Hotels add a 7.25% government tax to the bill, and most add a 10% service charge or a per-diem dollar equivalent in lieu of tips. Other extra charges sometimes include a 5% "energy surcharge" (at small guesthouses) and a 17% service charge (at most restaurants).

A $78 airport-departure tax and a $8.25 airport-security fee are built into the price of your ticket, as is a 16-passenger facility charge, whereas cruise lines collect $60 in advance for each passenger, again, normally included in the price of the ticket.

TIME

Bermuda is in the Atlantic time zone. Bermuda observes daylight saving time (from the second Sunday in March to the first Sunday in November), so it's always one hour ahead of U.S. eastern standard time. Thus, for instance, when it's 5 pm in Bermuda, it's 4 pm in New York, 3 pm in Chicago, and 1 pm in Los Angeles. London is four hours, and Sydney 14 hours, ahead of Bermuda.

TIPPING

Tipping in Bermuda is fairly similar to tipping in the United States. A service charge of 10% (or an equivalent per-diem amount), which covers everything from baggage handling to maid service, is added to your hotel bill, though people often still tip a few extra dollars. Most restaurants tack on a 17% service charge; if not, a 17% tip is customary (more for exceptional service).

TIPPING GUIDELINES FOR BERMUDA	
Bartender	$1 to $3 per round of drinks, depending on the number of drinks
Bellhop	$2 per bag, depending on the level of the hotel
Dive Instructor	5% to 10% of the total trip
Gas Station Attendants	$2
Grocery Baggers	$1 to $2 a bag
Hotel Maid	$10 at lower-end accommodations, $20 at higher-end accommodations
Porter at Airport	$1 per bag
Taxi Driver	15%, but round up the fare to the next dollar amount
Waiter	17%; nothing additional if a service charge is added to the bill

TOURS

SPECIAL INTEREST TOURS
GARDEN AND WILDLIFE TOURS

Free 75-minute guided tours of the Botanical Gardens depart from the visitor center Wednesday, Thursday, and Friday at 10:30 am weather permitting.

The Garden Club of Bermuda offers a unique experience of visiting local gardens. Tours are $100 for four people, $25 for each additional person.

Byways Bermuda offers personalized off-the-beaten-path tours of Bermuda for $100 per person for a six-hour tour.

For the adventurous, have Ashley Harris of Hidden Gems of Bermuda Limited take you cliff jumping or cave swimming. These tours are truly off the beaten path.

Contacts Botanical Gardens. ☎ 441/236–5902. **Byways Bermuda.** ☎ 441/535–9169 ⊕ www.bermudafootsteps.com. **Garden Club of Bermuda.** ☎ 441/232–1273 ⊕ www.gardenclubbermuda.org. **Hidden Gems of Bermuda Limited.** ☎ 441/236–1300 ⊕ www.bermudahiddengems.com.

HISTORICAL AND SOCIAL TOURS

The Bermuda Tourism Authority (BTA) publishes brochures with self-guided tours of Hamilton, St. George's, the West End, and the Railway Trail. Available free at all Visitor Information Centres and at hotels and guesthouses, the brochures also contain detailed directions for walkers and cyclists as well as historical notes and anecdotes. The BTA also coordinates walking tours of Hamilton, St. George's, Spittal Pond Nature Reserve, the Royal Naval Dockyard, and Somerset. The tours of Hamilton and St. George's, as well as most of the Royal Naval Dockyard tours, take in historic buildings, while the Spittal Pond and Somerset tours focus on the island's flora.

Bermuda Lecture Tours are run by witty British transplant Tim Rogers who has lived in Bermuda for more than a decade. Rogers leads exceptional walks (and seated talks) about various Bermuda topics that other historians or guides sticking to their textbooks may be hesitant to discuss. His humorous and conversational tours cover intriguing historical material on piracy, local ghosts and lore, and the island's more interesting geological and architectural features. A 90-minute walking tour costs $80 per couple and $10 extra for each additional person. Special group rates are also available.

Segway Tours of Bermuda offers a historical tour of the Royal Naval Dockyard aboard a Segway—an electric two-wheel vehicle. The machines are the only vehicles that can tour the National Museum of Bermuda. Sites include the Clocktower Mall, Casemates Prison, the Victualling Yard, the Glassblowing and Rum Cake Factory, and the Sail Loft. The 90-minute tour includes a brief orientation to the vehicle and costs $80. Tours depart daily at 10, noon, 2, and 4.

Contacts Bermuda Lecture & Tours.
☎ 441/238-0344 ✉ trogers@northrock. bm. **Bermuda Tourism Authority** (*BTA*) .
☎ 441/296-9200 ⊕ www.gotobermuda.com. **Segway Tours of Bermuda.** ☎ 441/236-1300 ⊕ www.segway.bm.

TAXI AND MINIBUS TOURS

For an independent tour of Bermuda, a taxi is a good but more expensive alternative to a group tour. A blue flag on the hood of a cab indicates that the driver is a qualified tour guide. These cabs can be difficult to find, but most of their drivers are friendly and entertaining—they sometimes bend the truth for a good yarn—and well informed about the island and its history. Ask your hotel to arrange a tour with a knowledgeable driver.

Cabs seat four or six, and the legal rate for island tours (minimum three hours) is $40 per hour for one to four passengers and $55.50 per hour for five or six passengers. Two children under 12 equal an adult.

Taxi and Minibus Tour Operators Bee-Line Transport Ltd. ☎ 441/293-0303. **Destination Bermuda Ltd.** ☎ 441/292-2325,

⊕ www.destinationbermuda.bm. **Island Taxi Services.** ☎ 441/295-4141 ⊕ www.bermudaislandtaxi.com.

■ VISITOR INFORMATION

Have all your questions answered about what it's like to be a visitor to Bermuda by getting in touch with the island's Tourism Authority. If you are heading to St. George's in the East End, the St. George's Foundation can help you find your way around the Old Town.

Contact Bermuda Tourism Authority.
☎ 441/296-9200 in Bermuda, 800/223-6106 in U.S. ⊕ www.gotobermuda.com. **St. George's Foundation.** ☎ 441/297-8043 ⊕ www. stgeorgesfoundation.org.

ONLINE TRAVEL TOOLS

One of the best Bermuda websites is Bermuda-online, which offers information on every aspect of life on the island, from history to transportation. The Tourism Authority's website is especially helpful during the initial stages of vacation planning. Bermuda.com has a great search engine and links to a number of Bermuda-related Web pages, plus listings. To keep up with current affairs, the island has one daily newspaper: *The Royal Gazette*. To find out about nightlife offerings, visit Nothing To Do In Bermuda, which will prove that there's lots to do in Bermuda, if you know where to look. And if you want to check out the types of people you will be partying with, take a look at the photos on the Black and Coke and Bermy Net websites.

Bermuda.com ⊕ *www.bermuda.com.* **Bermuda Online** ⊕ *www.bermuda-online. org.* **Bermuda Tourism Authority** ⊕ *www. gotobermuda.com.* **Bermy Net** ⊕ *www. bermynet.com.* **Black and Coke** ⊕ *www. blackandcoke.com* **Nothing To Do In Bermuda** ⊕ *www.nothingtodoinbermuda. com.* **The Royal Gazette** ⊕ *www.royalgazette.com.*

INDEX

PHOTO CREDITS

NOTES

NOTES

Fodor's BERMUDA

Editorial: Douglas Stallings, *Editorial Director*; Margaret Kelly, *Senior Editor*; Alexis Kelly, Jacinta O'Halloran, and Amanda Sadlowski, *Editors*; Teddy Minford, *Content Editor*; Rachael Roth, *Content Manager*

Design: Tina Malaney, *Design and Production Director*; Jessica Gonzalez, *Production Designer*

Photography: Jennifer Arnow, *Senior Photo Editor*

Maps: Rebecca Baer, *Senior Map Editor*; Mark Stroud (Moon Street Cartography) and David Lindroth, *Cartographers*

Production: Jennifer DePrima, *Editorial Production Manager*; Carrie Parker, *Senior Production Editor*; Elyse Rozelle, *Production Editor*; David Satz, *Director of Content Production*

Business & Operations: Chuck Hoover, *Chief Marketing Officer*; Joy Lai, *Vice President and General Manager*; Stephen Horowitz, *Director of Business Development and Revenue Operations*; Tara McCrillis, *Director of Publishing Operations*; Eliza D. Aceves, *Content Operations Manager and Srategist*

Public Relations and Marketing: Joe Ewaskiw, *Manager;* Esther Su, *Marketing Manager*

Writers: Robyn Bardgett, Amy Peniston

Editor: Jacinta O'Halloren

Production Editor: Carrie Parker

Production Design: Liliana Guia

34th Edition

ISBN 978-1-64097-010-6

ISSN 0192–3765

All details in this book are based on information supplied to us at press time. Always confirm information when it matters, especially if you're making a detour to visit a specific place. Fodor's expressly disclaims any liability, loss, or risk, personal or otherwise, that is incurred as a consequence of the use of any of the contents of this book.

SPECIAL SALES

This book is available at special discounts for bulk purchases for sales promotions or premiums. For more information, e-mail SpecialMarkets@fodors.com

ABOUT OUR WRITERS

 Born and raised in Bermuda, **Robyn Bardgett** actually considers herself a city girl at heart and, while she loves a day spent out on the boat enjoying Bermuda's aquamarine waters, she also has nothing against a cold, gray day exploring her favorite city, London. Despite her love for the "Old Smoke," Robyn is fiercely protective of her Bermudian heritage and her beautiful island home. She currently lives in Bermuda with her boyfriend, children, and dog, Biggles, and is a freelance copywriter.

 Amy Peniston is a Bermuda-born freelance web designer, writer, and content creator. She contributes regularly to *The Bermudian* magazine in addition to building websites and running social media marketing campaigns. She also teaches students worldwide through her online courses on Udemy. In her free time, Amy combines her passion for fitness and love for Bermuda by creating and sharing workout videos on her YouTube channel, amy dot. For Amy's full portfolio, visit ⊕ *www.amypeniston.com*.